ADVANCE PRAISE FOR *ALL ABOUT DRIPs AND DSPs*

Too often, DRIP investment advice is about how to buy stocks cheaply instead of what stocks to buy. George Fisher makes sure that the reader knows both.

> —Dennis Fertig, editor-in-chief, *Your Money* magazine

All About DRIPs and DSPs provides a no-nonsense approach to getting the maximum yield from your investments. It's based on data and cold facts.

> —George Harmon, professor of business journalism, Medill School of Journalism, Northwestern University

All About DRIPs and DSPs is written for everyone. New investors will learn the right ways to plan for a solid financial future. Seasoned investors will also benefit from George's outlook on investment planning. All parents should give a copy of this book to their children the day they receive their first paycheck.

> —Jerry D. Conner, executive vice president, Foote, Cone & Belding

ALL ABOUT DRIPs AND DSPs

OTHER TITLES IN THE "ALL ABOUT..." FINANCE SERIES

All About Stocks
All About Bonds
All About Options
All About Commodities
All About Mutual Funds
All About Real Estate Investing
All About Your 401(k) Plan
All About Variable Annuities

ALL ABOUT
DRIPs
AND DSPs

The Easy Way to Get Started

GEORGE C. FISHER

McGraw-Hill

New York   Chicago   San Francisco   Lisbon   London
Madrid   Mexico City   Milan   New Delhi
San Juan   Seoul   Singapore
Sydney   Toronto

Library of Congress Cataloging-in-Publication Data

Fisher, George C.
   All about DRIPs and DSPs / by George C. Fisher.
      p. cm.
   ISBN 0-07-136993-7
   1. Dividend reinvestment   2. Employee ownership.   3. Stocks.   4. Investments.
I. Title.

HG4028.D5 F57 2001
332.63'22—dc21   00-069928

McGraw-Hill

*A Division of The **McGraw·Hill** Companies*

1 2 3 4 5 6 7 8 9 0   DOC/DOC   0 9 8 7 6 5 4 3 2 1

ISBN 0-07-136993-7

This book was set in 11/13 Palatino type by The Composing Room of Michigan, Inc. Printed and bound by R. R. Donnelley & Sons Company.

This publication is designed to provide accurate and authoritative information in regard to the subject matter covered. It is sold with the understanding that the publisher is not engaged in rendering legal, accounting, or other professional service. If legal advice or other expert assistance is required, the services of a competent professional person should be sought.
   —From a declaration of principles jointly adopted by a committee of the American Bar Association and a committee of publishers.

 This book is printed on recycled, acid-free paper containing a minimum of 50% recycled de-inked fiber.

McGraw-Hill books are available at special quantity discounts to use as premiums and sales promotions, or for use in corporate training programs. For more information, please write to the Director of Special Sales, Professional Publishing, McGraw-Hill, Two Penn Plaza, New York, NY 10121-2298. Or contact your local bookstore.

I would like to dedicate this book to my three daughters, Kelly, Lindsay, and Becky. May they actually read, understand, and implement these concepts.

CONTENTS

PREFACE

Reinvesting cash interest and dividends received into their original investments is a time-tested investment strategy. Successful investors believe the benefits of compounding increasing dividends offered through dividend reinvestment will result in improving long-term investment returns. The strategy of investing with Dividend Reinvestment Plans (DRIPs) is to locate top-quality companies currently favored by Wall Street experts as being good investments and whose stocks are currently selling at a discount or a small premium to the underlying future long-term growth of its corporate earnings. Managers of quality companies think and act like they own the company, when in reality it is all the shareholders combined who actually own the company through their shares of stock. When managers and investors have a common goal—increasing shareholder values—the results usually provide attractive investment returns for company shareholders.

All About DRIPs and DSPs is about a lot of good, old-fashioned common sense. Excellent long-term returns are available from companies whose corporate mission is to do just that—grow shareholder value. The goal of All About DRIPs and DPSs is not to uncover the next IBM or Microsoft, nor is it to trade excessively for a few dollars point spread. Rather the goal is to find great companies with solid profits selling at reasonable prices, as well as to retain ownership of the shares over the long term. Four out of every five initial public offerings of stock fail to make the long-term investor wealthy. For every Microsoft, there are four companies that lost money for their investors. All About DRIPs and DSPs believes that great companies, which have historically provided their stockholders with excellent long-term returns, offer the best opportunity to continue to do so in the future.

Because All About DRIPs and DSPs is easy to read and makes sense, it's appropriate for investors of all sizes and types—large and small, using a traditional brokerage firm, a discount house, an Internet broker, or using company investor-direct purchase plans or dividend reinvestment programs. DRIPs and direct investing is appropriate for young and old, the sophisticated and initial investor alike.

One added feature of DRIPs and direct investing is that it is somewhat conservative in nature. By concentrating on well-managed companies with proven investor returns over time, investors' portfolios will feature some of America's best companies. Quality companies offered at reasonable prices will always have an investor following.

According to the US Department of Commerce, more than 45 percent of all American families either directly, through personal holdings of stocks as investments, or indirectly, through holdings of stock in their employers' pension plans, are affected by the gyrations of the stock market. In addition, it is estimated that there are between 7 and 9 million DRIP and Direct Stock Plan (DSP) participants.

Chapter 1 explains what DRIP and DSP plans are, along with a brief history. DRIPs have several advantages, along with inherent disadvantages, versus broker or Internet investing tools. The benefits of dollar cost averaging are evaluated because these are key elements in DRIPs.

Chapter 2 offers a basic summary of the differences between stocks and bonds as investment vehicles. Six basic concepts for finding good DRIPs are offered.

Chapter 3 answers the question, "Why invest in the first place?" This chapter analyzes different types of financial accounts and reviews the benefits of tax-deferred investing, along with the use of custodial accounts. Compounding dividends, the future value of money, and inflation are discussed within the context of DRIP and direct investing as an investment tool.

Chapters 4, 5, and 6 explain how to research companies using various criteria. Corporate Mission Statements along with Corporate Ethics Statements are reviewed. Management can be easily evaluated by reviewing just a few specific financial ratios. Current market pricing is a reflection of investors' belief in the company's future potential, and comparing stock prices using such tools as the PEG ratio can assist investors in identifying timely DRIPs. Annual reports are explained because they are an excellent and relatively painless resource of investor information. Third-party resources, such as broker recommendations, are always an important tool in DRIP stock selection. With the advent of the Internet, personal finance information abounds, possibly confusing investors as to where to go and what to look for. We have provided a few website recommendations to get the beginning DRIP investor feeling comfortable.

Chapter 7 explains investment risk and how it may impact your portfolio.

Chapter 8 discusses how to buy stocks using DRIP and direct investing programs. Stockbrokers and synthetic DRIP programs provide investors with the ability to benefit from a dividend reinvestment strategy without buying direct.

Chapter 9 outlines the investment concepts of *asset allocation* and *portfolio diversification*. DRIPs are a proven tool used to accomplish these significant investing strategies.

Chapter 10 discusses the importance of bonds as an investment. Direct investing is even popular for buying US government bonds.

Chapters 11 and 12 analyze mutual funds as investment vehicles and how they may be bad for investors' financial health. DRIPs provide a great alternative to mutual funds. Building a diversified DRIP portfolio based on the age of the investor is discussed.

A glossary of DRIP and direct investing terms, along with a review of over 100 companies offering DRIPs and direct investing programs, are offered as appendixes.

The biggest mistake that beginning investors make is not to "get in the game." Too many Americans are not saving enough of their earned income or are sitting on the sidelines watching our country's longest economic boom fly past them. Some investors have far too much of their assets in cash, afraid of the loss of capital. Other investors have far too much invested in high-risk, over-speculative stocks. *All About DRIPs and DSPs* is written with these investors in mind.

Making money in the stock market has never been easy and is never guaranteed. Investors, especially new investors, should research their investment selections and have concrete reasons prior to making any investment. DRIPs and direct investing programs are important tools used by many successful investors.

ACKNOWLEDGMENTS

I would like to acknowledge the efforts of several close friends who reviewed this manuscript as a work in progress, stimulating and motivating me to continue. Alex Evarts was of untold assistance as my frontline proofreader. Jerry Connor and Greg Peabody eagerly offered their own unique perspectives. Bill Johnson helped keep me on a straight path concerning tax issues. Lindsay, my daughter, helped out during her college summer break, consistently reminding me that all investors, but especially beginning investors, need precise yet easy-to-read presentations. My brother, "Uncle Stephen," has been willing to play the part of my own personal Charlie McCarthy for years, and for that I am grateful. My father and grandfather have been lifelong mentors concerning successful investing and frugality. I would also like to thank the staff at McGraw-Hill Publishing, and especially Kelli Christiansen, for their support and efforts on my behalf. Most of all, I have to express my gratitude to my lovely wife of 25 years, Karen (affectionately referred to as "my bride"), for her never-ending love and support during this and all my projects.

People work hard to earn a living. Earning a decent wage, however, is not sufficient to really get ahead financially. No matter what our income, each one of us needs to be saving a portion of every paycheck. For some, the savings could be $25 a month, whereas for others it could be $2500. The two biggest excuses for not establishing a regular saving and investing plan is either "I can't afford to invest" or "I am afraid to lose my money."

In today's economic environment, we cannot afford not to save and invest. With inflation increasing 3 percent to 4 percent annually, the cost to just stay alive goes up every year. Social Security will be a dubious source for retirement income for today's college students. In most household budgets, there are discretionary spending items. There are things we buy to make us feel good, like fast boats, or there are things to occupy our time, like golf or tennis. Some of every family's overall spending consists of frivolous items. There are some completely frivolous items in most household expenses, and it is from here that many families find their initial savings and investing seed money.

A small amount of money is all that is needed to begin investing, and one of the best opportunities for this seed money is Dividend Reinvestment Plans (DRIPs) and Direct Stock Plan (DSP) programs. Experienced investors use these opportunities. New investors use these opportunities. They both involve a desire to grow their nest egg in a steady, low-cost, investor-friendly manner.

What are DRIPs and direct investing programs? Both are direct investments by individual investors in companies, bypassing the traditional stockbrokers and investment firms. Both avoid annual management fees usually associated with mutual funds. Both are excellent tools for either small or large investors. Both are excellent for the careful investor who likes to do his or her own research and who buys stocks for the long term.

The amount of personal wealth generated over one's lifetime is directly related to two highly personalized concepts. The first concept is how much money is earned and how much is spent, saved, and invested. The second concept, directly impacting investment account balances, is which investment choices are made.

As an example, Calvin and Addy are identical twins. Raised in a small midwestern town, they went to the nearby state university and, at age 22, both became aeronautic engineers. Calvin and Addy worked side by side at the local airplane cockpit controls factory and have identical after-tax biweekly paychecks. Their identicalness, however, ends there. Currently age 42, the siblings have taken very different tracks concerning their personal finances and lifestyles.

Calvin loves to stop by the local high-priced coffee shop on the way to work each day, and he feels dapper in a new Volvo convertible, leased for $600 a month. He eats out at the local restaurants every day for lunch, usually "discussing business." Calvin enjoys watching HBO music specials and rents the latest DVD movies three times a week. In addition, Calvin has a fondness for travel to exotic destinations. Addy, in contrast, brings the last cup of coffee from home and drives around in a leased Jeep for $300 a month. Whenever the weather is nice enough, she eats a sack lunch outside at the local park; on other days, she hangs out at the company gym. Addy prefers gardening, watches old reruns on TV, and occasionally goes out for a burger and the movies. Addy owns a small, yet comfortable, second home down by the beach, and spends as much free time there are possible. When not occupied by the family, the beach house is available for rent, and the income covers much of the annual operating costs. Eventually the beach house will be used for her retirement.

Calvin and Addy's dad was very conservative with his money. As a Depression era child, their father taught them to save for their future. Calvin has been able to save 5 percent of earned income and invests only in safe, secure US government bond mutual funds, which pay a steady income of about 6 percent annually. With the income, Calvin buys more fund shares. Addy regularly saves 12 percent of earned income. She has a diversified portfolio of stocks and has realized an average return of 11 percent a year. Addy has also been reinvesting the dividends paid to shareholders by companies, buying more shares of stock with each quarterly dividend payment.

Seven years ago, at age 35, Calvin was saving at a rate of $2600 a year and had an investment account balance of $26,700. This year Calvin will set aside $5000 in savings. Calvin's account has grown into a nice nest egg; after 20 years, it has a current value of $172,000. Addy, at age 35, was saving at a rate of $6300 a year and had an investment account balance of $83,200. This year Addy will save $12,000 and currently has an even nicer nest egg of $258,000, also after 20 years.

As children, Calvin and Addy made a pact. They would each retire as soon as they had $1 million in the bank. At their current rate of savings and investing, Calvin will retire at age 67 with a $1 million investment account. Addy, however, will be able to retire almost 15 years earlier, having reached the $1 million goal at age 53.

Addy invests her annual savings in top-quality companies that have a history of increasing profits and dividends. She buys shares of stock in these companies, becoming a shareholder. Many companies reward shareholders by distributing a portion of the cash profits, and this distribution is called a *dividend*. As company earnings increase over time, management may elect to increase the amount paid in dividends. With this higher distribution, Addy chooses to buy more shares of stock, increasing the number of shares owned. Addy also adds optional cash payments to the dividend, increasing the number of shares purchased. Future dividend distributions are based on the number of shares owned; as the number of shares increases, so does the cash dividend distribution.

On January 1, 1989, Addy decided to invest in E'Town (stock symbol ETW), a small New Jersey water services utility company. Addy liked the steady income that high-dividend utilities usually pay. Addy also had researched the company and believed its management was capable of continuing to expand earnings and dividends over the next 10 years. Addy invested $600, after expenses for stock brokerage commission, and requested the broker deliver the stock certificate. She bought 20 shares at a market price of $30 a share. When the certificate came in the mail, Addy notified the company she was interested in enrolling in their DRIP program. Enrollment forms were mailed, completed, and returned to ETW, and Addy was added to the list of thousands of other ETW DRIP program participants.

In 1989, ETW paid their shareholders $1.95 in dividends for every share owned, and Addy received $39.00 in dividends for owning 20 shares. Addy decided to initially add $340 to the dividends received and to increase this optional cash contribution by 10 percent every year. Addy sent in a check for $340 from her annual savings plan, which was added to the dividend and used to buy an additional 12.72 shares. Each year ETW paid more cash dividends, and Addy added higher amounts from her savings plan. In 1994, Addy invested an optional cash payment of $500. During the first 5 years, Addy invested $2600 from the savings plan. ETW paid a 5-year total of $619 in dividends and the account would have owned 118.47 shares, worth $3600.

Addy continued buying more shares with ETW's dividend and invested slightly more each year. In mid-1999, Addy contributed almost $1000 from the savings plan. Addy owned 331.74 shares and was receiving $623 in annual dividends. In the fall of 1999, a French firm decided to purchase ETW for around $65 a share in cash, with the merger to be completed in the fall of 2000.

Addy's total investment over the previous 11 years amounted to $7940 from the savings plan and $2400 from dividends. Her shares are worth $21,480. Addy has realized an overall gain of 140.7 percent on the capital invested or an average return of 12.8 percent a year.

Addy is able to build financial wealth quicker than Calvin because of three basic differences. The first is the amount saved. Addy is able to save and invest more because of a determination to reduce personal expenses and increase the dollars available for investing. The second difference is in the choice of investments. Calvin chooses to invest in lower-return investments, which are inherently safer in risk. The downside of accepting a lower risk is that usually investors receive lower returns. Addy, however, was willing to accept a higher level of risk by investing in stocks and was rewarded with a higher rate of return. Addy was able to increase the annual profit generated by their respective investing plan almost twice as fast. The third difference is that Addy saved more of her income earlier. Over the years, with the investment power of compounding investment returns, her portfolio grew as the added savings each year earned greater amounts of income.

Addy's portfolio value also increased quicker through the investment strategy of buying more shares of stock with the dividend received. This investing tool is used by millions of investors to reach their financial goals faster.

There should be a reasonable amount of personal fear when it comes to choosing investments. If things don't work out, can the investor really afford to lose all, or even half, of his or her capital? The risk of choosing a bad investment can be mitigated by a better understanding of what moves markets and stock prices and by improving stock-selection criteria. Every investment chosen may not be a winner, and a truly diversified portfolio may have some losers among the stock positions. With a long-term investing outlook, declines in stock prices may provide excellent buying opportunities. Educated investors should be able to identify the difference between a company led by top-quality management whose current share price is undervalued and a company led by poor management whose share price, although down, may still be overvalued.

The one underlying fact concerning top-quality stock investments is that, since 1925, an investor with a 20-year time horizon has never lost money investing in the Standard and Poor's (S&P) Index of 500 large and diversified companies. Starting from 1925 to 1945 and calculating through the 1979 to 1999 20-year holding period, the S&P 500 Index would have returned a profit for every buy and hold investor. Although some 20-year periods provided more gains than others, over the past 75 years long-term investors have made adequate stock market returns. Any reasonable person can assume this trend would continue.

All About DRIPs and DSPs explains what DRIPs are and why they are becoming popular for both investors and companies. The book is focused on how to develop a diversified portfolio of stocks and bonds without paying stock brokerage commissions or annual management fees. It teaches you how to locate top-quality companies that should continue providing investors with more than acceptable investments returns. How to determine investment risk is discussed. Most investors do not need mutual funds and are paying dearly for the honor of having a money manager make all the investment decisions. The appendixes list over 100 companies that offer DRIPs or direct investing programs.

ALL ABOUT DRIPs AND DSPs

CHAPTER 1

What Are DRIPs and DSPs?

Key Concepts

- A Brief History
- Benefits of DRIP Investing
- DRIP Investing Disadvantages
- Costs Associated with DRIPs
- The Strategy and Advantages of Dollar Cost Averaging
- Overall DRIP and Direct Investment Strategy

The long-term accumulation of stock assets using **Dividend Reinvestment Plans (DRIPs)** is an investment strategy where company dividends are invested in additional shares of company stock rather than being paid in cash. DRIPs allow investors to add to the dividend, increasing the amount invested, without paying standard stock brokerage commissions. Some DRIPs buy and sell shares free of fees to the investor, whereas others charge small fees. Numerous companies reward shareholders by paying quarterly, semiannual, or annual cash dividends. As a return to shareholders of company profits, dividends are viewed as a powerful method to attract and develop shareholder loyalty. Over time, as corporate earnings increase, dividend payouts also should increase. Shareholders who elect to invest in additional shares of stock rather than cash dividends receive a double bonus: The shares received generate more dividends and the shares should increase in value over the long term. Many companies offer shareholders the opportunity to send in optional cash contributions (OCP) to be added to the next dividend payment, increasing their total dollars invested.

Originally, DRIPs required the investor to first buy some shares through a registered broker and to have the shares registered in the investor's name. Once the investor became a registered shareholder, with proof of ownership using an actual stock certificate, he or she was eligible to enroll in the company's DRIP. About 60 percent of DRIPs still have this requirement.

DRIPs have mutated since their initial rise in popularity during the 1960s. The DRIP strategy may include the ability to buy both the initial investment and the reinvested dividend shares directly from the company or its transfer agent, bypassing the commissioned middleman altogether. This is commonly called **Direct Investing,** which is officially known as **Direct Enrollment Stock Purchase Plans (DESPs)** or **Direct Stock Purchase (DSP).**

DRIP and direct investing strategies are a proven method of successfully building stock assets over the long term. According to the April 19, 1999, issue of *Barrons Financial Weekly*, every $100 invested in the S&P in 1925 would be worth $235,000 at the end of 1998, using the long-term strategy of reinvestment of dividends. However, the original $100 would have grown to about $9600, with the balance $225,400 coming from dividends and capital gains from additional stock purchased with those dividends.

A BRIEF HISTORY

For the past half century or so, numerous companies found it advantageous to issue new shares of stock rather than pay a cash dividend. A few of the early leaders in this type of offering were AT&T (T–1969), American General (AGC–1962), Dow Chemical (DOW–1970), and PPG Industries (PPG–1967). By presenting newly issued stock to current shareholders, companies were able to raise fresh capital without the required Securities and Exchange Commission (SEC) government filings and paperwork required for secondary stock offerings. Substituting newly issued shares for dividends was less expensive to the company than the costs associated with underwriting secondary offerings through the brokerage houses. In the economic and population boom of the 1960s, utility companies were consistently in need of new capital to build our country's basic infrastructure. Utilities discovered that current shareholders were excellent prospects for the sale of new stock, and they moved to motivate investors to enroll in their DRIPs. A few companies began offering discounts on the share price of up to 5 percent if existing shareholders would send in extra investment money, also known as OCPs. In other words, some utility companies would sell stock to their current shareholders for 5 percent less than the cost on the open market. This trend, although used by few companies today, offers DRIP investors the opportunity to buy investment assets at a discount, increasing long-term capital gains.

According to netstockdirect.com, a leading Internet DRIP resource, there are currently 115 companies that subsidize an investor's cost of stock purchases by offering discounts on their DRIPs. For example, Philadelphia Suburban Corp. (PSC), one of the largest investor-owned water utilities with over 1.8 million customers in the midwest and northeast, offers DRIP investors a discount on their dividend reinvestment purchases. PSC's formula is to charge 95 percent of the average high and low prices for 5 trading days prior to the investment date. An investor owning 49.28 shares in their DRIP program on April 1, 2000, would have received a dividend payment of $8.87, which would be used to purchase 0.52 shares at a transaction price of $16.96 per share. The market price on that day was $18.18, reflecting a DRIP purchase discount of $1.24 per share, or 6.8 percent. PSC's DRIP allows for initial direct investments of $500, OCP minimum of $50 a month and maximum of $30,000 a month, and the plan is free.

Why would a company want to have DRIP and direct investors? Because DRIP investors frequently are characterized as smaller investors compared with large mutual funds and asset-managed trust accounts. DRIP investors are frequently long-term thinkers and provide a more stable investor base. Many mutual fund money managers move in and out of a stock based on short-term goals and rewards, with a fickleness that reflects the emotions of the market. In contrast, long-term DRIP investors tend to dollar cost average their purchases, and many view a drop in a stock's share prices as an opportunity to increase their long-term share holdings rather than a time to sell.

Companies have also learned that individual shareholders can become a powerful new source of potentially loyal customers, and an expanding DRIP investor base can translate into higher company sales and profits. Some companies offer product discount coupons in their annual reports to encourage current shareholders to buy their products.

With DRIPs, stock ownership is registered in fractional shares because the dividend amount available for stock purchase is typically only a fraction of a share. This facilitates small dollar investments. Share ownership in a DRIP account is usually expressed up to three decimal places. It is not uncommon for small DRIP accounts to initially reinvest dividends that will purchase tenths of a share of stock. Many DRIP programs will accept as little as $10 to $25 for OCPs. For example, a $25 net investment in a $75 stock would equate to purchasing 0.333 shares, and a $5000 net investment in a $54 stock would equate to 92.592 shares. Future dividends are paid on the total shares owned on the Day of Record, including the fractional shares.

To participate in a company's DRIP, the investor must already be a registered shareholder of a minimum number of shares; typically just one share is needed. This is the only common thread throughout the field of DRIPs and direct investing. Once an investor is a registered shareholder, these companies allow enrollment in whatever program they offer.

For Internet users, NetStock Direct Corp offers the premiere on-line direct investing resource website at *www.netstockdirect.com*. Depending on the specific company's plan details, NetStock's no-fee service allows for automatic bank withdrawals to pay for DRIP purchases. Many companies at NetStock's website also allow DRIP investors to complete enrollment forms on-line. Investors then print the complete forms and mail them along with a check for their initial purchase.

Intimate Brands (IBI) is a recent newcomer to the world of DRIPs. Spun off by The Limited (LTD) in 1995, IBI is the leading specialty retailer of intimate apparel, beauty, and personal care products. IBI distributes products using the Victoria's Secret, Bath and Body Works, and White Barn Candle Company brand names. LTD still owns about 82 percent of all outstanding shares of IBI. To encourage shareholders to become customers, IBI includes discount coupons for lingerie and personal health care items in their annual

report. In the summer of 1999, IBI decided to offer a dividend reinvestment and direct investing program. IBI is a whiz at product
marketing, and the announcement of their DRIP program came
with much fanfare. IBI took out full-page advertisements in important newspapers like *The Wall Street Journal* and *The New York Times*,
with pictures of their famous scantly clad "Vicky Se's" models directing readers to the IBI Invest Direct link at their website or to an
800 phone number for their transfer agent. IBI's plan includes a minimum initial direct investment of $500 and minimum OCPs of $100.
Maximum purchases are currently set at $250,000 annually. There
are rumors that the IBI introduction of their DRIP program may
have set a record for attracting the most number of DRIP investors
in the shortest amount of time, although not particularly low in their
fee structure. During the first 60 days after the introduction of their
DRIP and direct investing plan, IBI's online DRIP enrollments and
requests for forms through NetStock Direct accounted for over 62
percent of all requests received during the first 6 months.

BENEFITS OF DRIP INVESTING

The primary benefits to DRIP investors revolve around the following investment philosophies:

- DRIPs allow small investments (or large investments if the
  investor is financially capable) to be invested regularly in a
  diversified portfolio of stocks that will grow into much
  larger amounts of money some sunny day in the future.
- DRIPs increase long-term investment returns. Compounding an increasing dividend, added to the discipline of regularly scheduled stock purchases or dollar cost averaging, is
  a superior recipe for accumulating long-term assets.
- DRIPs save on fees. DRIPs and direct investing programs
  save the cost of brokerage fees and the "hidden" costs of
  mutual fund asset-based management fees, and they avoid
  "phantom" capital gains tax exposure.

It has been proven that a one-time investment of $10,000 at age
20 will yield $1.35 million at age 65 based on an average 11 percent
annual return. Invest $38 a week over 40 years at 11 percent annual
return and it will also generate well over $1 million. Over the past

50 years or so, the S&P 500 Index has averaged a 12.5 percent annual return.

Now look at this in terms of reinvestment of dividends. According to Joseph Tigue and Joseph Lisanti, authors of *The Dividend Rich Investor*, a one-time investment of $1000 in the S&P 500 in 1980 would have been worth $4530 in 1995. However, if the investor reinvested the dividends into more shares, the same $1000 would have grown to $7940. Keep the dividends in your investment portfolio and the investment returns in real dollars will increase substantially. Optional cash payments to DRIP accounts of as small as $170 a month can grow into over $175,000 in 20 years and over $600,000 in 30 years, at a 12.5 percent annual return.

Reinvesting dividends is like an investment savings account. With any bank passbook, savings, or money market account, the cash balance earns interest that is added to the account, increasing the cash balance and increasing the interest earned in the next payment period. This is called *compounding of interest.*

DRIPs are the easiest method of transferring the power of compounding interest from passbook accounts to stock investments, but at more advantageous returns. Similar to crediting your passbook's cash balance with interest, the companies (or their transfer agents) buy additional shares of stock with your cash dividends, crediting these shares to your account. This higher share balance will generate higher cash dividends next payment period, which, in turn, is used to buy more shares. The cycle continues until the DRIP investor elects to withdraw.

An advantage of compounding dividend returns over compounding interest is the long-term impact of regularly increasing dividends and stock appreciation. Well-managed companies will reward long-term investors with dividend increases, either in cash or additional stock. As a means of returning company profits back to shareholders, top-quality management over time will not only increase corporate cash flow and earnings per share, but dividends as well. *The 2000 S&P Directory of Dividend Reinvestment Plans* lists over 247 companies offering DRIPs where dividends have been increased every year for 10 years since 1989. These include companies like AFLAC (AFL), Century Telephone (CTL), Disney (DIS), Federal Signal (FSS), Kimberly Clark (KMB), Pfizer (PFE), Pitney Bowes (PBI), and Walgreens (WAG).

The quickest way to find out how long it would take to double your money at a compounded constant return, use the Rule 72. Divide 72 by the anticipated yield and the answer is the number of years needed. For example, the value of an account holding a utility stock with a dividend yield of 7.2 percent, and no capital appreciation and no further dividend increases, will double in 10 years on just the compounding of the dividend (72 divided by 7.2 percent yield = 10). A 6.0 percent government bond will repay the entire face value in compounded interest over 12 years (72 divided by 6.0). In the same way, use Rule 115 to calculate the time it takes for money to triple. Divide 115 by the constant return rate. For example, the utility stock account would triple in 16.5 years (115 divided by 7.2 = 16.5) and the government bond in 19 years (115 divided by 6.0).

When an investor buys shares of stock over time, with a range of prices (both high and low) using the average cost of the stock, it is called *dollar cost averaging*. Because stock prices go up and down, investing $1000 every month for a year will typically purchase a different number of shares at different prices. With scheduled investments, such as this monthly example, the investor pays the average stock price for the investment period rather than risk market timing errors with a single purchase. DRIPs are best viewed as a cost-effective and flexible investing plan for implementing dollar cost averaging.

Many programs allow investors to have OCPs electronically deducted from checking or savings accounts. These bank-to-bank movements of your money are called *automated clearing house* (ACH) transfers or *electronic funds transfer* (EFTs), and they are easy to use. They facilitate the discipline of regular monthly investing. Based on an individual company's DRIP program, ACH investments can range from as little as $10 a month to as much as $20,000 a month.

DRIP programs do not charge annual management fees, asset-based fees, or advertising fees. If any, the only fees associated with DRIPs are collected when investments are bought or sold. With mutual funds, there is the special problem of "phantom capital gains," and these gains are considered taxable income for both the federal and state tax collectors. When a mutual fund sells a position for a gain, the capital gains tax liability is passed onto all fund investors and is reported to the IRS as taxable capital gains. This is known as "phantom capital gains tax exposure." Depending on the specific fund's situation, this annual phantom capital gains exposure could be substantial when reviewed from a long-term prospective. With DRIPs, the investor controls the timing of all capital gains by controlling when the stock is sold.

With most programs having low minimum investment requirements and with many plans offering very low transaction costs, DRIP investing is almost effortless for an investor seeking to develop a long-term, diversified portfolio. For as little as $3000 to $4000 in initial capital and $200 to $400 a month in OCPs, an investor is capable of accumulating one stock in each of the eight S&P industrial sectors.

DRIP INVESTING DISADVANTAGES

There are several investing quirks associated with DRIP and direct investing programs. First is the record keeping needed to properly calculate share purchases and costs to determine future taxable capital gains. Each dividend and OCP creates separate share purchases at specific prices. With the advent of computer spreadsheets, however, maintaining an acceptable log of DRIP purchases is fairly easy. A sample year 1999 DRIP investment log for 33 shares of Sears (S) with no OCPs is shown in Table 1–1.

T A B L E   1–1

Sears (S) Annual DRIP Statement for 33 Shares
as of January 4, 2000

Date	Div	Fee	OCP	Net	Price	Transaction Shares	Total Shares Held
Balance Forward							33.235
Jan 4, 1999	$7.64	$1	$0	$6.64	$43.416	0.153	33.388
April 1, 1999	$7.68	$1	$0	$6.68	$44.309	0.151	33.539
Aug 1, 1999	$7.71	$1	$0	$6.71	$46.119	0.145	33.684
Oct 1, 1999	$7.75	$1	$0	$6.75	$33.095	0.204	33.888
Jan 1, 2000	$7.79	$1	$0	$6.79	$31.167	0.218	34.106

Source: Sears Dividend Reinvestment Statement, January 4, 2000.

If OCPs were used, either automatic bank transfers or check, the amount invested would have been entered. Each DRIP statement usually includes all transactions since the first of the year, which makes log updates easy and not very time-consuming. Year-end annual DRIP account statements and a DRIP investment log should be kept with all tax records.

Second, a potential drawback is that DRIP programs trade shares on a specific date regardless of market price. For example, a company may purchase shares once a week on Tuesdays, once a month on the 15th day, or once a quarter on the dividend payment date. This precludes the choice of either overall market timing or stock price limit orders (buying shares at a specific predetermined price only). Selling or withdrawing from a DRIP frequently requires sending written requests. Shares are sold on the same timetable as the regularly scheduled DRIP purchases. OCPs waiting for investment in a DRIP account do not usually earn interest. These drawbacks should not be a problem if the investor is focused on long-term opportunities.

Third, there are minimum and maximum OCP dollar amounts. Although not commonly a problem, DRIP investors need to be aware of specific program limits. Some programs have very high maximum limits, such as $10,000 a month or over $200,000 a year, whereas others have OCP maximum limits as low as $1000 a month.

Dividends are considered taxable income and, just like earned income, the government wants its share. If an investor enrolls in a DRIP program where the cash dividends are reinvested, the income tax due will be paid from earned income. Although not usually a huge problem, some DRIPs allow for partial reinvestment of dividends. This means that an investor can reinvest a portion of the dividend and receive cash for the balance.

DRIPs are not for day traders, short-term traders, or investors with less than about a 3- to 5-year investing time frame. DRIPs are most popular with investors who are looking to make a long-term investment commitment to a specific management team, and whose goal is to reap potential capital gains from rising stock prices.

COSTS ASSOCIATED WITH DRIPS

DRIP fees are split into two major categories. DRIPs are segregated based on how the first shares are acquired. Either the investor buys these shares directly from the company (or its transfer agent) or from a broker.

Of the over 1600 companies offering DRIPs and direct investing options, more than 40 percent will sell the initial shares directly to the investor. These programs are called *direct stock purchase* (DSPs) or *direct enrollment stock purchase programs* (DESPs). With the easing in the mid-1990s of SEC rules regulating DRIPs and direct investing plans, more companies are allowing investors to purchase shares directly from them or their transfer agents.

Sixty percent of DRIPs require the investor to purchase initial shares elsewhere. The shares must be registered in the investor's name, and then the investor may enroll. These companies demand investors become a shareholder of record. To be a shareholder of record, investors need to purchase their initial investment through a broker and take physical delivery of the certificate of shares, thereby notifying the company that the investor is the shareholder. After enrolling, the investor sends any future OCPs directly to the company or to its agent. With these plans, there is initially a third-party broker commission along with a delivery of share certificate fee. This requirement makes the initial cost to establish these plans much higher than plans that allow for an initial direct investment. When returning the DRIP enrollment forms, an investor can include the stock certificate, and thus the number of shares is credited to the account.

For instance, Home Depot's (HD) DRIP program offers investors the option of sending directly to the company a minimum of $250 as an initial investment. HD purchases the initial stock for the DRIP accounts on the open market every week and sends a statement to the shareholders detailing their stock positions. In contrast, Honeywell (HON) requires an investor to be a registered shareholder of at least one share prior to enrolling in its DRIP program. To be a DRIP participant with Honeywell, an investor first needs to develop a relationship with a brokerage firm on-line, discount, or full service. There are minimum brokerage account balances and stock trade commissions along with share delivery fees associated with establishing an account through a broker. After the initial investment is purchased and the stock certificate has been received, the investor contacts HON and enrolls in its DRIP.

DRIPs are also categorized by whether a transaction fee is

charged. Once a DRIP is established, the program may levy a fee to purchase or sell shares. Almost half of all companies offer totally fee-free DRIPs, and there is no cost to the investor to purchase or maintain his or her DRIP investment. Companies that offer stock investing free of fees include some big names such as Coca-Cola (KO), Exxon-Mobil (EXM), Intel (INTC), and Pitney Bowes (PBI). Fee-free DRIP companies range in size from the giant conglomerates like Johnson and Johnson (JNJ) to small local banks like 1st Federal Bank (FFLC) in Florida. At last count, more than 750 companies offer fee-free DRIP programs.

Other DRIPs stipulate transaction fees for the purchase and sale of shares and may include some of the following costs:

- *Setup Fees*—$5 to $15 to establish a DRIP account
- *Termination Fees*—$5 to $15 to sell all shares and terminate the DRIP program
- *Commissions*—Fees vary per purchase or sell transaction. Some programs charge a flat per share fee ranging from $0.03 to $0.15 a share. Others charge a small percentage of the investment up to a maximum of between $2.00 and $25.00. Some charge both.

It is common for programs to charge as little as $1 per trade if the investor signs up for automatic ACH withdrawals. Some plans charge fees for termination only and some for each transaction. However, even a DRIP with relatively high fees can be an attractive and cost-effective method of accumulating shares of stock.

For example, Chicago Bridge and Iron (CBI), a Dutch company headquartered in the United States, builds oil terminals, cryogenic testing facilities, and large industrial complexes. As a Dutch company, CBI's shares are traded as American Deposit Receipts (ADRs), where one share on the New York Stock Exchange equals one share traded on the Dutch exchange. Also, as foreigners, U.S. citizens are subject to a 15 percent withholding on their dividends. CBI has a relatively high-cost DRIP program with a one-time $10 setup fee, a flat $5.00 fee per OCP, and a charge of 5 percent of the dividend up to a maximum of $5. There is a $0.10 per share commission and a $5 fee to terminate the plan. Minimum initial direct investment is $200. Minimum OCP is $50 a week and a maximum of $250,000 per week.

A DRIP investor who purchases CBI stock at a dollar cost average price of $16 per share and an annual dividend of $0.24, with a $250 initial investment and $250 a month ACH investment, would pay several different DRIP fees. CBI would charge the investor estimated first-year fees consisting of a one-time $10 setup fee, a $5 fee for the initial investment of $250, a $1.56 commission for the initial investment, a $5 fee for each monthly investment of $250, a $1.56 commission for each monthly investment, and a $2.43 fee (5 percent of dividend to a maximum of $5) per quarter for dividend reinvestment.

At the end of the first year, the investor would have invested $3250 and paid about $105 in DRIP fees (3.2 percent). If the investor had the financial ability to double the investment to $500 initially and $500 a month ACH, or $6500 the first year, CBI's DRIP fees would have been about $135 (2.0 percent). Had the investment goal been to accumulate $25,000 in CBI stock over a 12-month time frame using a $1000 initial investment and dollar cost averaging an OCP of $2000 a month, DRIP fees would be about $251 (1.0 percent). A one-time investment of $25,000 would carry first-year DRIP fees of $191 (0.7 percent). If there are no additional OCP investments, quarterly fees going forward for reinvestment of dividends would be $5. As with standard brokerage fees, the more dollars invested in CBI, the lower the purchase fees.

Some investors insist on investing only with companies charging no DRIP fees. Some avoid all high-fee DRIP programs. This is a bit like the tail wagging the dog. DRIP fees are an important consideration in stock selection, but the quality of management and anticipated future earnings and dividend growth should have a much greater impact on total investment returns.

THE STRATEGY AND ADVANTAGES OF DOLLAR COST AVERAGING

Dollar cost averaging is an investment technique that spreads investment dollars over time and rides the fluctuations of a stock's price up and down. It requires a discipline of maintaining long-term regularly scheduled investments. Instead of taking chances with market timing for specific stocks, the dollar cost averaging mechanism invests on a regular timetable. The investor's principal buys more shares when the stock is down and fewer shares when the stock advances. Much like an installment plan, dollar cost averaging with DRIPs allows investors to pay for either a predetermined goal of a specific number of shares or a reasonable dollar amount invested regularly over a specific time frame. For example, an investor wanting to own 100 shares of a stock could purchase 10 shares each quarter during the next 10 quarters. An investor may want to own $20,000 of a stock, regularly investing $1000 a month for 20 months.

As part of its blueprint, stocks are purchased during both weak and strong market cycles. Dollar cost averaging advocates the accumulation of shares in down cycles that later outperform those bought during strong market cycles. Tables 1–2, 1–3, and 1–4 outline the effect of a dollar cost averaging program during up markets, down markets, and volatile markets.

TABLE 1–2

Dollar Cost Averaging in Up Markets

Investment	Share Price	Shares Purchased	Total Shares Owned
$500	$10	50.00	50.00
$500	$16	31.25	81.25
$500	$20	25.00	106.25
$500	$20	25.00	131.25
$500	$32	15.63	146.88

TABLE 1–3

Dollar Cost Averaging in Down Markets

Investment	Share Price	Shares Purchased	Total Shares Owned
$500	$32	15.63	15.63
$500	$20	25.00	40.63
$500	$20	25.00	65.63
$500	$16	31.25	96.88
$500	$10	50.00	146.88

TABLE 1—4

Dollar Cost Averaging in Volatile Markets

Investment	Share Price	Shares Purchased	Total Shares Owned
$500	$32	15.63	15.63
$500	$20	25.00	40.63
$500	$16	31.25	71.88
$500	$20	25.00	96.88
$500	$32	15.63	112.51

As shown in Table 1–2, the total investment of $2500 purchased 146.88 shares with an average cost of $17.02 a share. The investor's average share cost is 15 percent below the average market price of $19.60 over the same time period. Due to buying more shares when a stock is cheaper, a dollar cost averaging portfolio will always have an average cost lower than the average market price.

The total investment of $2500 in a down market, as shown in Table 1–3, again purchased 146.88 shares, with an average cost of $17.02 and an average market price of $19.60. With the stock down in price and an average cost below the average market price, to break even on the investment principal the stock would have to rally to $17 for the dollar cost averaging investor rather than rallying to almost $20 to reach the average market price.

A dollar cost averaged $2500 investment in a volatile market (Table 1–4) would have purchased 112.51 shares with an average cost of $22.22 a share or 7.4 percent below the average market price of $24.00 a share, also creating additional gains.

Dividend reinvestment programs with an ACH bank transfer alternative provide a cost-effective tool for an automatic savings and investing plan using a long-term dollar cost averaging strategy. If an investor makes regular stock purchases, increased investment returns over the long term can become standard.

OVERALL DRIP AND DIRECT INVESTMENT STRATEGY

DRIP investing maximizes the benefits of compounding returns from both an increasing cash dividend and dollar cost averaging stock purchases. DRIPs are long term in nature, and direct stock purchases and sales are not usually efficient for short-term investors. The goal of DRIPs is to accumulate stock assets over the long haul and to build personal wealth one dividend payment and OCP at a time. Minimum long-term DRIP horizons should be in the range of 3 to 5 years, and many investors maintain a DRIP account for 35 to 50 years. It is not uncommon to establish a specific investment dollar or number of shares goal per DRIP account; when that is reached, OCPs are transferred to a new DRIP investment, letting the dividends of the initial stock selection continue to accumulate.

On April 14, 2000, the Dow Jones Industrial Average experienced its largest single-day point drop ever—falling 617 points. CNN's leading financial newscast, "MoneyLine," interviewed the chief economist for Merrill Lynch. When asked who was doing the selling, the chief economist replied, "It was not the little guys and it's not the long-term investor. Our studies of stock market corrections over the past 30 years indicate that 55 percent of long-term investors do nothing. Twenty percent of long-term investors add to their stock positions during market corrections, and only 25 percent sell positions." The point drop, by and large, was not caused from DRIP investors unloading their shares. DRIPs and direct investing programs have become the ultimate investing tool for the buy and hold investor.

The most popular alternative to DRIPs and direct investing is to buy a mutual fund and forget about it. Many investors do not make the time to research investing opportunities and depend on fund managers, but at a cost. Have you ever wondered why there are over 7000 mutual funds listed in *The Wall Street Journal* and other financial newspapers? The answer is simple: We live in a capitalist society, and the mutual fund asset management business is extremely profitable. Asset managers thrive off the annual fees investors pay them based on the current value of their investment. As the account values increase over the years due to higher additional contributions, dividends, and capital gains, so do the annual management fees.

DRIP investing offers much lower transaction costs than most mutual funds without asset-based management fees. DRIP investors find they are putting more of their hard-earned money to work for them. With low minimum monthly and relatively high maximum OCPs, DRIPs and direct investing options are an easy method of developing a diversified portfolio of both stocks and bonds, regardless of whether the investment is $100 or $100,000. Much like the most popular of funds, long-term investors should have exposure to all industrial sectors and invest in both stocks and bonds. It is easy to develop a list of top-quality diversified companies offering DRIPs with no ongoing purchase fees and allowing investors to purchase the initial shares direct. This list includes: Bell-South (BLS), a telecommunications company and one of the "Baby Bells"; Connecticut Water Service (CTWS), a water utility company serving the northeast; McGraw-Hill (MHP), publisher of this book; 3M (MMM), a consumer products giant; Pfizer (PFE), a leading pharmaceutical company; and Washington Mutual (WM), the largest savings and loan institution in the United States.

It is important to select all investments carefully. With long-term investing, well-managed companies that focus on improving shareholder value are preferred to incubator start-up firms with no real cash flow, profits, or dividends. Benjamin Graham is considered by many to be the Father of Value Investing. Warren Buffett, the multibillionaire from Omaha, is his most famous student. Graham believed that well-managed companies provide the best long-term investment returns over the long haul. Although every investor may not agree with most of the investment commandments preached by Graham, they provide a useful yardstick in measuring an investor's own experience. Our favorites are:

- Be an investor, not a speculator
- Understand the difference between price and value
- Rake the market for bargains
- Don't expect every decision to be perfect
- Rule #1: Diversify with stocks and bonds
- Rule #2: Diversify with a wide range of stocks
- When in doubt, stick to quality
- Be patient
- Think for yourself

With these simple guidelines, a DRIP investor can easily build a rewarding long-term investment portfolio.

TABLE 1-5

Johnson Controls Dividend Reinvested, Annual OCP $200

Year	Avg. Price	Div. Rate	Div. Paid	OCP	Total $ Invested	Shares Bought	Shares Owned	Value	Capital Invested
00	$57.68	$1.09	$214.33	$200	$414.33	7.08	203.59	$11,756	$3,400
99	$64.50	$1.00	$190.57	$200	$390.57	6.06	196.63	$12,683	$3,200
98	$43.13	$0.92	$167.49	$200	$367.49	8.52	190.57	$8,219	$3,000
97	$36.13	$0.86	$148.28	$200	$348.28	9.64	182.05	$6,578	$2,800
96	$23.75	$0.82	$129.99	$200	$329.99	13.89	172.41	$4,095	$2,600
95	$29.50	$0.78	$115.31	$200	$315.31	10.69	158.52	$4,676	$2,400
94	$23.13	$0.72	$97.19	$200	$297.19	12.85	147.83	$3,419	$2,200
93	$18.50	$0.68	$81.44	$200	$281.44	15.21	134.98	$2,497	$2,000
92	$12.68	$0.62	$61.47	$200	$261.47	20.62	119.77	$1,519	$1,800
91	$13.50	$0.62	$49.99	$200	$249.99	18.52	99.15	$1,339	$1,600
90	$14.38	$0.60	$38.43	$200	$238.43	16.58	80.63	$1,159	$1,400
89	$18.88	$0.58	$30.16	$200	$230.16	11.08	64.05	$1,209	$1,200
Initial Share Purchased		52.97					52.97		$1,000
Profit: Total Capital Investment		$3,400							
Total Profit		$8,356							
% Gain		245%							
Total Dividend Received		$1,304							

Source: Value Line Investment Survey.

17

TABLE 1-6

Apache Corp Dividend Reinvested, Annual OCP $200

Year	Avg. Price	Div. Rate	Div. Paid	OCP	Total $ Invested	Shares Bought	Shares Owned	Value	Capital Invested
00	$55.50	$0.28	$75.38	$200	$275.38	4.96	274.19	$15,218	$3,400
99	$19.25	$0.28	$71.44	$200	$271.44	14.10	269.23	$5,183	$3,200
98	$33.13	$0.28	$69.16	$200	$269.16	8.12	255.13	$8,452	$3,000
97	$38.38	$0.28	$67.21	$200	$267.21	6.96	247.00	$9,480	$2,800
96	$26.88	$0.28	$64.46	$200	$264.46	9.84	240.04	$6,452	$2,600
95	$23.25	$0.28	$61.31	$200	$261.31	11.24	230.20	$5,352	$2,400
94	$25.00	$0.28	$58.42	$200	$258.42	10.34	218.96	$5,474	$2,200
93	$21.38	$0.28	$55.08	$200	$255.08	11.93	208.63	$4,460	$2,000
92	$13.38	$0.28	$49.85	$200	$249.85	18.67	196.70	$2,632	$1,800
91	$12.25	$0.28	$44.26	$200	$244.26	19.94	178.02	$2,181	$1,600
90	$15.25	$0.28	$39.86	$200	$239.86	15.73	158.08	$2,411	$1,400
89	$8.50	$0.28	$32.76	$200	$232.76	24.72	142.36	$1,210	$1,200
							117.64		$1,000

Initial Share Purchased 117.64

Profit: Total Capital Investment $3,400

Total Profit $11,818

% Gain 347%

Total Dividend Received $666

Source: Value Line Investment Survey.

TABLE 1-7

SunTrust Bank Dividend Reinvested, Annual OCP $200

Year	Avg. Price	Div. Rate	Div. Paid	OCP	Total $ Invested	Shares Bought	Shares Owned	Value	Capital Invested
00	$60.50	$1.42	$353.44	$200	$553.44	9.14	258.04	$15,612	$3,400
99	$70.50	$1.38	$333.05	$200	$533.05	7.56	248.90	$17,548	$3,200
98	$69.25	$1.00	$235.06	$200	$435.06	6.28	241.34	$16,713	$3,000
97	$50.00	$0.93	$210.96	$200	$410.96	8.22	235.06	$11,753	$2,800
96	$34.50	$0.83	$179.16	$200	$379.16	10.99	226.84	$7,826	$2,600
95	$26.00	$0.74	$149.77	$200	$349.77	13.45	215.85	$5,612	$2,400
94	$23.25	$0.66	$124.37	$200	$324.37	13.95	202.40	$4,706	$2,200
93	$21.50	$0.58	$101.17	$200	$301.17	14.01	188.45	$4,052	$2,000
92	$18.13	$0.52	$82.60	$200	$282.60	15.59	174.44	$3,163	$1,800
91	$12.00	$0.47	$64.31	$200	$264.31	22.03	158.85	$1,906	$1,600
90	$10.50	$0.43	$48.65	$200	$248.65	23.68	136.83	$1,437	$1,400
89	$10.68	$0.39	$36.51	$200	$236.51	22.14	113.14	$1,208	$1,200
Initial share Purchased				93.63			93.63		$1,000

Profit Total Capital Investment	$3,400
Total Profit	$12,212
% Gain	359%
Total Dividend Received	$1,891

Source: Value Line Investment Survey.

19

EXAMPLES OF LONG-TERM DRIP INVESTING

Assume an investor decides to initially invest $1000 in 1989 in three different DRIP programs, to reinvest all dividends, and to add an additional OCP of $200 a year to each. This investor chooses Johnson Controls (JCI), a leading manufacturer of automobile interiors and auto parts; Apache Corp (APA), a mid-size oil exploration company; and SunTrust Banks (STI), a southeastern regional bank. Tables 1–5 to 1–7 outline the DRIPs in each stock from 1989 to 2000.

In these three stocks, the individual initially invested $3000 and over the next 12 years contributed an additional $10,200 for a total capital contribution of $13,200. The portfolio is worth $42,586 ($11,756 in Johnson Controls, $15,218 in Apache Corp, and $15,612 in SunTrust Banks) and is generating $642 a year in dividends, offering a current portfolio yield of 1.6 percent. Since establishing the DRIP programs, the investor has received over $3800 in dividends, and the current cash dividend yield based on the capital contributed would be about 4.6 percent, respectable by most standards.

If the investor had been a really high roller back in 1988 and had the financial resources to invest $10,000 combined and $2000 annually in JCI, APA, and STI, the capital invested in each DRIP account would have been $34,000, for a total capital contribution of $134,000. The portfolio would be worth over $424,200 ($117,200 in Johnson Controls, $151,500 in Apache Corp, and $155,500 in SunTrust Banks) and generating $6400 a year in dividends. The total dividends received over this period would have equaled almost $40,000.

CHAPTER 2

Stocks, Bonds, and Six Steps for Successful DRIP Investing

Key Concepts

- What Are Common Stocks, Corporate Bonds, Preferred Stocks, and Government Bonds?
- Compounded Annual Rates of Return by Decade
- Six Basic Steps to Successful DRIP Investing

Companies live or die based on two line items found in their financial statements: operating cash flow and working capital. *Operating cash flow* is the amount of cash produced by operating the specific business, whereas *working capital* is the amount of cash on hand to invest in the business for market expansion, capital improvements, and new product development. To generate additional capital, companies can either offer to sell equity, or ownership, in the company or to borrow using loans. The instruments used to sell equity are called *stocks*. Loans sold to investors are called *bonds*. Bond investors can be individuals, bank investment portfolios, and life insurance companies. The following is a brief description of each. For more detailed information, refer to two sister books, *All About Stocks* and *All About Bonds*.

COMMON STOCKS

Companies are either private or public. Generically, private companies are those that are owned by a small number of individuals or organizations and whose assets are not readily available for sale to the general public. Most small businesses are examples of private companies. For instance, investors have a very hard time investing in the local Ma and Pa Lumber Yard because the assets are controlled and owned by Ma and Pa. In contrast, public companies offer their assets for sale or for collateral to the general public either as business partners or lenders. A company may decide that the general public wants to invest in its business and will issue shares of common stock as the means to attract public capital. The company determines its value as an organization, which consists of its assets less its liabilities, and offers shares to anyone willing to buy. The share certificates represent ownership in the assets of the company and can be transferred among investors. Home Depot (HD), operating up the street from Ma and Pa, is a public company interested in having its assets owned by the general public. Once the shares are sold through an initial public offering (IPO) and if there is sufficient interest, the shares are then traded among investors. The company may sell new shares to the general public, generating additional capital, which is called a *secondary offering*.

A shareholder owns a specific percentage of all net assets and can lay claim to company profits. For example, on January 1, 2000, HD had 2.3 billion common stock shares outstanding, revenues of $38 billion, net assets of about $12.7 billion, and net income of $2.3 billion. One share in HD represented 1/2,300,000,000 of HD's net assets, about $5.52 in assets and $1.00 in earnings. In reality, the company usually retains the majority of net profits not distributed in dividends. HD's management decided to reward shareholders and return a portion of the $2.4 billion generated in operational cash flow in 1999. HD paid $255 million in dividends to its 195,000 shareholders, which amounted to $0.113 a share. HD paid its dividend in cash, but sometimes a company may choose to reward shareholders by paying dividends in more shares. This is called a *stock dividend* and usually amounts to less than 25 percent of the number of shares owned prior to the stock dividend.

As the earnings and net assets of the company grow through profitable business dealings, so should the value of the shares. However, there is a point where the company has made so much money per share that its share price gets quite high and may be unattractive to new investors. For example, stocks selling at $53 a share are considered more attractive to a wider audience of investors than stock selling at $53,000 a share. Most investors prefer to own 1000 shares valued at $53 each rather than 1 share at $53,000. This is in part psychological because the large dollar share price can sometimes be daunting, but mainly it is for ease of liquidity. It is far easier to buy or sell half a 1000-share position than to sell half of a 1-share position. When the shares reach a market price that management considers unattractively high, they may elect to complete a *stock split.* A stock split increases the company's number of shares outstanding and gives each current shareholder additional shares based on current holdings. The individual investor has the same value in the company, but the value is spread over more shares as the market price per share usually decreases by the ratio of the stock split.

For example, an investor purchasing 100 shares of HD on January 3, 1997, at the market price of $50 a share would have experienced three different stock splits by the beginning of 2000. HD split their stock three for two in July 1997. Shareholders, including those with DRIPs, on the Stock Split Date of Record owned three shares after the split for every two shares held before the split, including fractional shares. One hundred shares of HD became 150 shares. HD was trading at about $60 before the split, so 100 shares were worth about $6000. After the stock split, HD traded at $40 a share, and the 150 shares represented the same dollar value as before. With additional shares issued at no added capital investment to the investor, the average cost per share for all shares was reduced by one third. In July 1998, HD again split its stock, but this time two for one. The 150 shares became 300 shares. In December 1999, HD once more split its stock three for two, and the 300 shares became 450 shares. Between January 1997 and January 2000, an HD investor would have experienced a 450 percent increase in the number of shares owned, and the average cost paid for those shares was reduced from the original purchase price of $50 a share to $11.19. On January 2, 2000, HD stock was trading at $69, and the original $5000 investment had grown to $31,100. Had HD not split its stock, based on market valuations, the original shares purchased at $50 would have been trading at around $311 a share.

As an owner in the company, no matter how many shares owned, every shareholder typically has the right to vote on various issues that affect a company. Usually based on the annual meeting of stockholders, investors are offered the chance to vote by proxy. The vast majority of common stock comes with voting rights. There may be instances, however, where the company has issued two classes of stock, "A" and "B" shares, where only holders of "A" might have the right to vote. With companies offering more than one class of stock, it may be preferable to own the same class as management, which is usually the voting class.

CORPORATE BONDS

Companies can also generate capital by borrowing money, either from a financial institution or the public. Money borrowed directly from the bank is commonly called a *loan*, whereas selling a loan to investors is called a *bond*. Interest and principal payment terms for loans are controlled by the bank; by contrast, the company controls the terms of the interest and repayment of bonds. Like bank loans, the terms of a bond cannot be changed without the consent of both the bond issuer and bondholder. In the case of HD, the company had about $750 million in long-term debt outstanding at the end of 1999. Approximately $250 million was owed to financial institutions and $500 million to the general public. An investor could lend money to HD by buying one of its notes or bonds, which would pay a predetermined amount of interest. The principal is stipulated to be repaid at a certain date, called the *bond maturity date*. As with any lending relationship, the company may use its assets as collateral for the loan. Investors in the bonds have ownership rights to the assets designated as collateral in case of default. Bondholders are not owners of the company and have no voting privileges.

PREFERRED STOCKS

Preferred stocks are a hybrid security that combines the steady income feature of bonds with the equity feature of common stocks. In common stocks, the dividends are not predetermined by the terms of the investment, and management can increase or decrease common stock dividend rates at will. Preferred stocks, in contrast, usually have a fixed dividend rate, much like a bond, that does not fluctuate. The fixed dividend of a preferred stock is a key distinguishing feature of preferred stock and makes it a relatively stable investment. Preferred stocks may not have a claim on profits and assets of the company depending on the terms.

Many preferred stocks carry the option for management to convert to common shares at a predetermined exchange rate. These are called *convertible preferred* stocks. For example, Sea Containers (SCR.B) is a large lessor of shipping containers for international ocean-going vessels and an operator of ferries and luxury hotels. In the early 1990s, SCR.B generated an additional $109.7 million in working capital by issuing new preferred stock with an annual dividend of $4.00 a share, convertible at an exchange rate to 2.73 shares of common. The preferred stock traded at around $60 a share. In 1998 the company decided to redeem the preferred issue, and shareholders received 273 shares of SCR.B common stock for every 100 shares of preferred stock. The annual dividend rate for the common stock was only $0.70 a share, compared with the $4 dividend per share paid to the preferred stockholders. The company saved cash flow by paying $1.91 in common share dividends ($0.70 times 2.73 shares from the conversion) where they had been paying $4 in preferred dividends.

Another major difference among common stocks, preferred stocks, and corporate bonds is their position in the pecking order for repayment if there is a liquidation or bankruptcy. Banks and financial institutions are the first to get repaid. Next the bondholders are eligible for their share. Different series and levels of bonds and the specific terms of each determine the order for disbursement. Preferred stockholders are next in line. Common stockholders get the balance, which, in a bankruptcy case, is usually not even enough money to call your broker.

Unlike bonds, preferred dividends are accounted for on the corporate financial statement as dividends, not interest. Interest is deductible from operating earnings before calculating income taxes. Preferred stock dividends, like common stock dividends, are paid with after-tax dollars, making preferred stock dividends more expensive to corporations than bond interest. Companies do not usually prefer to issue preferred stock due to this difference. Unlike common stockholders, preferred shareholders do not have a shareholder's vote.

GOVERNMENT BONDS

As is common knowledge, the United States is the world's largest debtor nation. Our government owes over $5.8 trillion. The general public owns $3.7 trillion of our nation's debt through ownership of US Treasury bills, notes, and bonds. The balance of the debt is owed to foreigners and other US government agencies, such as the Social Security Administration. In the case of government bonds, which are readily available for the smaller investor, individuals can lend money to the US government, which issues a bond certificate along with a promise to pay regularly scheduled interest payments. The terms of the bond require repayment of principal at some specific date in the future. Considered the investment benchmark for both capital preservation and relatively risk-free returns over the long term, US Treasury debt is fairly stable in price and offers interest yields that are both safe and secure.

Investors have many bond maturity or repayment choices when selecting bond investments. The time frame for bond investing is based on both the nature of the investment (10-year bonds should be bought with the goal of holding for 10 years) and the length of time until the funds are needed.

COMPOUNDED ANNUAL RATES
OF RETURN BY DECADE

For financial needs greater than 10 years in the future, stocks have proved to generate higher returns over corporate and government bonds or short-term money market accounts and Treasury bills. According to Ibbotson Associates' book, *Stocks, Bonds, Bills and Inflation, Edition 2000,* Table 2–1 lists 10-year compounded annual returns by decade. The data are based on investments made at the beginning of the decade and held until the end.

With the exception of the 1970s, the compounded return for S&P 500 Index over a decade period has outpaced government bonds, corporate bonds, and inflation. The average annual 10-year compounded return, adjusted for inflation, for the S&P 500 Index was 9.6 percent over the past five decades. When adjusted for inflation, bonds experienced negative returns in the 1950s, 1960s, and 1970s. During the past 50 years, only in the 1980s and 1990s did bonds provide investors with positive inflation-adjusted returns.

TABLE 2-1

Compounded Annual Rate of Return by Decade, Dividends and Interest Reinvested

	1950s (%)	1960s (%)	1970s (%)	1980s (%)	1990s (%)
S&P 500 Index	19.4	7.8	5.9	17.5	18.2
Small Cap Stocks	16.9	15.5	11.5	15.8	15.1
Long Term Corporate Bonds	1.0	1.7	6.2	13.0	8.4
Long Term Gov't Bonds	0.1	1.4	5.5	12.6	8.8
Gov't T Bills	1.9	3.9	6.3	8.9	4.9
Inflation	2.2	2.5	7.4	5.1	2.9

Source: Ibbotson Associates, *Stocks, Bonds, Bills and Inflation, Edition 2000.*

SIX BASIC STEPS TO SUCCESSFUL DRIP INVESTING

DRIP and direct investing can be as simple or as complicated as the investor chooses. A DRIP investment portfolio for one investor may involve a $50 per month automatic withdrawal to one or several DRIP programs, whereas another investor may own over 50 DRIPs and send in OCPs to selected companies. All investors, regardless of past performance or sophistication, need to review these basic DRIP investing steps. Because investing is an ongoing and fluid process, an annual review of goals and performance is required for optimum returns. Over time, an investor will develop a pattern of successful investing. Like all great pursuits, however, it begins with the first step.

1. *Pick a Goal, Any Goal.* The first step is to determine a worthy financial goal, which should not be a difficult task. An easy goal is building assets for retirement, as the quicker the assets build, the sooner retirement can begin. The goals can be as serious as investing for a future generation's education expenses, or as frivolous as saving for a larger sailboat. The goals should be realistic and obtainable, with the savings rate necessary for achievement falling within annual earned income restraints.

2. *Reflect and Educate.* With the world of investment alternatives always expanding, every investor needs to focus on

stock selections that fall within their personal risk-related comfort levels. Generally speaking, most investments can be categorized as *aggressive* (more risk, more expected returns), *moderate* (average risk, average expected returns), or *conservative* (low risk, lower expected returns). If a speculative investment, whose value swoons and soars in price, keeps the investor awake at night, it may be time to rethink the risk criteria of the selection process. On the other side of the spectrum, a money market account may not provide the returns necessary to reach the financial goal within the time frame desired. Common stock returns have historically outperformed bonds and money market accounts, but bonds and money market accounts provide less risk. Within the scope of stocks, the individual choices are virtually limitless. It is important to consistently update our knowledge of new social and business trends, as both provide investment opportunities. No business or investment selection operates in a vacuum, and overall economic factors can greatly affect investment returns.

3. *Research Specific Companies.* DRIPs are long-term investments, and uncovering companies with excellent management should be the primary focus. Within every industry, there are well-managed and not-so-well-managed companies. Because the development and implementation of successful business strategies and action plans to grow profits and dividends will ultimately determine the value of an investment, the best management will offer the best long-term returns. There are several easy methods of comparing management performance, such as operating cash flow and return on equity, within the array of financial numbers available to all investors.

4. *Develop Diversified Portfolio.* The one common theme from leading financial advisors is the need to diversify every investor's portfolio. Having 12 different Internet start-up companies or owning several mutual funds with the same top-10 stock holdings is not considered diversification. Within broad categories of investment choices and industrial sectors, the success of a diversified portfolio lies in ownership of each category.

5. *Take the Plunge, Get in the Game.* After developing goals, savings budgets, and a list of specific investments, the investor investigates the easiest, lowest-cost means of acquiring the asset. It may be direct from the company, direct from the US Treasury Department, or through a broker.

6. *Keep Up.* Although DRIPs are long term in nature, it is not usually a good idea to enroll and then put the account statement in the back of the closet, not to see the light of day for years to come. The company will send quarterly and annual reports, which should be read and analyzed. At least annually, dust off the portfolio and refigure asset allocation, overall portfolio performance along with individual stock returns. Revisit each specific financial goal and determine the progress toward accomplishment. If one sector of the portfolio has outperformed others, resulting in an overweighing in the overall portfolio, rebalance to a more equal allocation.

EXAMPLE OF MONTHLY INVESTMENT IN WAL-MART

An individual enrolls in the DRIP program offered by Wal-Mart (WMT), the largest discount retailer, in January 1998 and has $200 a month automatically withdrawn from a bank account. Wal-Mart has been an excellent long-term growth stock. As long as the consumer-spending sector of the economy remains strong, WMT should continue to do quite well. WMT is starting to aggressively expand overseas, opening its first of 10 stores in the United Kingdom. On the first of every month, WMT's transfer agent electronically withdraws $200 and buys stock, and quarterly dividends are reinvested.

Table 2–2 outlines the value of the DRIP account from January 1998 to March 1999.

The investor would have contributed $3000 and the DRIP account would have been worth $4550. Total fees paid by the DRIP investor would have been $15, to make 15 different purchases over a 15-month time frame.

Wal-Mart
Monthly Investment $200

Date	Price Per Share	$ Invested	DRIP Fees	Div. Paid	Shares Bought	Shares Owned	Value	Total $ Invested	Average Cost Per Share
Mar-99	$93.44	$200.00	$1		2.130	48.703	$4550.65	$3000	$61.60
Feb-99	$84.75	$200.00	$1		2.348	46.573	$3947.05	$2800	$60.12
Jan-99	$82.00	$203.34	$1	$3.34	2.468	44.225	$3626.43	$2600	$58.79
Dec-98	$77.75	$200.00	$1		2.559	41.757	$3246.62	$2400	$57.48
Nov-98	$73.67	$200.00	$1		2.701	39.198	$2887.86	$2200	$56.13
Oct-98	$66.56	$202.68	$1	$2.68	3.030	36.497	$2429.09	$2000	$54.80
Sep-98	$60.50	$200.00	$1		3.289	33.466	$2024.73	$1800	$53.79
Aug-98	$65.04	$200.00	$1		3.060	30.177	$1962.71	$1600	$53.02
Jul-98	$68.84	$201.94	$1	$1.94	2.919	27.118	$1866.86	$1400	$51.63
Jun-98	$57.74	$200.00	$1		3.446	24.199	$1397.32	$1200	$49.59
May-98	$55.30	$200.00	$1		3.599	20.753	$1147.58	$1000	$48.19
Apr-98	$53.06	$201.07	$1	$1.07	3.771	17.154	$910.13	$800	$46.64
Mar-98	$49.88	$200.00	$1		3.990	13.383	$667.55	$600	$44.83
Feb-98	$45.14	$200.00	$1		4.408	9.393	$424.04	$400	$42.58
Jan-98	$39.92	$200.00	$1		4.985	4.985	$199.00	$200	$40.10

Source: *www.quicken.com.*

Why Invest in the First Place?

Key Concepts

- Pay Yourself First
- How to Categorize Long-Term Financial Needs
- The Advantages and Disavantages of Tax-Deferred and Custodial Accounts
- Compounding Dividends and Dollar Cost Averaging in Action
- Inflation and DRIP Investing

Don't listen to your kids. Money does not grow on trees. Money does, however, grow like trees. Imagine a sunny but barren corner of your backyard. You have two choices: Either do nothing or plant a tree and some flowers. If you choose the former, the corner will always be bright, but unattractive. If you choose the latter, you will have set a goal to improve the appearance of that specific corner of your property. To accomplish this goal, you need to first learn about the various types of trees and flowers that will thrive within the parameters of the location. Your choices should also fit your gardening style: Do you enjoy gardening or is it a chore, ranking right up there with trips to the dentist? Do you pay someone else to do your gardening for you? The selection of the specific trees and flowers has options, too. Do you want a plant that requires a lot of maintenance, or is a maintenance-free plant important? You can either buy a tree and some flowers or grow them from seed. Usually, the older and more mature the plants, the more costly they are.

After much consideration, you may chose a 6-foot Hawthorne tree surrounded by colorful daylilies having various blooming times. With this list, you shop the local nurseries, thumb through a few catalogs, and maybe even search on-line looking for the best bargains. You then plant them, fertilize them, water them, and weed them. Over the years, the Hawthorne flowers profusely. In the fall, its red berries fall to the ground and sprout new trees. The daylilies multiply and are divided several times, spreading more color under the tree. After several growing seasons, you would have achieved your goal of improving the appearance of the corner of the property.

Growing personal wealth is much akin to growing the Hawthorne tree and daylilies. Both the investor and gardener need to research their various options and factor in their personal lifestyles. The gardener needs to buy the initial tree and plants or even the seeds. An investor needs to buy an asset—stocks, bonds, or even a money market account. Similar to the volunteer trees that sprout at the base of the Hawthorne, top-quality companies sometimes spin off assets to shareholders in the form of new companies, expanding the shareholders' asset base. For optimum performance, the gardener needs to spend time every growing season cultivating, fertilizing, and weeding, and the investor needs to maintain his or her knowledge of investment choices and overall market/economic factors. As with the gardener who constantly stunts plant growth by annual pruning, an investor who withdraws dividends and interest will realize smaller account balances in the future. If properly cultivated and sustained, personal wealth, Hawthorne trees, and daylilies will grow into things of beauty.

We all have current and future financial needs. It is a basic fact of life. We need a roof over our head, food on the table, and clothes on our backs. If married, your spouse and children also have the same basic needs. Increasing levels of education often lead to improved lifestyles and increasing incomes. Someday we all want to stop working for a living and either do it for fun or do something else. However, each of these have one common thread—they all cost money. Earned wages, bonuses, and commissions, either through an employer or as a self-employed individual, provide us with income to pay our monthly bills and, hopefully, have a bit left over. Granted, some years there is a bit more left over than others. If we are extremely lucky, we may fall into inheritance, game show winnings, or some other type of financial windfall.

The decision-making process for a gardener is much like that for an investor. A basic gardening choice needs to be made—do nothing or spend a few hours and a few dollars a year improving the appearance. With personal finances, investors have similar basic decisions concerning what happens to the bit of income left over or the lump sum monetary windfall. Do you do nothing and spend it or do you attempt to build on that extra capital? We have to assume you chose the latter or you would have put this book down by now.

Investors' financial goals usually fall into several well-known categories. These include saving to pay for short-term expenses, investing to build a family financial foundation and financial safety net, investing for a specific expense for a specific time in the future, and investing to generate income for retirement living expenses. The first step in achieving any financial goal, however, is to set aside the *seed* capital.

In other words, pay yourself first.

PAY YOURSELF FIRST

All income comes from either people at work or from capital at work. The ability to earn an income and to generate personal capital is one of our greatest individual assets. Earned income is the reward for people at work, whereas dividends, interest, and capital gains are the rewards of capital at work. If an investor saves 12 cents from every dollar of earned income and achieves a 10 percent annual return, in just over 6 years the account would be worth 1 year's income. All too often, savings for future needs get lost in the pile of today's monthly bills. However, it is important to begin the habit of saving and investing 12 percent of your income. Over time, the funds saved are allocated to different accounts achieving specific financial goals. The easiest method of paying yourself first is to have DRIP ACH automatic withdrawals scheduled immediately after each pay period. As a financial goal is obtained, a regular savings and investing plan can begin funding the next financial goal.

REGULAR SAVINGS PLANS CREATE SEED MONEY

Investors should maintain a steady savings plan from earned income. As income grows over the years, so does the annual amount saved and invested. Even if investment choices underperform the historic return for the S&P Index, this seed money can grow into a substantial portfolio. Let us assume an investor begins a career at age 23 with an income of $15,450. At age 28, earned income is $26,866; at age 33, $48,559; at age 38, $70,458; at age 43, $106,214. Twenty-five years later, at age 48, earned income is $166,302. Table 3–1 outlines a 12 percent annual savings plan at an 11 percent annual return.

Over a 25-year career, the investor had saved $205,882. At an 11 percent annual return, the account balance would be worth over $630,000.

What if the individual was not as frugal and only saved 8 percent of earned income? The first-year investment would have been $1236. At the same 11 percent return, the account would have been worth $92,880 at age 38 and $402,480 at age 48. Although about one-

T A B L E   3–1

Annual Investments Based On 12 Percent Savings Rate of Earned Income and an 11 Percent Annual Return

Age	Income	12% Savings Rate	Value of Account at 11% Annual Return
23	$15,450	$1,854	$2,058
28	$26,866	$3,224	$18,251
33	$48,559	$5,827	$56,990
38	$70,458	$8,455	$139,320
43	$106,214	$12,746	$299,139
48	$166,302	$19,956	$630,720

third smaller than the previous account balance from saving 12 percent of income, capital contributed was $68,628 less over the 25-year period.

RETIREMENT

The financial requirements for retirement are vastly different for different people. However, retirement centers around one simple fact: The quality of life in retirement is directly linked to the amount of assets produced through saving and investing over the long term. Always stash away at least the minimum IRA contribution allowed by the government. In an Individual Retirement Account (IRA) or an employer-sponsored 401(k) retirement account, dividends, interest, and capital gains accumulate tax-deferred, and money always grows faster when account balances are not annually reduced by paying taxes. The first $38 of every weekly savings plan should be sent right to your IRA or 401(k) account. All other savings and investments come second. The compounding of increasing dividends on a tax-deferred basis is a very attractive benefit of DRIP investing for retirement needs.

SHORT-TERM EXPENSES

Every investor should have a money market or savings account with a balance of between 6 months and 1 year of income. This can be used for foreseeable future expenditures such as replacing the old dishwasher, paying for a vacation, or making a down payment on a new car. Short-term savings accounts can also be used in case of a heath issue or unforeseen accident. Possibly earned income is seasonable and a savings plan may assist in evening out income peaks and valleys. Savings accounts should be safe and secure and have ease of access and liquidity. Banks, credit unions, and savings and loans are popular for this type of savings account. Interest rates are very low, and savings accounts usually yield between 3.5 percent and 5.0 percent. Second in importance only to tax-deferred retirement investments, short-term expense accounts tend to insulate long-term investments against premature selling. When the old jalopy finally bites the dust, with an adequately funded short-term expense account, an investor should not have to sell long-term stock investments for the relatively small down payment.

FAMILY FINANCIAL FOUNDATION AND FINANCIAL SAFETY NET

Much like a well-built house stands on a great foundation, an investor's overall personal financial strategy should be the long-term accumulation of high-quality assets that can be either liquidated when necessary or retained to increase personal wealth. Investing to build a financial foundation and financial safety net should be a fundamental necessity for every family. The objective should be to have a minimum of 1 or 2 year's income saved for those unforeseen and catastrophic events, like uninsured flood damage, a medical procedure not covered by insurance, or loss of your job. Building a basic financial foundation at any age is as easy as opening an account at your local stockbroker, discount house, or otherwise enrolling in several DRIP programs. The investment goals of these accounts are long-term capital gains and increasing dividends. DRIP accounts are long-term tools investors use to build a basic financial foundation.

SPECIFIC EXPENSE AT A SPECIFIC TIME IN THE FUTURE

As an investor gets older, income should increase. As income goes up, the ability to save and invest more each year also goes up. After a retirement account, a short-term savings account, and financial foundation accounts have been funded and have grown into a total value equaling about 1.5 to 3 years' income, an investor should begin analyzing other future expenses. These may include a second home that can be used during retirement years or future college expenses for children and grandchildren. Different from the basic financial foundation, investing for a specific expense for a specific time in the future usually entails a specific monetary goal, such as $100,000 in 20 years. Monthly contributions can be diverted from accounts whose goals have been met to new accounts focused on these specific new goals. DRIPs and direct investing should be part of the financial plan developed to reach these specific goals.

SEPARATE ACCOUNTS

It is common for an investor to have several active financial accounts. By segregating accounts by financial goal, it becomes easier to track the progress of achieving that goal and to stay the course. With the advent of electronic bank withdrawals and ACH transfers, it is easy to have $1000 invested in five different investments or even $50 a month in each of 10 separate DRIP accounts. For example, a typical family with three kids may have the following accounts:

- Money market account
- IRA
- Family foundation
- Custodial account—child A
- College account—child A
- IRA account—child A
- Custodial account—child B
- College account—child B
- IRA account—child B
- Custodial account—child C
- College account—child C
- IRA account—child C

Within each of these accounts, there may be multiple DRIP investments generating quarterly statements. This may seem like an abundance of accounts and a maze of record keeping. In practice, however, separating accounts by use helps attain that specific goal. Each account has a different specific purpose, and it is far easier to determine how you are progressing toward your goals of funding specific future expenses if money for each expenditure is kept separate. Maintaining a simple log by account, either computerized or manual, of all investments makes for easy organization. Maintaining a series of spreadsheets, especially with a computer, takes just a few minutes a month. With the profusion of financial websites on the Internet, portfolio tracking by account becomes a snap.

This is not a new concept. It is not uncommon for families to keep several large manila envelopes marked for specific expenses. One envelope is labeled *Utility Bills*, another *Rent*, and another *Food*. With every weekly paycheck, these families first deposit money into a savings account for their financial foundation and then place specific amounts of money into each envelope. When each bill is due, there is sufficient money in each envelope to cover it. Families know at any given moment how they are positioned to pay each bill coming due. Updating this theory for the new millennium, how better to determine whether you have sufficient funds to pay $10,000 to $30,000 per year for college tuition than to have that money in specified college fund accounts?

TAX-DEFERRED ACCOUNTS

The government has only six methods of motivating the general population to act in a specific way. These six methods are to mandate or legislate, create a penalty or reward, and levy taxes or remove taxes. Taxes are not only a mechanism to transfer wealth from the citizens to the government, but also become a tool to encourage society to accomplish specific goals. When developing personal financial objectives and action plans to achieve those objectives, tax implications should be considered. Both federal and state governments love to collect taxes from investors. Dividends are fully taxable as a component of adjusted gross income. All interest received or accrued is also fully taxable, except tax-exempt state or municipal bonds. Both are taxed at the same rate as earned wages and salaries. Uncle Sam loves bull stock markets because of higher capital gains tax revenues. The difference between an investment's gross cost, including transaction fees or commissions, and the net proceeds, deducting fees, and commissions, represents the capital gain and is taxable at a current federal rate of 20 percent, if the asset is held more than 12 months. The government taxes capital gains from assets held less than 12 months the same as earned income and salaries, which in most instances is higher than 20 percent.

Our politicians have decided that college education and retirement funding are worthy financial goals and offer tax breaks on their investments. The government wants us to be saving for our retirement needs and for our own or our offspring's higher education expenses. To assist the population in reaching these goals, taxes are greatly reduced for investments set aside for these specific purposes. There are various tax breaks for investors to fund traditional IRAs, Roth IRAs, 401(k) Programs, and Educational Savings Accounts. In all of these programs, income taxes are not levied when dividends or interest are received. Also capital gains are not taxed at the time of realization. Depending on the specific tax-deferred program, taxes are collected when the funds are withdrawn, allowing these accounts to increase in value at a faster rate.

There are many excellent books and articles available at the bookstore, the library, or over the Internet about the advantages and disadvantages of each type of tax-deferred program. Our goal here is not to review the work of others, but to provide a brief overview as to how these programs generically work and how DRIP and direct investing may play a role in each account. For example, a sister book, *All About Your 401(k) Plan*, offers informative insight into employer-sponsored defined contribution retirement programs. Suffice it to say, any and all tax-deferred accounts should be utilized whenever possible.

TRADITIONAL, ROTH IRAs, AND 401(K)s

In general, every American taxpayer is eligible to establish an IRA. A qualified taxpayer can deduct from taxable adjusted gross income contributions of up to $2000 per year to a traditional tax-deferred IRA, subject to limitations if also an active participant in a 401(k) plan. The traditional IRA is not annually taxed on its dividends, interest, or capital gains, and the investor's tax exposure is limited to when the funds are disbursed. The IRS regulations, however, impose mandatory annual disbursements beginning by age 70½. The required minimum traditional IRA distribution triggers a taxable event.

In 1997, Congress passed revisions to the traditional IRA rules and this updated alternative is called a *Roth IRA*. Roth IRAs offer investors the option of setting aside up to $2000 a year, but the contribution is not tax deductible. The Roth IRA allows the accumulation of dividends, interest, and capital gains free of current taxes, and allows tax-free distribution to the investor. The account is required to be open more than 5 years, and the investor is to be at least 59½ years old for disbursements to qualify for favorably tax treatment. There are no required minimum distributions with a Roth IRA account. It may be advantageous for current traditional IRA investors to rollover their assets into a Roth IRA. This decision, however, should not be made without either expert tax advice, or adequate research, to determine the current tax liability of early withdrawal and rollover of a traditional IRA.

Employer-sponsored 401(k) retirement programs allow employees of a company to save for their own retirement. Contributions are deducted from their paychecks prior to calculating withholding taxes. The pretax contribution is invested on the employees' behalf and is intended to remain in the account until age 59½. Many companies encourage enrollment in their 401(k)s by matching a portion of the employee's contribution. For example, the company may contribute 50 cents for every dollar of employee contribution. The employee owns the 401(k), and all funds are in the employee's name. Dividends, interest, and capital gains accumulate without exposure to current taxes. Distributions are taxed as with a traditional IRA.

As the government tries to wean Americans off a dependency on Social Security as our primary retirement fund, maximum contributions to IRA accounts will be raised in the future. This will encourage more investors to save using tax-deferred accounts. It is anticipated that the $2000 maximum contribution will be increased to $5000 soon. A $5000 annual contribution to a tax-differed account returning 8 percent annually would grow to $570,000 in 30 years. That same contribution earning 11 percent annually could increase to over $1 million in 30 years.

EDUCATIONAL SAVINGS ACCOUNT

In the mid-1990s, the government began to encourage higher education by making it easier to pay postsecondary education expenses. Much like the Roth IRA, the Educational Savings Account, also known as an Education IRA, allows for tax-advantaged contributions of up to $500 a year per account specified for college expenses. Interest, dividends, capital gains, and distributions are tax-free provided they are used to pay for postsecondary education expenses. Although not sounding like much, a $500 annual contribution earning 11 percent tax-deferred for 18 years will grow to almost $28,000. This is far from a 4-year ride at an Ivy League college, but it will pay a big chunk of a state university diploma. In this day and age, a college education is a requirement to really get ahead, and it is expensive. The ability to pay tuition for even lower cost community colleges and state universities is still a prerequisite for attendance. There are loans, scholarships, and grants, in addition to work-study programs. A $500 annual tax-advantaged savings plan per child, started when each child is born, may make the difference of a lifetime. The Education IRA account benefits are phased out as the parents' adjusted gross income exceeds $150,000 for a married couple filing jointly and is eliminated when the adjusted gross income exceeds $160,000 for the same couple. Accounts must be distributed when the beneficiary reaches age 30 or it can be rolled over to a member of the beneficiary's family, such as their children.

BENEFIT OF TAX-DEFERRED ACCOUNTS

The basic benefit of a tax-deferred account is that its balance grows faster than an account that is subject to annual deductions for income taxes. For example, compare two portfolios with a $10,000 balance, identical income, and capital gains, but one is tax-deferred and one is not. The portfolios are well diversified with a combination of bonds, growth, value, and income-producing stocks, with an average current yield of 2.5 percent. The capital gains of each portfolio increases by 10 percent a year, for a total portfolio return of 12.5 percent, which is in line with the historic return of the S&P 500 Index. Fifty percent of the portfolio value is traded once every 6 years to diversify assets, creating an average portfolio turnover of 8.3 percent a year and triggering a capital gain once every 6 years. The investor files tax returns as a joint married couple and has an average lifetime annual adjusted taxable income of between $43,850 and $105,950. This would equate to a 28 percent income tax bracket using the year 2000 IRS tax table. If the investor happened to live in a state where income is subject to a 5 percent income tax rate, the total annual income tax liability would be 33 percent. The long-term federal capital gains tax is 20 percent. Table 3–2 estimates the value of both a taxable and a tax-deferred account after deducting for federal taxes only.

An investor at age 28 with an IRA account of $10,000 would have a tax-deferred account worth $1,583,000 at age 71. That same $10,000 invested in a taxable account, based on these assumptions, would be worth $903,700 at age 71. The investor would have paid almost $57,000 in income tax on dividends and interest received and

T A B L E   3–2

Value of $10,000 Invested, 10 Percent
Annual Capital Gains, and 2.5 Percent
Current Yield

Year	Tax-Deferred Account	Taxable Account
1	$11,250	$11,180
5	$18,020	$17,467
10	$32,473	$28,943
15	$58,518	$48,059
20	$105,451	$79,943
30	$342,433	$232,713
40	$1,111,990	$646,723

$63,000 in capital gains tax. Not only did the investor transfer $120,000 from his personal wealth to the government over the last 43 years; he also missed out on a lifetime's worth of dividends and capital gains that would have been generated.

Had the investor averaged less than $43,000 a year in taxable income and lived in a state with a 6 percent income tax, the annual tax exposure would be 21 percent (15 percent for the feds and 6 percent for the state). The taxable account would grow by a relatively modest amount due to a lower tax liability and would be worth $977,000 at age 71. In contrast, an investor with a lifetime average taxable income between $105,950 and $161,450 and living in a 6 percent income tax state would have a taxable account balance of about $815,991. This represents a taxable account balance of just a bit more than half the tax-deferred account.

What better way to celebrate the birth of a grandchild than to establish an IRA in that newborn's name? Fund it with a one-time diversified conservative portfolio of $1000 in stocks. At a tax-deferred return of just 8 percent a year, the IRA will grow to almost $150,000 when the grandchild reaches age 65.

WHERE TO HOLD YOUR IRA ACCOUNTS

There are few times when a stockbroker's services are preferred to DRIPs and direct investing. Tax-deferred accounts are one of those exceptions. For accounts that include strict government regulations, it is best to maintain those with a third party, partially for the burden of recordkeeping and proof of compliance. Almost all brokers offer tax-deferred accounts. Although purchase and sell transaction costs are higher than investing directly with the company through an OCP, most brokers offer the service of reinvesting all dividends, usually at no charge. The strategy of reinvesting dividends is not limited to just companies or their transfer agents offering a DRIP or direct investing plan. Use the broker's dividend reinvestment service whenever possible. Most tax-deferred accounts are charged an annual fee, ranging from $35 to $50. By having all IRA assets in one account, multiple account fees are avoided. A tax-deferred account at a broker also opens up all the broker's services to the investor as a client. These include the broker firm's research and investment commentaries, representing services that should be important to individual investors. With the advent of account access through the Internet, an investor with an IRA at Merrill Lynch has free on-line access to their entire library of research—free. What better method to augment an investor's independent research for a taxable investment than to include a major brokerage house's analysis.

Some DRIP programs offer the option to establish an IRA. These include Bell Atlantic (BEL), Intimate Brands (IBI), Lucent Technologies (LU), SBC Communications (SBC), Sears (S), and Wal-Mart (WMT). However, it is common to have each separate DRIP IRA account charge a $35 annual fee. A portfolio of 10 different DRIP IRA accounts could generate up to $350 a year in fees, whereas that same investment at a major brokerage firm, with dividends reinvested, would incur one flat annual fee of $50.

CUSTODIAL ACCOUNTS

Custodial accounts are established for minor persons under the ages of 18 to 21. Custodial accounts are similar to Trusts in that assets, including stocks, are under the direction of a person other than the beneficial owner. Trusts are historically more expensive, time-consuming, complicated, and more legally regulated. There are two sets of regulations concerning custodial accounts: the Uniform Gifts to Minors Act (UGMA) and the Uniform Transfer to Minors Act (UTMA). The UGMA was adopted in 1956, and the UTMA is an updated and expanded version. Because the laws governing custodial accounts are established by each state, it is important to check the regulations of the state in which the account was originally opened, either by contacting a lawyer, a stockbroker, or the state directly. The primary intent of custodial accounts is to make the transfer of assets to children or grandchildren easier. The custodian manages the assets for the benefit of the minor, and title passes to the minor when they become of legal age, usually 18 to 21 years old. It is important to remember that any asset transferred into a custodial account immediately becomes the property of the minor. The person who initially funds the custodial account may decide to manage the assets or that responsibility can be passed along to another. Disbursements from custodial accounts are permissible provided they are exclusively for the benefit of the minor. Dividend income and capital gains are taxable to the minor at the parents' tax rate until the minor is 14 years old. After reaching age 14, the tax liability is calculated on the child's income at normal rates, which is usually lower than the parents' tax rate.

Custodial accounts have several uses. The first is as a planning tool for college expenses. Separate custodial accounts for each child assist in saving for college. Segregating assets and placing some in the minor's name will help focus on the goal. The second most popular use of custodial accounts is for estate planning. Some investors may wish to give their money away before they die. The gift tax regulation allows each taxpayer to give anyone up to $10,000 a year without incurring a tax liability for either party. Custodial accounts can act as a recipient for those funds. For example, if an investor and their spouse transferred $10,000 each to a custodial account, at the end of 10 years, $200,000 would have been passed from one generation to another. Any appreciation of the assets over the $200,000 gift has also skipped estate tax. Annual gifts per grandparent of up to $10,000 per grandchild to custodial accounts are a great method of transferring wealth using a generation-skipping strategy.

The disadvantage of custodial accounts deals with three basic problems. The first is, once an asset is transferred, there is no taking it back. The assets legally belong to the minor. The law requires all custodial accounts to be terminated once the minor is considered a legal adult. Title of the assets pass directly to their control, and the beneficiary can then legally sell all the assets. They may have an urge to buy a VW Bug and drive the 17,845 km Pan American Highway from Prudhoe Bay, Alaska, crossing the Andes mountains just north of Santiago, Chile, and continuing to its end at Parque Nacional, Lapatia Bay, Tierra del Fuego, Argentina. They can, it's their money. The second drawback is custodial accounts count as assets of the minor when applying for college financial aid. Large custodial accounts may disqualify a minor for college scholarships, grants, and possibly some student loans. If the purpose of custodial accounts does not include college education expenses, further research should be done to determine whether custodial accounts would interfere with other college-funding options. Custodial accounts cannot be used for basic parental support of the minor. For instance, custodial accounts should not be used for child support in the case of divorced parents. Any distributions found to have been used for child support will become taxable income to the adult.

COMPOUNDING DIVIDENDS AND DOLLAR COST AVERAGING IN ACTION

For long-term investors, the concepts of *compounding increasing dividends* and *dollar cost averaging* become powerful tools for increasing personal wealth. According to *Stocks, Bonds, Bills and Inflation: Historic Returns 1926–2000* by Ibbotson and Singuefield, since 1926, only twice were there negative compounded annual returns for 10-year holding periods for the S&P 500. Negative years were recorded for the periods 1929 to 1938 and 1930 to 1939. Since 1931, during every 10-year period, common stocks provided investors a positive compounded rate of return. For 5-year holding periods, negative compounded rates of return occurred only seven times. These years were 1927 to 1931, 1928 to 1932, 1929 to 1933, 1930 to 1934, 1937 to 1941, 1970 to 1974, and 1973 to 1977. There has never been a negative compounded rate of return for common stocks held for a 20-year time period. In other words, since 1926, an investor with a 20-year investment horizon has always made a profit buying the S&P 500 Index and compounding the annual dividend returns. The easiest method of compounding stock investment returns is through dividend reinvestment. By way of the DRIP account, the investor automatically enrolls in a dollar cost averaging strategy.

The Dividend Rich Investor by Joseph Tigue and Joseph Lisanti calculated an investor's compounded returns, as if it were a DRIP

TABLE 3-3

1-, 5-, 10-, and 15-Year Returns for S&P
500 Ending 12/31/95, Compounded vs.
Not Compounded

Time Period	Compounded Return (%)	Not Compounded Return (%)
1 year	38	34
5 years	115	85
10 years	300	191
15 years	694	353

Source: Joseph Tigue and Joseph Lisanti, *The Dividend Rich Investor.*

account, for the S&P 500 for 1, 5, 10, and 15 years ending December 31, 1995, and compared these results with a non-DRIP portfolio. Table 3–3 outlines their findings.

The histories of three very different stocks provide stark examples of these strategies in action. Hawaiian Electric (HE) is the local electric utility for the Hawaiian Islands. Over the years, HE has maintained strong financial management and is considered one of the best conservatively managed electric companies in America. The geographic service area, mainly a few islands in the middle of the South Pacific Ocean, has challenged HE's revenue and profit growth. As a popular tourist destination for Asians and with the weakness in their economies in the late 1990s, the Hawaiian economy has not been as strong in recent years and HE stock has traded in a narrow range in the $30s. However, HE has historically offered regular dividend increases and an above average dividend yield. Table 3–4 outlines a one-time $10,000 investment in HE and its performance between 1988 and 1999, with dividends reinvested at the annual median market price.

In the 12 years since the DRIP was established, the initial investment of $10,000 has grown to $25,665. This represents a 13 percent annual overall return and is in line with the historic returns of the S&P 500. The stock price, however, only provided a 1.7 percent average annual gain. The balance was realized by the dividend increasing from $1.95 a share to $2.48 a share and by buying more

TABLE 3-4

Hawaiian Electric Dividend Reinvested, Annual OCP $0.

Year	Avg. Price	Div. Rate	Div. Paid	OCP	Shares Bought	Shares Owned	Value
99	$36.00	$2.48	$1654	$0	45.95	712.91	$25,665
98	$39.50	$2.48	$1556	$0	39.40	666.96	$26,345
97	$37.20	$2.44	$1436	$0	38.63	627.56	$23,345
96	$36.40	$2.41	$1331	$0	36.57	588.93	$21,437
95	$35.95	$2.37	$1228	$0	34.16	552.36	$19,857
94	$33.20	$2.33	$1128	$0	33.98	518.20	$17,204
93	$35.45	$2.29	$1041	$0	29.38	484.21	$17,165
92	$39.70	$2.25	$968	$0	24.40	454.83	$18,057
91	$33.65	$2.21	$892	$0	26.53	430.44	$14,484
90	$33.65	$2.17	$823	$0	24.47	403.91	$13,592
89	$34.85	$2.07	$741	$0	21.27	379.44	$13,224
88	$29.75	$1.95	$655	$0	22.03	358.17	$10,655
Initial Share Purchased						336.13	$10,000

Profit: Total Capital Investment $10,000
Total Profit $15,665
% Gain 156.6%
Dividend Received $13,458

Source: Value Line Investment Survey.

shares with the higher payout. Over the years, the number of shares owned increased from the initial 336 to 712 shares, growing the annual cash dividend from $655 to $1654. After 12 years, the original $10,000 investment is now generating a 16.5 percent annual cash return. The total cost of the shares, including dividends, yields about 7.5 percent. Because the price of the stock was mostly stable, the dollar cost average of all the shares, including the cost of the shares purchased with dividends, is $32.90, 7.2 percent below the average market price of $35.27.

A $10,000 investment in Merck & Company (MRK), in contrast, would produce much higher capital gains. Merck is the leading US manufacturer of pharmaceuticals and introduced several blockbuster new drugs in the 1990s. In addition, Merck acquired Medco, the largest pharmaceutical managed care company, further expanding its sales and profits. Table 3–5 outlines a one-time $10,000 investment in MRK and its performance between 1988 and 1999, with dividends reinvested at the annual median market price, adjusted for stock splits.

MRK has been one of the stellar Wall Street winners. A $10,000 DRIP investment would have grown to $81,006, for an average 59 percent annual return. Dividends increased an average of 26 percent a year. Had the dividends not been reinvested, the original 919 shares would be worth just over $62,000. The $8600 in dividends reinvested in MRK stock added $11,000 in capital gains. The average cost per share, including dividends, is $15.52. Although the current dividend yield is a seemingly paltry 1.6 percent, after 12 years

TABLE 3–5

Merck & Company Dividend Reinvested, Annual OCP $0

Year	Avg. Price	Div. Rate	Div. Paid	OCP	Shares Bought	Shares Owned	Value
99	$67.58	$1.12	$1320	$0	19.45	1198.67	$81,006
98	$73.38	$1.12	$1300	$0	17.73	1179.13	$86,525
97	$58.75	$0.95	$1085	$0	18.48	1161.41	$68,223
96	$45.38	$0.85	$953	$0	21.01	1142.92	$51,866
95	$35.25	$0.71	$780	$0	22.15	1121.91	$39,547
94	$20.13	$0.62	$661	$0	32.86	1099.76	$22,138
93	$18.25	$0.57	$589	$0	32.31	1066.90	$19,471
92	$20.50	$0.52	$524	$0	25.59	1034.59	$21,209
91	$26.50	$0.46	$456	$0	17.22	1008.99	$26,738
90	$15.25	$0.39	$377	$0	24.73	991.78	$15,125
89	$12.00	$0.32	$301	$0	25.12	967.04	$11,606
88	$10.88	$0.27	$248	$0	22.81	941.93	$10,248
Initial Share Purchased						919.11	$10,000

Profit:	Total Capital Investment	$10,000
	Total Profit	$71,006
	% Gain	710.1%
	Dividend Received	$8,600

Source: Value Line Investment Survey.

of increasing dividends, the original investment is yielding 10.2 percent.

Another example is GATX (GMT), a leading financial services company specializing in leasing railroad, aircraft, and telecommunications equipment. In the winter of 2000, Warren Buffett, America's leading value investor, increased his stake in the company to 15 percent. A similar $10,000 investment in GMT in 1988 would have grown to $37,702. Then $8546 in dividends would have been reinvested and the DRIP account would be generating $1148 a year in dividends. The stock more than doubled in price, rising from $14.25 to $35.00 a share, along with a more than doubling of the dividend from $0.50 to $1.10. GMT's average annual return based on the initial $10,000 is 23 percent.

Increasing dividends and compounding their growth can make a huge difference in expanding DRIP account balances. By dollar cost averaging the dividend reinvestment, more shares are purchased during periods of lower stock prices. In these examples, there were a few years of stagnant or lower stock prices. The additional shares purchased with higher cash dividends gave the account a real boost when stock prices began to rise over time.

THE TIME VALUE OF MONEY

People usually earn money not only for the basic necessities of life, but also because they like to spend it. As a nation of consumers, Americans need to be assured that delaying consumption and immediate gratification will eventually result in greater consumption or more gratification some day in the future. One method investors can use to justify delaying immediate consumption is to calculate the time value of investing rather than spending money. There is a rather simple formula used to calculate the value of a specific investment at a level rate of compounding returns over a specific time period.

That formula is Future Value = Present Value times ([return rate per period + 1] times the power of the number of compounding periods). For example, in plain English, the future value of $1000 in 5 years at a compounded rate of 5 percent is $1276.28 or $1276.28 = $1000 (.05 + 1) to the 5th power, or $1276.28 = $1000 (1.2762815). Using this formula, investors can calculate the future value of specific investments based on a belief of anticipated future returns. The formula works in reverse as well. For instance, an investor wanted to know the amount of a lump sum investment it would take in 1982 to pay the estimated $140,000 for 4 years at an Ivy League college today at a 12.5 percent annual return. The formula is $140,000 = Investment Value x (1 + 0.125) to the 18th power. The answer is $18,700. In other words, $18,700 invested in 1982 at a compounded rate of return of 12.5 percent would equal the $140,000 it may take to attend an expensive, private university for 4 years. Using the same calculation, if your child decides to take a fifth year at the same expensive university, you had better have invested $21,003 in 1982 instead.

The time value of money is also important when calculating the timing of a tax-deferred contribution. Any contribution during the year to an IRA account is credited to that year's income tax calculation (actually investors have until April 15 of the following year to make their contribution). Making an IRA contribution at the beginning of the year rather than at the end of the year will positively impact the future balance. Table 3–6 is a comparison of numerical factors used to calculate total returns based on investing the same amount of money at the beginning of the year versus at the end of

TABLE 3–6

Total Return Factor for Comparison of Investing at the Beginning versus End of the Year, 15 Percent Compounded Return

Year	Beginning	End	Year	Beginning	End
1	1.1500	1.0000	10	23.3493	20.3037
2	2.4725	2.1500	15	54.7175	47.5804
3	3.9934	3.4725	20	117.8101	102.4436
4	7.7537	6.7424	25	244.7120	212.7930
5	10.0668	8.7537	30	499.9569	434.7451
6	10.0668	8.7537	35	1013.3457	881.1702
7	12.7268	11.0668	40	2045.9539	1779.0903

Source: www.hec.ohio-state.edu.

the year, if the investment were aggressive in nature with a 15 percent average annual rate of return.

In other words, if $2000 were invested every January 1, after 40 years, the investment would be worth $4,091,907, at an aggressive average of 15 percent compounded annual return. The same $2000 invested on December 31 of each year would be worth $3,558,180 after 40 years. By investing in December rather than the preceding January, the investor misses the first year's return. The difference between these two examples is the value of the first year's capital gains and dividends, compounded over 40 years.

The choice to procrastinate contributing to IRA accounts until the last minute could be a half-million-dollar mistake. This is additional proof that DRIP investing is much like voting in Chicago—it's best to do it early and often.

INFLATION AND DRIP INVESTING

One of the basic goals of investing money is to beat future cost increases of the items we are delaying purchasing today. We all know what inflation is: It is rising prices over time for the same goods or services. For instance, a $0.15 cup of regular coffee (not the overpriced fancy variety from the upscale coffee shops) in 1969 may cost $0.99 to $1.50 in 1999. Phrased another way, an equal amount of $1000 in 1969 dollars would be $4655 in 1999 dollars. Inflation impacts investing in several ways. Investment returns are usually not calculated in inflation-adjusted terms. Inflation-adjusted calculations are also known as the real rate of return. If a long-term portfolio returns 12.5 percent, while the long-term inflation rate was 4 percent, the real rate of return would be 8.5 percent (12.5 − 4.0 = 8.5). After taking into consideration annual cost increases for items we buy every day, the portfolio's value gained 8.5 percent in annual purchasing power. Investments made in 1959 would have to be worth a minimum of 5.725 times more in 1999 just to keep up with inflation. There are many websites, such as *westegg.com/inflation*, that provide inflation index factors used for historic real rates of return calculations.

When comparing or calculating projected or historic rates of investment returns, keep in mind the inflation backdrop for those times. For instance, the 1988 investment of $10,000 in Hawaiian

Electric increased in value to $25,665 by 1999. The Inflation Index Factor for that same period was approximately 1.366, or the initial $10,000 needs to grow to $13,666 just to keep up. HE rewarded investors with a 13 percent nonadjusted return and a real rate of return of 10 percent. Merck, in contrast, had a real rate of return of 41.1 percent over the same 12 years.

Inflation tables are easy to read and understand, and they are a very powerful tool in calculating real personal portfolio gains. There are two ways to analyze money adjusted for inflation. An investor can compare a specific amount of money today and calculate what that would have been worth in previous years, or how much a specific amount in previous years would be worth today. For example:

An equivalent amount of $1000 in 1959 would be worth $5600 in 1999 dollars,

An equivalent amount of $1000 in 1969 would be worth $4655 in 1999 dollars,

An equivalent amount of $1000 in 1979 would be worth $2482 in 1999 dollars,

An equivalent amount of $1000 in 1989 would be worth $1366 in 1999 dollars.

The reverse equation to the prior list is:

$1000 in 1999 would have been worth $731 in 1989,

$1000 in 1999 would have been worth $402 in 1979,

$1000 in 1999 would have been worth $214 in 1969,

$1000 in 1999 would have been worth $178 in 1959.

When calculating future financial goals, it is important to attempt estimating the future cost associated with that goal. For instance, the future cost of a college education for a newborn, if inflated at the same rate as overall inflation from 1979 to 1999, could cost 2.295 times more than today. An Ivy League college costing around $32,000 a year today may cost as much as $73,440 in the year 2019. Thus, $8000 today for annual in-state tuition at the state university may cost $18,360 a year 20 years from now, following the experience of overall inflation during the past 20 years.

Inflation also impacts investment choices by requiring minimum levels of return. For instance, if current inflation is at 3.5 percent and a long-term Treasury bond is yielding 5.8 percent, the current real rate of return to an investor is 2.3 percent. A passbook account at your local savings and loan that offers 4.5 percent interest is providing a real rate of just 1 percent. A utility company stock with a 7 percent dividend will provide a 3.5 percent inflation adjusted return. If a dividend is increased more than the inflation rate, the investment is gaining in its real rate of return. GATX (GMT) paid a $0.50 annual dividend in 1989 and a $1.10 annual dividend in 1999, for an average annual dividend increase of 12.0 percent. With an Inflation Index Factor of about 1.366 during that same time frame, the original $0.50 dividend would have to be enhanced to $0.66 to maintain purchasing parity. With its dividend increases to $1.10, GMT has provided long-term investors with an increasing real rate of return from its dividend yield. GMT's stock valuation over the same time frame also rose from a split-adjusted price of $14.40 to $36.00. Some of this capital gain came from greater investor interest in GMT as an excellent investment in terms of real rates of return. Long-term investors search for top-quality companies with increasing corporate earnings that allow for dividend increases exceeding the inflation rate.

As outlined previously, *Barron's Financial Weekly* calculated the 1998 value of $100 invested in the S&P 500 in 1925. Thus, $100 in 1925 would be worth $932 in 1998 dollars, adjusted for inflation. Without reinvesting dividends, the value of the S&P 500 investment would have grown to about $9600. After considering the effects of inflation, the value rose $8568, or 85 times the original investment. However, when a dividend reinvestment plan was added, the total value of the account would have grown to about $235,000. Adjusted for inflation, a DRIP for the S&P 500 would have increased by approximately 225 times the original $100. Long-term investors find that a sure-fire way to beat inflation over time is to invest in stocks offering dividend increases that are growing faster than the inflation rate.

CHAPTER 4

How to Research Stocks, Part I: Management and Stock Price Analysis

Key Concepts

- Long-Term Earnings and Interest Rate Trends Drive Overall Market Trends
- Stocks Versus Bonds
- Evaluating Company Management Using Corporate Mission, Annual Letter to Shareholders, and Ethics Statements
- Evaluating Company Management Using Financial Numbers
- Management Evaluation Rules of Thumb
- Financial Numbers in Action
- Market Capitalization
- Stock Price Evaluation Tools
- PEG Ratios and Their Importance in Stock Price Evaluation
- Stock Valuation Rules of Thumb
- Overall Comparisons for Lucent Technologies, Merck, Federal Signal

The only reason to make any monetary investment is to produce a profit some time in the future. We do not buy stocks for their recreation value or because they will improve our health. We buy stocks to satisfy our personal need to continually improve our standard of living. To grow our long-term personal wealth sufficiently to meet our future financial goals and requirements, profits from our investments are imperative. Profits can be either in capital gains or increasing dividends. The bigger the long-term returns, the faster we reach our goals. Researching investment choices is a key ingredient to better portfolio returns.

The goal in studying companies and their stock prices is to identify the best long-term prospects for future investment gains. The best candidates should be established companies in expanding industries led by efficient management. These companies should be leaders in their industry, most ranking in the top three in market share. Industry leaders can affect, rather than respond to, competitive pricing policies and have market leverage, with new products having immediate brand awareness. Industry leaders will usually generate greater corporate cash flow to finance business expansion and product development. The specific industry need not be large, and the company products may focus on viable niche markets.

Many investors become skittish when it comes to the research step in selecting stocks. It is far easier to listen to your neighbor and the gossip around the water cooler or pass the job off to a mutual fund money manager. Stock research is considered by most investors as being just a tad above getting pecked in the head by a flock of crows, but it need not be. With an array of financial information available to the average investor, it is easy to be confused about which financial numbers are important and what each means. With the appearance of start-up Internet companies in the 1990s as an investment selection, and with investors purposely discarding fundamental financial analysis as an investment tool, confusion concerning financial information became more prevalent. Once an investor understands how to read and compare financial statements and is no longer intimidated by what could be considered as a confusing list of statistics, financial information becomes the heart of investment research. With the advent of the Internet and proliferation of financial websites, stock research for the typical investor has become much quicker and easier.

There are many different investment philosophies and strategies. A quick trip to the library or bookstore will reveal as many different investment approaches as there are authors. Some are based on short-term trading of stocks that are in fashion and demonstrating great short-term upward price momentum. Some focus on buying stock in companies currently in bankruptcy and waiting for a turnaround. Others preach the benefits of technical analysis over fundamental analysis. Most important in any investment study is developing a personal comfort level with the approach. Pick investments that match the investor's lifestyle. If the investor does not want to be glued to a computer screen, then short-term trading may not be appropriate. If an investor worries about tomorrow's market performance even before today's market closing bell has sounded, then speculative issues may not fit that investor's personality.

DRIPs and direct investing are usually preferred tools for long-term buy-and-hold investors seeking additional capital gains realized by the compounding of increasing dividends. Research, therefore, should be focused on long-term investments that offer both capital gains potential from rising stock prices and dividends that should consistently increase over the years. Long-term stock gains are usually associated with increasing corporate earnings, which are the direct result of management's ability to implement sound long-term business strategies and action plans.

The stock market as a whole reacts to many different factors. These factors include economic growth, interest rates, productivity, and wage growth. Over the past 50 years, the trend for the market has been up, as demonstrated by the S&P returns of an average of 12.5 percent annually. Within the overall trend of the market, individual investments react to individual factors, such as earnings, cash flow, dividends, and long-term performance of management.

There will always be fads and trendy investments. In the 1970s, it was oil services providers; in the 1980s, it was biotech companies; and in the 1990s, it was Internet.com companies. With these fads come excessive speculation and stock market gambling. Investment decisions are no longer based on fundamental corporate long-term trends, but rather on the hopes that some other speculator will be willing to pay a higher price, creating the capital gain. Some speculative market trends do have investment merit, such as biotech and the Internet, but within the world of speculative investing, basic fundamental research is all but forgotten. DRIP and direct investing will, by nature, focus on established companies, most of which are in the mainstream of Wall Street. Within the framework of established companies with proven management and real earnings, cash flow, and dividends, there can be exposure to the latest fad or trend. DRIP investors, through their careful research and focus, can uncover top-quality companies with existing profitable businesses that are expanding into these hot market segments.

For example, the ability to buy US postage stamps on the Internet is a time- and money-saving service that is of great interest to small businesses and consumers. In 1999, Internet start-up companies E-Stamp (ESTM) and Stamps.com (STMP) were the first to be approved by the US Postal Service to offer US postage stamps over the Internet. Using software provided by these companies at their websites, consumers can print the required postage directly on to envelopes, reducing trips to the post office. Pitney Bowes (PBI), the leader in the mailing industry with annual revenues of over $4 billion and cash flow of $750 million, was a Johnny-come-lately, and their approval was several months later. Investors desiring stock portfolio exposure to this fast-growing market gobbled up the IPOs of both STMP at $15 a share in the summer of 1999 and ESTM at $23 in the fall of 1999. PBI was trading around $60. Both STMP and ESTM were projected to lose money in 1999—up to $-2.90 a share each. PBI, in contrast, rewarded shareholders with $2.31 a share in earnings along with $1.76 in dividends, and both are anticipated to grow at a 13 percent clip over the next few years. STMP roared to a height of $90 a share, but then crashed back to its offering price of $15, all within 9 months. ESTM had a worse fate—rising to $43 and then plummeting to $4 in 6 months, and its CEO quit in May 2000. With some overall market and specifically technology stock weakness, PBI's price fell from $60 to around $40 during the same period. The PBI DRIP investor would be dollar cost averaging their investment with the accruing dividends while the ESTM investor would be sulking with a huge capital loss.

Over the next few years, PBI should make substantial inroads into the Internet postal market, increasing revenues and profits. Pitney Bowes is anticipated to garnish at least 30 percent of the on-line postage business by 2005, which could add up to $300 million to top line revenues. With an entire package of web-based shipping and direct marketing products available to small businesses, PBI expects to package their new "PitneyWorks" services to new E-postage customers. PBI is another good example of a "brick and mortar" company moving to become "click and mortar." As investors begin to realize these revenue and profit gains, PBI's stock price should rebound accordingly.

It is important to conduct stock research to determine not only the financial strength of the company and its earnings potential, but also to evaluate management's ability to deliver increasing shareholder value.

LONG-TERM EARNINGS AND INTEREST RATE TRENDS DRIVE OVERALL MARKET TRENDS

Corporate earnings and the value investors place on each dollar per share of those earnings are one major factor in stock market trends and specific stock performance. The S&P 500 Index rose from 330.40 in 1990 to 1469.25 in 1999. Combined operating earnings per share for the companies in the Index also rose from $22.65 to $51.68. In dollar terms, operating profits increased from $150 billion to $426 billion. Two investment forces were at work to fuel the bull market of the 1990s. First, corporate earnings were growing fast, and the value investors were willing to pay for those rising profits also rose. Based on the S&P 500 Index in 1990, investors were willing to pay $14.59 (330.30 divided by 22.65) in share price for each dollar of earnings per share; in 1999, that same dollar of corporate earnings fetched $28.43 (1429.25 divided by 51.68) in share price. In other words, investors were willing to pay a price to earnings ratio for the S&P 500 Index, also known as the PE, of 14.59 in 1990 and a PE of 28.43 in 1999. As stock investing became more popular and as general overall personal wealth increased with the booming economy in the 1990s, investors' demand for stocks increased and the PE expanded. Assuming investors in 1999 paid a PE ratio the same as in 1990, the higher earnings alone would have driven the Index to 754, providing investors with a 128 percent gain for the decade.

STOCKS VERSUS BONDS

There is extreme competition for every new investment dollar, with the largest competitive instrument to stocks being bonds. Bonds, especially safe and secure US Government bonds, provide investors with a benchmark to judge competitive investment returns. Interest rates are controlled by the Federal Reserve and are monetary tools the government uses to accelerate or cool the economy. Usually interest and inflation rates move together. Inflation increases due to strong economic growth and interest rates generally tend to rise to slow growth and bring it and inflation into balance. For example, in the 1970s, inflation ran rampant, rising to around 14 percent. Then through a severe economic slowdown caused by rising interest rates, inflation fell to around 4 percent. The average inflation rate for the 1970s was 7.4 percent—well above the 2.5 percent in the 1960s. The return for the S&P Index declined while long-term government bond returns increased, with stocks rising 5.9 percent versus 6.2 percent for bonds. During the 1980s and 1990s, inflation continued to subside, registering a 5.1 percent average increase in the 1980s and 2.9 percent during the 1990s. Interest rates dropped accordingly, and stocks again outperformed bonds in the 1980s by 15.5 percent versus 13 percent and in the 1990s by 18.2 percent versus 8.4 percent.

As interest rates rise to fight inflation, bond yields also rise, attracting investors' capital out of stocks and into bonds. If investors can realize a 7 percent to 8 percent secure return by buying a government bond, many will do so. However, with low inflation and low interest rates of 4.5 percent, investors will prefer the potentially larger returns offered by stocks. Rising corporate earnings, low inflation, and low interest rates will always drive the stock market higher, whereas slowing earnings, rising inflation, and increasing interest rates will lower stock market returns.

DRIP investors with a diversified portfolio of stocks and bonds should be better insulated against overall market declines than an investor who is focused on just one industry, such as technology. Through dollar cost averaging of regular investments, a DRIP and direct investor can profit from temporary market declines by buying more shares when the stock or bond is down. Although few can accurately predict future stock market movements, DRIP investors benefit from the long-term growth trends of both the markets as a whole and of specific company fundamentals.

EVALUATING COMPANY MANAGEMENT USING CORPORATE MISSION, ANNUAL LETTER TO SHAREHOLDERS, AND ETHICS STATEMENTS

Within the backdrop of rising or falling interest rates and general economic activity, DRIP investors should be searching for companies whose management has consistently increased corporate profits and dividends. As the market as a whole climbed in the 1990s due to increasing earnings and dividends, so did the stock price of most individual companies. The bull market of the 1990s can be characterized as the rising tide that lifted all boats. The extent of an individual company's capital gain, however, is directly related to management's ability to generate long-term profits. As the caretakers of investors' capital, management's primary goal should be to increase revenues and profits for the benefit of all shareholders. There are several ways to evaluate management's commitment to shareholders. The first place to look for management's directive is to review the Corporate Mission Statement. Usually adopted by the board of directors, a mission statement is a few-sentence guideline stating the purpose of the corporation's existence. As the stated corporate purpose, management is judged by how well it performs using the mission statement as a yardstick. Shareholders deserve a place in every public company's Corporate Mission Statement. If increasing shareholder value is not one of the stated purposes of the company, then it can be assumed that it is not a primary focus for management.

PepsiCo (PEP), the large soft drink and snack foods company, has an excellently written mission statement. The PepsiCo mission statement is:

> PepsiCo's overall mission is to increase the value of our shareholder's investment. We do this through sales growth, cost controls and wise investment of resources. We believe our commercial success depends upon offering quality and value to our consumers and customers; providing products that are safe, wholesome, economically efficient and environmentally sound; and providing a fair return to our investors while adhering to the highest standards of integrity.

Coca-Cola (KO), PepsiCo's arch rival, has a mission statement that is very simple and direct. The first two sentences are "Our mission is to maximize share-owner value over time. In order to achieve this mission, we must create value for all constituents we serve, including consumers, our customers, our bottlers, and our communities."

Briggs & Stratton (BGG) is the largest US manufacturer of small horsepower gasoline engines by dollar revenue. Their Corporate Mission Statement is also quite simple, although a bit wordier:

We will create superior value by developing mutually beneficial re-
lationships with our customers, suppliers, employees and communities. We will enhance our brand equity and leadership position by developing, manufacturing at a low cost, marketing and servicing high
value power for a broad range of power products. In pursuing this
mission, we will provide power for people worldwide to develop
their economies and improve the quality of their lives and, in doing
so, add value to our shareholders' investment.

Tecumseh Products Company (TECU.A, TECU.B) is the largest
manufacturer of compressors for refrigeration and second largest
manufacturer of small horsepower gasoline engines by revenue.
Compared with the previous three examples, Tecumseh Products is
not as investor friendly. Because their Corporate Mission Statement
is not available at their website, we contacted the Investor Relations
and Human Resources Departments. After consultation with the legal staff, Tecumseh Products declined our offer to participate in this
project by supplying a copy of its Corporate Mission Statement. We
are unable to analyze it for a commitment to its shareholders. If
Tecumseh Products is as uncooperative toward all potential investors as it was to this author and potential investor, I would be
suprised to see the word *shareholder* in its mission statement. The
PepsiCo, Coca Cola, and Briggs & Stratton Corporate Mission Statements were available to the general investing public at their company websites.

In addition to the Corporate Mission Statement, the Annual
Letter to Shareholders from the Chairman will also give astute investors insight into the priority that management gives to increasing shareholder value. Written as the first few pages of a Corporate
Annual Report, the Letter to Shareholders should include not only
how the company increased shareholder value during that specific
year through higher revenues, EPS, and operating cash flow, but
also the strategies and action plans needed to continue doing so in
the future. Look for words such as *shareholder* or *company owners*,
and how often the chairman refers to the corporate mission of providing investors with exceptional returns. PepsiCo's Chairman and
Chief Executive Officer's 1999 Letter to Shareholders specifically
discussed their stagnant share price within the context of the consumer products industry underperforming and out of favor with investors, and it included the steps PepsiCo management is taking to

remedy the situation. Coca-Cola's 1999 Letter to Shareholders described a difficult year that resulted in disappointing financial results and a reshuffling of management. The last sentence is very focused: "Our mission is to create value for you (the shareholder), and we will do just that." Briggs & Stratton and Tecumseh Products' 1999 Letter to Shareholders does not mention the concept of shareholder value nor does it acknowledge shareholders' existence.

PepsiCo has a small investor-friendly DRIP program, with only one drawback—the investor needs to be a shareholder of record of minimum 5 shares. Once enrolled, the minimum OCP is $25 and the maximum is $5000 a month. The plan is free of fees, with the company paying all administrative fees and brokerage commissions. After purchasing shares from a broker and paying the usual broker fees for stock certificate distribution, the PepsiCo investor is eligible to enroll in their DRIP. PepsiCo has one class of common stock, owned and controlled by the individual voting shareholders. In contrast, Tecumseh Products does not offer a DRIP program, and has two classes of stock, A and B—one having voting rights and the other not.

Let us assume that, beginning in 1990, a net $2000 initial investment and a net annual $2000 OCP were made in both PEP and TECU.A at the median annual market price from 1990 to 1999. Dividends were reinvested annually, directly with PepsiCo and through a stockbroker's DRIP service for Tecumseh Products. PEP spun off their restaurant division, consisting of Kentucky Fried Chicken, Pizza Hut, and Taco Bell, to shareholders in 1997. Each shareholder received 1 share of Tricon Global Restaurants (YUM) for every 10 PepsiCo shares owned. The investor would have received 109.7 shares of YUM, worth an additional $3300. During the 1990s, neither investment could be considered a stellar choice. Although one company was focused on increasing shareholder value, the other did not acknowledge its importance. Table 4–1 compares the returns by each, adjusted for stock splits, as of December 31, 1999.

Although PEP and TECU.A are in very different industrial sectors and are of vastly different size and market capitalization, it is not a coincidence that the company focused on providing shareholder value far surpassed the company that may not directly state that as a corporate goal.

TABLE 4-1

10-Year Return: PepsiCo and Tecumseh Products,
1990 to 1999

	PepsiCo	Tecumseh
Investment	$22,000	$22,000
Shares originally purchased 1990	174.67	74.35
Shares held in 1999	1240.64	714.13
Value as of Dec. 31, 1999	$45,035	$28,315
Value of Tricon Global spin-off	$3,300	NA
Dividends reinvested	$3,144	$4,918
Profit	$26,335	$6,315
10-year return on investment	119.7%	28.7%
10-year average annual return	11.9%	2.8%

A Corporate Ethics Statement may reveal interesting aspects about the quality of management. Jack Welch, outgoing CEO of General Electric (GE), carries around in his pocket a laminated card printed with the company corporate ethics. Breaking any of these rules is cause for immediate employment termination from GE. If a company is strict on employee ethics, it is usually also concerned about its shareholders as well. Companies with unethical business practices are not usually very appealing investments to shareholders.

Both Corporate Mission Statements and Corporate Ethics Statements should be available from the company. Contact Shareholder or Investor Relations and request a copy or visit the company website because they are sometimes listed. The Letter to Shareholders is included in every annual report, and most annual reports are now also available at the company website. If shareholders are not mentioned in the Mission Statement and in the Annual Letter to Shareholders, and if there is no Corporate Ethics Statement, it may be time to find a company with more focused management.

EVALUATING COMPANY MANAGEMENT USING FINANCIAL NUMBERS

Seven financial numbers can measure management's long-term effectiveness of increasing shareholder value: earnings per share growth, dividend per share growth, operating cash flow growth, return on equity (ROE), return on assets (ROA), debt to equity ratio, and Standard and Poor's Equity Ranking. Combined, these provide an overall picture of management's ability to increase the value of investors' capital. With an investor's long-term view, these financial numbers should be reviewed as 5- and 10-year averages and as a comparison with the respective industry's averages.

Earnings per share (EPS) is the amount of net profit generated by the company divided by the number of shares. Growth in EPS comes from either more income or fewer shares. As corporate profits and cash flow exploded in the 1990s, companies used their cash to expand their businesses and buy back shares, both of which contributed to higher EPS. According to Michael Sivy, Columnist for *Money Magazine,* in 1998 alone, U.S. corporations repurchased $209 billion worth of their stock. Reducing the numbers of shares outstanding will cause a rise in EPS even with flat net profits. Investors should evaluate not only the EPS, but also net profit and the number of shares outstanding. An excellently managed company will not only demonstrate consistency in earnings growth over at least a 5-year period, but its EPS growth rate should equal or exceed its industry peers.

Dividend per share is the amount of cash or stock paid by the company to its shareholders. As with EPS, it is important to review the dividend history for the past 5 years, along with anticipated future growth. Many investors review the payout ratio or the ratio of dividends to earnings. For example, if a company earns $1.00 a share and has a $0.20 dividend, the payout ratio is 20 percent. The company reinvests the cash flow not paid to investors in the form of dividends. Some industries have historically higher payout ratios, such as utilities. Others, such as high tech, tend to retain the majority of profits to reinvest. Most companies try to maintain a certain payout ratio range, allowing for dividend increases to match earnings increases.

Operating cash flow is the amount of cash generated by operating the business. Every business requires a positive operating cash flow to remain a viable long-term investment. Some investors believe that operating cash flow per share is a more important indicator of company value than earnings. Research should focus on the growth of operating cash flow over the past 5 to 10 years. There are several accounting components of corporate cash flow. These include cash flow from operating activities, cash flow from investing activities (including business acquisitions, divestitures, and marketable securities), and cash flow from financing activities (including loan proceeds and repayment, dividends, and foreign exchange rate adjustments). The most critical is the operating cash flow because it accurately identifies the profitability of management's performance.

Return on equity (ROE), and *return on assets* (ROA) are considered efficiency ratios for evaluating management accomplishments. These numbers reveal to investors how efficiently management utilizes the assets at their disposal. The higher the ROE and ROA, the more money management has earned from stockholders' investments. ROE, which is similar to return on investment (ROI), is calculated by dividing net income, before nonrecurring items, by the book value or stockholders' equity. This ratio measures how much profit the company squeezes from every dollar of investor's equity capital. High return on equity ratios may be the result of a high return on assets, extensive use of debt financing, or both. ROA is calculated by dividing net income, before nonrecurring charges, by total corporate assets. ROA evaluates how well management profits from all its assets, such as manufacturing plant and equipment, inventory, and cash on hand. Higher return on assets can be attributed to higher profit margins or higher asset turnover, such as inventory. Older assets that have depreciated over the years and are carried on the books at a low cost will skew ROA ratios a bit higher.

Debt-to-equity ratio is used to evaluate the amount of corporate leverage through debt financing. Debt to equity evaluates total debt to book value or stockholders' equity. A company that has expanded through leveraging their assets at the bank and has a high debt-to-equity ratio will have higher interest expense and larger debt repayment than a company with no debt. Companies with low debt-to-equity ratios will have less debt service exposure during times of rising interest rates.

Standard and Poor's Equity Ranking, also known as the *quality ranking*, is an easy and effective means to categorize management's performance. Defined in the 1998 Directory of Dividend Reinvestment Plans,

> Growth and stability of earnings and dividends are key elements in S&P's common stock rankings. Our computerized scoring system is based on per-share earnings and dividend records of the most recent ten years. This period is considered sufficient time to measure secular growth, to capture indications of basic changes in trends as they develop and to encompass the full peak-to-peak range of the business cycle. Basic scores are computed for earnings and dividends, then adjusted as indicated by a set of predetermined modifiers for growth and stability within the long-term trend and cyclicality. Adjusted scores for earnings and dividends are then combined to yield a final score.

S&P equity ranking are as follows:

A+	Highest	B+	Average	C	Lowest
A	High	B	Below Average	D	In Reorganization
A−	Above Average	B−	Low	NR	Not Ranked

S&P equity ranking focuses on the two items most valued by investors: consistency and stability in earnings growth along with consistency and stability in dividend growth. This ranking is a powerful tool in evaluating long-term performance of management in these two important attributes. Although specifically designed not to be a stock market pricing tool, S&P's rankings can provide additional insight used in the stock-selection process. Using their ranking as a guide, why would an investor desire to place capital with a management team having a 10-year record of achieving below average gains in shareholder value?

Earnings per share information is available through most financial newspapers. Anticipated EPS growth rates can be found in publications such as *Value Line*, usually available at the Business Resource Desk of the local public library, or by subscription to *First Call* or on-line at financial research sites such as *www.zacks.com*. Dividend growth per share is available in *Value Line*. Annual operating cash flow numbers are available from each company's annual report or on the Internet. Many publications offer "cash flow" or "cash flow per share" data. However, it is important to check what accounting elements are included. Did the company increase its cash by issuing more common stock, by borrowing more capital, or by selling assets? Most overall cash flow figures not directly taken from the annual report, or specified as "operating cash flow," should be assumed to mean total corporate cash flow, including operating, investing, and financing activities. Return on equity (ROE), return on investment (ROI), and return on assets (ROA) are often available from the annual report and are published in *Value Line* and on the Internet. Comparisons of specific company financial numbers to industry averages are available on the Internet at many financial websites. S&P equity rankings are found in their stock reports, also at the library.

MANAGEMENT EVALUATION RULES OF THUMB

As rules of thumb, DRIP and direct investors should look for companies whose management has provided investors with:

- Above industry average earnings growth rates,
- Maximum 65 percent dividend payout ratio and dividend yields at or above the current yield of the S&P 500 Index,
- Dividend growth rates at or above industry average,
- ROE and ROA 12 percent to 15 percent or higher and above industry average,
- Debt-to-equity ratios in the 35 percent to 50 percent range; and
- S&P equity ranking B+ (average) and higher.

Within the framework of these management analysis tools, each investor needs to find a personal comfort level. A more aggressive investor may not be bothered by high debt-to-equity ratios if management provided excellent ROE and ROA ratios, demonstrating the ability to squeeze profits from its highly leveraged assets. Conservative utility investors may focus on EPS growth, dividend growth, and payout ratios. Financial ratios do not exist in a total vacuum, so be sure to compare management's performance with those of its competitors. Not all investment choices will fall within every limit outlined earlier. It is important to research the combined information because it should have an impact on investors' long-term investment returns.

FINANCIAL NUMBERS IN ACTION

Let us assume an investor has cash to invest and, after reviewing his or her portfolio of common stocks, realizes there are two industrial sectors not currently represented. To balance the portfolio, the investor determines that noncyclical companies are needed, such as nonalcoholic consumer beverages, and cyclicals, like capital goods. The investor desires the steady growth and defensive nature of noncyclical sector investments and wants more direct exposure to the ebbs and tides of the overall economy offered by the cyclical sector. After reviewing several companies in each sector, the selection is whittled down to four companies: PepsiCo (PEP) versus Coca-Cola (KO) and Tecumseh Products (TECU.A) versus Briggs and Stratton (BGG). Table 4–2 is a comparison of the financial numbers available through the Internet and at the public library as of March 2000.

Based on Table 4–2, the following conclusions could be made concerning PepsiCo versus Coca-Cola: Both PEP and KO's last 5-year EPS growth rates were well above industry average, but KO earnings grew faster. PEP's revenues are about 70 percent from its Frito Lay snack foods division, whereas the majority of KO's revenues are from its soft drink business. Wall Street analysts anticipate KO to continue to excel in EPS growth over PEP over the next 5 years. PEP generated greater cash flow per share in 1999, but its growth rate has lagged during the previous 5- and 10-year periods. KO takes an edge with dividend increases both realized in the last 5 years and anticipated in the next 5 years. PEP's projected dividend growth rate is below industry average. Payout ratios for both are below industry average, creating the potential for larger dividend increases in the future, especially from PEP. KO's payout ratio is quite high and may be a restricting factor in its future dividend growth. In all measurements of management efficiency, KO wins hands down and surpasses industry averages. Long-term debt at KO is almost 50 percent higher than PEP and also above industry average. All in all, KO appears to be a better-managed company

TABLE 4–2

Financial Comparisons: PepsiCo, Coca-Cola, Tecumseh Products, Briggs & Stratton

	PEP	KO	Industry Average	TECU.A	BGG	Industry Average
Stock price	$36	$47		$46	$38	
1999 revenues	$20.3 billion	$19.9 billion		$1.8 billion	$1.5 billion	
1999 operating income	$2.8 billion	$3.9 billion		$195 million	$180 million	
1999 EPS	$1.37	$0.98		$6.99	$4.54	
2000 anticipated EPS	$1.39	$1.45		$6.60	$5.23	
2001 anticipated EPS	$1.58	$1.76		$7.25	$5.52	
Last 5-yr. EPS avg. growth rate	4.6%	5.2%	1.1%	4.9%	5.1%	12.0%
Next 5-yr. EPS avg. growth rate	13%	15%		10%	8%	
1999 operating cash flow	$3.2 billion	$3.8 billion		$163 million	$113 million	
1999 cash flow per share	$2.06	$1.80		$10.57	$8.36	
Last 10-year avg. cash flow growth	11%	17%		6%	12%	
Next 5-yr. avg. cash flow growth	6%	8%		8%	10%	

1999 dividend per share	$0.54	$0.64		$1.28	$1.20	
Dividend yield	1.4%	1.3%	1.3%	2.7%	3.3%	1.6%
Last 5-yr. avg. dividend growth	8.8%	10.4%	11.7%	−2.0%	5.1%	5.9%
Next 5-yr. avg. dividend growth	6.5%	9.0%		5.5%	3.5%	
Payout ratio	39%	65%	75%	22%	19%	17%
ROE 5-yr. average	23.3%	50.0%	39.2%	11.7%	22.2%	17.1%
ROA 5-yr. average	7.2%	19.9%	14.96%	7.4%	10.6%	8.0%
ROI 5-yr. average	9.6%	36.7%	26.47%	9.0%	14.4%	10.9%
Long-term debt to equity	0.45	0.66	0.40	0.02	0.28	0.58
S&P equity ranking	A	A		B+	A−	
Mission statement includes stockholders	Yes	Yes		Not available	Yes	

Sources: S&P stock reports—Feb/March 2000, *Value Line Investment Survey—*May **2000,** *zacks.com, multexinvestor.com, aol.com/personalfinance.*

than PEP, providing investors better EPS growth rates, better cash flow generation, and better returns on their assets and equity. However, KO will probably underperform in dividend growth and, due to its leverage, may be more susceptible to higher interest expense if interest rates climb. Both PEP and KO carry the identical S&P equity ranking of "A" for high consistency in earnings and dividend growth.

Based on Table 4–2, the following conclusions could be made concerning Tecumseh Products versus Briggs & Stratton: Both companies generated EPS growth rates worse than industry averages over the past 5 years, but TECU.A is anticipated to accelerate its future EPS growth faster than BGG. Like PEP, TECU.A generated greater cash flow per share in 1999 than BGG, but averaged half the cash flow growth of BGG over the past 10 years. In addition, BGG is anticipated to continue generating higher cash flow growth over the next 5 years. Dividend increases for both were below industry average, but TECU.A actually cut its dividend an average of 2 percent a year over the past 5 years. Regarding management's efficiency ratios of ROE, ROA, and ROI, BGG not only outperformed TECU.A by a wide margin, but also beat industry averages, like KO. Both TECU.A and BGG have little debt, with TECU.A being almost debt-free. Overall, an investor can conclude that BGG is a well-managed company and has delivered better shareholder returns on investors' equity, assets, and investment. S&P ranks BGG above average in returning shareholder value via consistency in earnings and dividend growth, whereas TECU.A ranks as an average performer.

MARKET CAPITALIZATION

Each company with publicly traded stock is assigned a total value by investors based on the price they are willing to pay for its shares. *Market capitalization* is defined as the current value of a company derived by multiplying the number of shares outstanding by the market price. For example, PepsiCo has 1.444 billion common shares outstanding and Coca-Cola has 2.471 billion shares. Based on a market price of $36 for PEP and $47 for KO, the respective market capitalization would be $51.9 billion for PEP and $116.1 billion for KO. Tecumseh Products has 25 million shares outstanding of both Class A and Class B combined. At a market price of $46, TEUC.A has a market capitalization of $1.150 billion. Briggs & Stratton has 23 million shares and, at a market price of $38, is valued at $874 million in market capitalization. Companies are often classified based on their market size. Although there is not a hard-and-fast rule, generally market capitalization is categorized as follows:

Large capitalization (large-cap stocks)	over $5 billion
Medium capitalization (mid-cap)	$500 million to $5 billion
Small capitalization (small-cap)	$150 million to $500 million
Very small capitalization (microcap)	below $150 million

The larger the capitalization, the more liquid the investment. With 2.471 billion shares outstanding, investors will buy and sell KO stock every day. Small-cap companies with fewer shares and less investor interest may not trade every day.

HomePort Bankcorp (HPBC), the only locally managed bank on the island of Nantucket (off the coast of Cape Cod, Massachusetts), is a very profitable, niche market, microcap stock. Based on 1.8 million shares and an April 2000 market price of $23, HPBC has a market valuation of just $41 million. HPBC's stock does not trade every day because there are not always buyers and sellers. During April 2000, KO had an average daily volume of shares traded of 6.2 million shares, whereas HPBC's average daily volume was just 1000 shares. It would be easier and more efficient to buy and sell 5000 of KO than 5000 shares of HPBC. Large-cap stocks are usually considered established, well-known companies with strong brand awareness. Many conservative investors will focus on only large- and mid-cap stocks, whereas more aggressive investors may prefer small- and microcap stocks.

Smaller capitalization stocks may have more price volatility, and the stock price demands of the buyers or sellers may not be readily met. With fewer shares and more illiquid markets, small-cap stock share prices are sometimes characterized as having higher highs and lower lows. If a specific small company suddenly finds favor on Wall Street and there is a flurry of buying activity, share prices can quickly move to overvalued levels. Likewise, if a small-cap company finds itself out of favor and there is a rush to sell shares, its stock price may reach undervalued levels.

Management should be evaluated using the same criteria regardless of the market capitalization. Even small companies can have great management. For example, HomePort Bancorp has two branches and another under construction. The number of ATM machines can be counted on one hand or one foot. The service area of the bank is the small hook-shaped island of Nantucket (meaning "land far out to sea" in Wampanog Native American) about 3 miles wide and 15 miles long. Resting 30 miles off the coast of Cape Cod, Massachusetts, HPBC's service area is limited, and this could be considered a severe hindrance to revenue expansion. However, HPBC's management should be the envy of the banking industry. According to the company's first-quarter 2000 report, HPBC has $300,000 in nonperforming assets (a.k.a. problem loans) from a loan portfolio of $267 million. Potential problem loans of only 0.11 percent of its total loan portfolio are far below the industry average. HPBC's achievements have been stellar, providing investors ROE and ROI of 19.7 percent, almost 25 percent higher than industry average. Five-year average operating profit margins were 37 percent higher than industry average, and its 5-year average net profit margins were 45 percent higher than average. In 1999, EPS were $2.75 and are anticipated to grow to $3.10 in 2000 and $3.45 to $3.65 in 2001. During the past 5 years, EPS have grown an average of 18 percent a year. Long-term EPS growth rate is expected to slow a bit—to 13 percent over the next few years. The current dividend is $1.00 annually; with the stock trading around $23, it provides a comfortable 4.4 percent yield. The dividend represents a 30 percent payout ratio, which is a bit higher than average. Institutions like mutual funds and trust accounts own 22 percent of all outstanding shares, which is about half the industry average. With a small float, an increase in institutional interest could have a positive impact on its share price.

HomePort Bancorp's Corporate Mission Statement is entitled, "A Commitment to Our Community." HPBC's mission is

> to help our customers achieve their personal and business goals . . . by offering sound advice and a wide range of financial products. To help our employees reach their full potential . . . while providing an

unsurpassed level of service to our customers. To help our community by being the best corporate citizen in town . . . consistently working to protect our unique quality of life. To help our depositors and investors enjoy a high level of financial security . . . by continuing to operate in a sound fiscal manner.

HPBC is an excellent example of superior management squeezing every dollar of profit from the capital investors make available to them.

A diversified portfolio of DRIP companies should have exposure to investments in all market capitalization categories. Although a portfolio may not be equally weighted in all categories, some small-cap exposure is preferred.

STOCK PRICE EVALUATION TOOLS

Quality of management is only one area of investment research. Once top-quality companies are identified, the investor needs to determine whether the current stock price and dividend yield are satisfactory to provide adequate future investment returns. In addition, it is helpful to develop an understanding of the company's following on Wall Street.

The *PE ratio* is probably the single most important ratio for an investor. At any given moment in the trading day, it loudly barks out exactly what investors are willing to pay for each dollar of corporate earnings. Generally, stock prices are driven by supply and demand. With only a finite number of shares available to investors, although quite large for some companies, a stock price is set by what an investor is willing to pay and what a seller is willing to receive. The more investors believe a specific company's management will outperform its competitors, the higher the demand for its stock as an investment, and so its share price rises. Likewise, if there is a sudden turn for the worse and management fails to deliver on investors' expectations, the demand will shrivel up, and the stock price will plummet. Within each industrial sector, the PE ratio investors are willing to pay differs based on both the earnings growth of that sector and the level of interest by investors. The PE ratio is so significant an investment tool that most newspapers list it along with the stock price and the dividend yield.

The PE is derived from dividing the current stock price by its earnings per share. Returning to previous examples, the S&P 500 Index traded at a PE ratio of 14 at the beginning of 1990. Investors were willing to pay $14.38 for every dollar of per-share earnings of all the companies comprising the Index. At the end of 1999, investors were willing to pay $28.43 for the same dollar of earnings, and the market Index traded at a PE of 28. In the 1990s, investors drove the stock market higher not only because of growing corporate earnings, but also by expanding the PE ratios they were willing to pay. At the height of the Internet investing frenzy, having a *.com* after your name was more important than how much operating cash flow or earnings per share were generated. PE ratios, if calculable at all, sometimes reached 1000. In March 2000, Yahoo! (YHOO), the leading Internet search engine, traded at a price of $250 a share and is anticipated to earn $0.35 a share for all of 2000. This would mean investors buying Yahoo! stock at $250 a share would have paid a year 2000 PE ratio of 750 times earnings.

With the examples of PepsiCo, Coca-Cola, Tecumseh Products, Briggs & Stratton, and HomePort Bancorp, Table 4–3 outlines the

TABLE 4–3

PE Comparisons: PepsiCo, Coca-Cola, Tecumseh Products, Briggs & Stratton, HomePort Bancorp

	PEP	KO	TECU.A	BGG	HPBC
Stock price	$36	$47	$46	$38	$23
1999 PE ratio	25	47	7	8	8
5-yr. high–low PE	91–18	54–29	17–6	24–5	15–8
5-yr. median PE	54	42	11	14	12
Industry PE ratio	56	56	18	18	12
Industry 5-yr. high–low PE	65–26	65–26	31–13	31–13	34–10
Industry 5-yr. median PE	45	45	22	22	22
Sector PE ratio	31	31	18	18	20
S&P 500 PE ratio	35	35	35	35	35

Source: www.zacks.com.

PE ratio for each based on the stock prices as of March 2000 and earnings for the year 1999.

Partially due to its superior management as reflected in the efficiency numbers, investors are currently willing to pay almost twice as much per dollar of 1999 corporate earnings for KO than PEP, as demonstrated by KO's PE of 47 versus PEP's PE of 25. KO is trading toward the top of its 5-year PE range, whereas PEP is closer to its bottom of the range. In addition, PEP is trading at about half the current industry PE ratio and its median PE for the past 5 years. KO may have better management, but PEP is a better stock value based on comparison of the respective current PE ratios. TECU.A and BGG are neck to neck based on current and industry average PE ratios, but BGG is trading much lower than its 5-year median ratio, like PEP. BGG is not only more focused on increasing shareholder returns than TECU.A, also demonstrated by its efficiency factors, but it also represents a better investment value. HPBC is an excellently managed company that is trading at the low end of every PE category, representing great long-term value.

Investors are willing to pay more for each dollar of earnings for a fast-growing company than for a slow-growing company. However, high-PE stocks carry a higher risk that the share price could plummet if investors' expectations are not met. Just one below-par quarter, or even the hint of one, will send a high flyer crashing to the ground. Low-PE stocks carry a lower risk of falling much in price due to earnings or dividend disappointments. Due to the already low expectations of investors, however, a low PE may indicate that investors have little faith in management's ability to deliver on its earnings promises.

Dividend yield is the amount of the dividend divided by the stock price; it indicates the annual cash return to the investor. A $1 annual dividend on a $10 stock represents an annual dividend yield of 10 percent. One goal of DRIP investing is to find companies with adequate dividends to reinvest, as well as the opportunities to increase its dividends over the long term. Because dividends are a return to the shareholder of corporate profit, there must first be earnings with which to pay dividends. Usually, increasing earnings will allow management to continue raising its dividends while maintaining or increasing its payout ratio. Investors want a consistent

TABLE 4-4

Dividend Comparisons: PepsiCo, Coca-Cola, Tecumseh Products, Briggs & Stratton, HomePort Bancorp

	PEP	KO	TECU.A	BGG	HPBC
1999 annual dividend	$0.54	$0.64	$1.28	$1.20	$1.00
1999 dividend yield	1.4%	1.3%	2.7%	3.3%	4.4%
Avg. 5-yr. dividend yield	1.4%	1.0%	2.7%	2.5%	5.6%
Avg. 5-yr. dividend growth	8.8%	10.4%	-2.0%	5.2%	-22.0%
Industry 5-yr. avg. yield	1.0%	1.0%	1.3%	1.3%	1.7%
Industry 5-yr. div. growth	11.7%	11.7%	5.9%	5.9%	18.0%
Payout ratio	36%	65%	23%	19%	30%
Industry avg. payout ratio	75%	75%	17%	17%	25%

Source: www.zacks.com.

pattern of increasing dividends no matter how small initially. Many investors search for both dividend yields in excess of the S&P 500 Index and good dividend growth. With the run up in the S&P Index during the 1990s, it currently yields about 1.3 percent annually, which is very small by historic terms. Investors should compare dividend yields and growth rates with the company's competitors to evaluate its overall dividend performance. Table 4–4 shows dividend comparisons for PEP, KO, TECU.A, BGG, and HPBC.

Both PEP and KO offer about the same current yield. The current yield for KO is slightly above its 5-year average. PEP's yield is right on target. KO has increased its dividend annually more than PEP. Although seemingly small, the difference in the 5-year growth rates can create huge differences over the long term. During the last 5 years, PEP has increased its dividend by 76 percent, or for every dollar of dividends received in 1995 the investor now receives $1.76. KO has increased its dividends by 108 percent over the last 5 years, and $1.00 then equals $2.08 now. Both have payout ratios below industry average, with PEP's ratio leaving plenty of room to grow. BGG offers a better dividend yield than TECU.A, both on a current basis and compared to its 5-year average. BGG increased its dividends almost as much as its peers, whereas TECU.A cut its dividend. TECU.A's payout ratio is a bit higher than industry average, which may crimp its ability to raise dividends in the future.

HPBC currently yields an attention-getting 4.4 percent and historically yields about 2.5 times the industry average. According to John Sweeney, CFO of HPBC, in the past 5 years, the company found its bank capitalization ratio to be quite high at around 20 percent, and therefore management decided to return some capital back to the shareholders in the form of one-time special dividends. This continued until the bank's capitalization ratio was a more industry-normal 8.5 percent. These special dividends, however, cause the average dividend growth for the past 5 years to indicate the dividend was cut by 22 percent. When contacted, the company was very informative concerning these one-time dividends. This demonstrates the value of further investigation when financial numbers may seem askew.

Price-to-sales ratio is another method of evaluating the value of current stock pricing. Made popular by James O'Shaughnessy in his book *What Works on Wall Street,* the concept of comparing price with sales is to locate companies whose current market price represents good value based on a low price-to-revenue ratio. The formula is simple: current price per share divided by revenues per share. Some investors believe this is as important a ratio as the PE. The price-to-sales ratio will assist in identifying strong companies that may be experiencing temporary earnings difficulties, and the subsequent PE ratio will make that investment look expensive. Coca-Cola is a good example. In 1999, KO reshuffled management, laid off workers, and generally restructured its management responsibilities. This caused a one-time charge against operating earnings, reducing EPS. This is now reflected in a high PE ratio for KO. When price to sales are compared, however, this one-time shortfall becomes a non-event. There are two primary weaknesses with relying solely on a PE comparison as an evaluation of stock value. The first is that sales per share do not fluctuate as much as earnings per share, providing a more stable comparison. Second, if a company has no earnings and is operating at a loss, the PE ratio is inconsequential. Price-to-sales ratios vary based on the industry analyzed. Industries with low revenue growth, low earnings growth, and low profit margins will have historically a lower price to sales ratio. Likewise, indus-

TABLE 4-5

March 2000 Price-to-Sales Ratio: Pepsi-Co, Coca-Cola, Tecumseh Products, Briggs & Stratton, HomePort Bancorp, with Industry Averages

	Price to Sales	Industry Average
PEP	2.8	4.7
KO	6.1	4.7
TECU.A	0.5	1.5
BGG	0.5	1.5
HPBC	1.8	1.7

tries with high earnings growth and margins will have higher ratios. As a rule of thumb, stocks that are traded at a price-to-sales ratio of 10 or greater are considered very expensive. The price-to-sales ratios for these companies are listed in Table 4–5, along with current industry averages.

Using the price-to-sales ratio, PEP represents a better value at $36 than KO at $47, both on an individual company and industry average comparison. TECU.A and BGG are both trading substantially below industry average, and HPBC trades right at the industry average.

Broker recommendations are available over the Internet or from a stock brokerage firm. Several companies publish a consensus view of all broker recommendations. Usually broker recommendations are rated 1 to 5, with 1 being a strong buy recommendation, 3 being a neutral recommendation, and 5 being an outright sell recommendation.

With the sharp drop in revenues from stock trading commissions, brokerage firms have turned to investment banking as a larger source of revenues. With this larger importance of revenue generated from companies actually followed by the brokerage firm, the lines of demarcation between independent broker research and investment banking are evaporating. Over time, companies plan on mergers, sell bonds, or possibly issue more shares with a secondary offering of stock. Merchant bankers and stock brokerage firms make a fee on these and other corporate services. With many executive compensation packages revolving around stock options, what CEO in his or her right mind would favor a brokerage firm with a sell rating on its stock? It is in the best interest of the brokerage firm to maintain a positive investment recommendation for companies that it is soliciting for investment banking business. According to the June 2000 issue of *Smart Money Magazine,* the historic separation between brokerage house investment research and investment banking has become blurred. Before the rush to collect millions of dollars in Internet IPO fees, the investment research staff was much more independent and less pressured for positive recommendations. Although not attempting to paint the entire profession of broker research in a negative light, a strong dose of realism is required when relying on a single brokerage for advice.

Some investors feel that a bottom broker recommendation of 4 or 5 is meaningless, and that one must use the first three categories only. According to Chuck Hill, director of research at First Call Inc., of the 28,500 company ratings currently tracked, fewer than 1 percent are rated either a 4 or 5 or sell recommendations. Although there are no hard statistics, Hill believes that 15 to 20 years ago, sell recommendations ran somewhere around 5 percent to 10 percent of all recommendations. Of the 28,500 investment opinions, currently there could be about 285 stocks with sell recommendations, down from 1425 to 2850 considered normal two decades ago. If these broker recommendations were truly unbiased, there should be as many sell or underperform as buy recommendations, relative to the overall direction of the market. However, Hill believes the present 100-to-1 ratio of overall buy to sell recommendations is out of balance for an unbiased resource.

If the bottom two categories develop into meaningless recommendations and are dropped from the categories, then a 1 becomes a buy recommendation, a 2 becomes a hold recommendation, and a 3 becomes a sell. Although not considered an automatic sell signal, if the consensus of brokerage firms rates a stock a 3, investors may want to investigate other opportunities.

Zacks.com is a leading provider of broker recommendation consensus numbers on the Internet. First Call/Thompson Financial Corp also provides the same type of information by subscription, in

TABLE 4-6

March 2000 Consensus Broker Recommendation
and Number of Analysts: PepsiCo, Coca-Cola,
Tecumseh Products, Briggs & Stratton,
HomePort Bancorp

	Median Recommendation	Industry Average	Number of Analysts
PEP	1.30	2.13	22
KO	1.92	2.13	20
TECU.A	1.00	2.18	2
BGG	1.75	2.18	4
HPBC	2.00	1.95	1

Source: www.zacks.com.

print, or over the Internet. By reviewing consensus recommendations, rather than just one firm's analysis, an investor acquires a better overall understanding of the current feeling of all brokerage
house recommendations. Both First Call and Zacks list in-depth information about the recommendations, such as the number of analysts that follow the company, whether the latest earnings report
was in line with expectations, revisions of recommendations for the
past 7 and 30 days, along with consensus EPS growth rates.

Table 4-6 lists the median consensus recommendations as of
March 2000, as reported in *zacks.com,* for the previous examples.

PepsiCo has a higher buy recommendation from the 22 brokers
that follow the company than Coca-Cola has from its 20 brokers.
Tecumseh Products is also rated higher on the buy–sell scale than
Briggs & Stratton. There are very few analysts, however, following
Tecumseh, Briggs & Stratton, and HomePort Bancorp. To feel comfortable with a consensus, some investors like to see a minimum of
seven analysts' recommendations. Is a consensus recommendation
of only two brokerage firms, both potentially competing for additional investment banking fees, really a true Wall Street view of the
overall long-term investment opportunities offered by management?

PEG RATIOS AND THEIR IMPORTANCE IN STOCK PRICE EVALUATION

There is one more ratio that is revealing when determining the long-term investment value of a company based on its current stock price and management's ability to grow earnings—the PEG ratio. The PEG compares the current price-to-earnings ratio with the company's anticipated long-term EPS growth rate. The goal of this ratio is to determine whether a stock is selling at a premium to the underlying growth rate of earnings. When the current PE equals the long-term EPS growth rate, the PEG would equal 1.0. If the stock were selling at a current PE ratio of half the long-term growth rate, the PEG is 0.5; and if the stock traded at a PE of twice the underlying growth rate, the PEG would be 2.0. The strategy of researching PEG ratios is a belief that a company's fair value should be close to its long-term earnings growth potential. When a company is trading at a PEG of 2.0 or higher, investors are paying a huge premium to future earnings growth. Many investors believe the best time to buy a company's stock for the long term is when it is undervalued. Investors who follow the PEG strategy are most intrigued when a company is trading at half or less of its long-term growth rate, or at a PEG of 0.5 or less.

The PEG formula is current price divided by current EPS divided by the anticipated EPS growth rate. For PEP, the PEG would be 36 divided by 1.37 divided by 13, or 2.0. In contrast, KO would have a PEG calculation of 47 divided by 0.98 divided by 15, or 3.1. According to the PEG strategy, PEP is a much better stock value at its current price. Although PEP could be considered overvalued with a PEG of 2.0, it is still below KO's even more overpriced PEG of 3.1. Some investors prefer to use forward earnings estimates rather than the most recent actual earnings. The belief is that last year's corporate earnings are already reflected in the current stock price; with DRIP investing being long-term in nature, next year and the year after are of most interest. Using forward earnings estimates, Table 4–7 outlines the various PEG ratios for the previous examples.

When anticipated earnings are used for the PEG calculations, several interesting comparisons are revealed. Based on current PE and PEG ratios, PEP stock at $36 may be considered a better value than KO at $46. In just a few short years, however, if PEP and KO

TABLE 4-7

PEG Calculations: PepsiCo, Coca-Cola, Tecumseh
Products, Briggs & Stratton, HomePort Bancorp

	PEP	KO	TECU.A	BGG	HPBC
Price	$36	$47	$46	$38	$23
EPS growth rates	13%	15%	10%	8%	13%
1999 EPS	$1.37	$0.98	$6.99	$4.24	$2.75
2000 EPS	$1.39	$1.45	$6.60	$5.23	$3.10
2001 EPS	$1.58	$1.76	$7.25	$5.52	$3.45
1999 PEG	2.0	3.1	0.6	1.0	0.6
2000 PEG	1.9	2.2	0.7	0.9	0.6
2001 PEG	1.7	1.7	0.6	0.8	0.5

Source: *zacks.com.*

achieve investor expectations and their respective earnings estimates, both would have the same PEG and would be equal in price
to earnings growth comparisons. Although TECU.A has a current
edge in the PEG ratio over BGG, during the next 2 years, the advantage may be expected to dissipate. Looking ahead, HPBC is undervalued using the current stock price and year 2001 earnings estimates.

STOCK VALUATION RULES OF THUMB

When analyzing current stock valuations to determine the best
long-term DRIP investment, focus on the following:

- A PEG ratio of 1.0 is desirable, and a PEG of 0.5 or less is
  considered an excellent value;
- The PEG should be within industry averages;
- The current PE ratio should be closer to the bottom of the 5-
  year range and below the median of its 5-year PE range;
- Current PE should be below the current industry median;
- There should be a consistent pattern of increasing divi-
  dends with a low payout ratio;

- Dividend growth and dividend yield should be above industry averages;
- Price to sales should be less than 10 and below industry averages; and
- Broker recommendations should be taken with a grain of salt, but should be rated 2.5 or better.

Keep in mind potential conflicts of interest, especially with less than seven analysts' recommendations.

OVERALL COMPARISONS FOR LUCENT TECHNOLOGY, MERCK, FEDERAL SIGNAL

Lucent Technologies (LU) is the leading designer, developer, and manufacturer of telecommunications equipment systems, software, and miscellaneous products. Spun off by AT&T in early 1995, at a split-adjusted price of $7.40 per share, LU is the old "Bell Labs" and accounted for much of the innovative history of AT&T. LU was a stellar winner in the last half of the 1990s. As the most widely owned stock in America, LU represents an important portion of many investors' portfolios. Merck (MRK) is a leading US manufacturer of pharmaceuticals. With the expiration of many blockbuster drug patents in the next few years, some investors are concerned that MRK may experience slower revenue and profit growth going forward. Federal Signal (FSS) is the leading producer of fire engines, ambulances, and street sweepers. FSS also leads the industry in manufacturing consumable tools for manufacturing metal stamping dies, in addition to safety-warning devices such as sirens and horns. Table 4–8 lists comparisons, adjusted for stock splits, of these three companies in very diverse industries.

Management Analysis

The following analyzes management of LU, MRK, and FSS:

| *Average EPS Growth Rates vs. Industry Average* | LU's EPS growth rate is about half of industry average, MRK's EPS is also about half of industry average, and FSS's EPS growth rate is almost equal to industry average. |

TABLE 4-8

Comparisons: Lucent Technologies, Merck, Federal Signal

	LU	Industry Average	MRK	Industry Average	FSS	Industry Average
Stock price	$56		$68		$20	
1999 revenues	$38.5 billion		$32.7 billion		$1.0 billion	
1999 operating income	$4.5 billion		$8.6 billion		$106 million	
1999 EPS	$1.10		$2.45		$1.25	
2000 anticipated EPS	$1.26		$2.79		$1.50	
2001 anticipated EPS	$1.53		$3.06		$1.75	
Last 5-yr. EPS avg. growth rate	36.8%	30.3%	15.8%	17.6%	4.2%	14.6%
Next 5-yr. EPS avg. growth rate	20%	31%	12%	24%	12%	14%
1999 operating cash flow	−$1.2 billion		$6.1 billion		$57 million	
Price to cash flow	32	37	22	30	10	27
Last 10-yr. avg. cash flow growth	11 % (5 yr.)		16%		14%	
Next 5-yr. avg. cash flow growth	18 %		11%		9%	
1999 dividend per share	$0.08		$1.16		$0.76	
Dividend yield	0.1%	0.2%	1.7%	1.3%	3.7%	1.1%
Last 5-yr. avg. dividend growth	NM	7.2%	14.0%	11.5%	11.9%	11.0%
Next 5-yr. avg. dividend growth	13%		12%		5%	
Payout ratio	6%	5%	42%	34%	56%	38%
ROE 5-yr. average	6.4%	7.0%	37.2%	35.5%	20.5%	20.2%
ROA 5-yr. average	3.5%	5.1%	16.9%	16.2%	8.1%	4.4%
ROI 5-yr. average	2.4%	2.9%	21.4%	24.0%	16.0%	9.3%
Long-term debt to equity	0.55	0.28	0.29	0.28	0.39	1.23
S&P equity ranking	NR		A+		A+	
PE ratio	49	55	26	33	15	39
5-yr. PE high–low	76–17	92–21	37–19	55–19	23–11	45–15
5-yr. PE median	46	56	28	36	17	30
Current price to sales	4.5	15.6	4.7	7.6	0.8	4.0
Broker consensus	1.8	1.6	2.0	1.7	1.8	1.6
Number of brokers	37		32		4	
1999 PEG ratio	2.3		2.3		1.3	
2000 PEG ratio	2.0	1.8	2.0	1.1	1.2	0.9
2001 PEG ratio	1.6		1.8		0.9	
Market cap	$184 billion		$156 billion		$911 million	
Mission statement includes shareholders	Yes		Yes		Yes	

Sources: S&P stock reports—Feb/March 2000, *Value Line* Investment Survey—May 2000, zacks.com, multexinvestor.com, aol.com/personalfinance.

Maximum 65 percent Dividend Payout Ratio and Dividend Yield versus Industry Average	All three companies either equal or exceed their respective industry averages, with FSS currently yielding an impressive 3.7 percent.
Dividend Growth versus Industry Average	All three companies exceed industry averages. With an extremely low dividend of just two cents a quarter and its short trading history, LU's dividend history is not meaningful.
ROE, ROA 12 percent to 15 percent, and better than Industry Average	LU is much less than the 12 percent to 15 percent target, but within the industry average, and MRK's mirrors its industry average. FSS's ROA and ROI are almost twice the average.
Debt to Equity	LU and MRK fall within acceptable range, and FSS carries substantially less debt than its peers.
S&P Equity Ranking	LU does not have the 10-year trading history required to be included. MRK and FSS carry the highest ranking of A+.
Mission Statement Includes Shareholders	Investors are included in all three Corporate Mission Statements.

Stock Value Analysis

The following compares the stock values of LU, MRK, and FSS:

PEG Ratio	LU and MRK are trading at twice the underlying profit growth rate, which should be considered expensive but in line with their respective industry averages. FSS is trading at a slight premium to its long-term EPS growth rate, which is acceptable.

Current PE Ratio	All three stocks are trading at their median PE ratios of the last 5 years. They also have historically traded at a discount to the industry average, with FSS trading at about half its peers.
Price-to-Sales Ratio	All three trade at comfortable discounts to their respective industry averages, with FSS trading at about one-quarter of its peers.
Consensus Broker Recommendation	All three are about equally liked on Wall Street and are rated just a tad below their peers.

All three companies would be acceptable DRIP investments. Although somewhat overpriced, both LU and MRK are leaders in their industries and should continue to offer investors adequate returns. FSS, although highly leveraged, offers investors a good current dividend yield that should continue to increase at an acceptable rate. Based on price-to-sales and PE ratios, FSS at $20 a share is currently a bargain within its industry.

The research required to gather the prior information took approximately 2 hours on-line and 1 hour at the local public library. All the information needed to adequately research potential investment choices are readily available to any and all investors willing to exert the smallest amount of effort. To do less prior to putting your hard-earned capital to work could be considered in the category of gambling or playing portfolio Russian Roulette rather than long-term investing.

Author's Note: During the writing of this book, HomePort Bancorp accepted an acquisition offer from Seacoast Financial Corp for $36 a share in cash. Seacoast Financial realized the strategic market strength of HPBC is its home-grown, local business approach. Seacoast Financial will operate the bank as a separate subsidiary and will leave lending decisions on the island of Nantucket.

CHAPTER 5

How to Research Stocks, Part II: Reading an Annual Report

Key Concepts

- Annual Report's First Section—Letter to Shareholders, Pretty Pictures, and Financial Highlights
- Annual Report's Second Section—Management's Discussions and Cash Flow
- Annual Report's Third Section—Report of Independent Auditors and Board of Directors
- Proxy Statements and Notice of Annual Meeting

There are several resources an investor can use while researching potential stock investments. Some are straight from the company, in the form of a detailed business summary in the annual report and proxy statement. Quarterly reports provide investors with interim financial information. As a shareholder of a publicly held company, you are entitled to receive at least one report every year informing you of the financial status of your company. Most companies will also send quarterly statements to their shareholders. The annual report is usually much more detailed and is audited by an outside accounting firm. Quarterly financial statements are not usually audited and may be subject to revisions when audited. Quarterly reports are designed to update current shareholders on important events, rather than present a complete financial review. In addition, the company is required to submit more explicit reports on a quarterly basis to the Securities and Exchange Commission (SEC) outlining the financial results of the company. The SEC 10Q report is filed on a quarterly basis and a 10K on an annual basis. Although an annual report is considered an unofficial document, the SEC reports are the comprehensive official reports of company activity. SEC reports are available at *www.sec.gov/edgarhp.htm.* If you are not a shareholder, annual reports are usually available for the asking. Contact the Investor Relations Department and request a copy. With the advent of the Internet, the vast majority of companies offers quarterly and annual reports at their websites and they are available for download. Direct company website links are available through most financial websites. For example, *www.netstockdirect.com* easily links viewers to their desired company websites by simply identifying the company by either name or stock ticker symbol.

Annual reports vary in length. The Harley Davidson's (HDI) 1999 annual report is 99 pages, Merck's is 62 pages, and HomePort Bancorp's is 38 pages. An annual report contains a wealth of information and should be read by every shareholder and potential investor. Not only does it tell the story of the company's products or services, but it also details the most recent annual financial results and historical data. The annual report includes a letter to shareholders written by top management. As discussed previously, an astute investor can evaluate management's commitment to its shareholders partially by the tone of the annual letter. The annual report will discuss operational details of each business segment and includes management's assessment of the business. The financial information provided includes not only sales and profits, but also important statistics such as number of shares outstanding, stock incentive plans for employees and management, and members of the board of directors.

Annual reports can be somewhat controversial. Some investors and Wall Street pundits believe they are nothing more than corporate hype aimed at the investment and financial community. Most people either do not bother to read annual reports or do not understand the information presented. Due to its relative difficulty in being comprehended, annual reports are ignored by all but a few shareholders. Most new investors do not review the latest annual report prior to investing. However, the information found in most annual reports should be considered basic for long-term DRIP investors.

According to SEC regulations, all companies with over 500 shareholders and $1 million in assets are required to publish an annual report within 90 days of year-end. As a shareholder, the annual report comes automatically to the investor's mailbox and provides a relatively effortless means to review the performance of both management and the investment in their stock. With most companies ending the year December 31, annual report season is usually the following March.

Very little is written in most investment guides about annual reports. Nearly all give this important research tool just a cursory acknowledgment. John Downes and Jordan Elliot Goodman, in *Barron's Financial and Investment Handbook, 5th Edition,* wrote the best synopsis of an annual report on page 89: "Weekend sailors know an axiom that if you can understand a dinghy you can sail a yacht. It's all in grasping the fundamentals. Annual reports are the yachts of corporate communications, and in full regalia they can be as formidable as they are majestic." Drafted from the combined efforts of accountants, lawyers, marketers, and executives, annual reports are targeted to a variety of audiences—stockholders, potential stockholders, security analysts, lenders, customers, and employees. However, they are essentially financial statements consisting of an income statement and a balance sheet.

There is a movement afoot, especially with smaller companies, to offer a slimmed down version of an annual report. These shorter versions are simply a repackaged annual 10K report filed with the SEC. As a regulatory filing, 10K reports are more difficult to read and are substantially less shareholder-friendly in their presentation.

Harley Davidson (HDI) is the largest US manufacturer of heavyweight motorcycles. HDI is a very well-managed company with a rich corporate history and brand awareness envied by many in business. Mr. Paul Dean, editorial director of *Cycle World* magazine, was most descriptive in his portrayal of Harley Davidson's loyal following: "Do you know of any other product that will cause people to tattoo its name on their bodies?"[1] In 1999, Harley Davidson produced over 183,000 motorcycles and had a 49 percent market share in North America, 6 percent share in Europe, and 19 per-

TABLE 5—1

Selected Financial Data, Harley Davidson

	HDI	Industry
ROA 5-year average	12.6%	9.7%
ROI 5-year average	16.3%	13.4%
ROE 5-year average	23.9%	18.1%
Long-term debt to equity	0.23	
Dividend increase 5-year average	20%	
Payout ratio	9%	
1999 operating cash flow	$416 million	
Shares outstanding	303 million	
Market cap	$12 billion	

Source: zacks.com.

cent share in Asia Pacific in the 651cc and higher niche market. Harley Davidson's analysis as of May 2000, with industry averages, is listed in Table 5–1.

Harley Davidson's Corporate Mission Statement is very focused, but not as investor-friendly as some. "We fulfill dreams through the experience of motorcycling, by providing to motorcyclists and to the general public an expanding line of motorcycles and branded products and services in selected market segments." However, the first two lines of the 1999 Letter to Shareholders more than makes up for this oversight.

> Dear Fellow Shareholders: It is my privilege to share with you in the Annual Report the results of Harley Davidson's 14th consecutive record year of financial performance. Our consistent growth has had a clear benefit to investors—a shareholder who purchased $10,000 of Harley Davidson stock when we first went public in 1986 would be a millionaire today—for many, a dream come true. In what follows, we hope to show you not only how Harley Davidson inspires, cultivates and shares the dream of motorcycling with our customers, but also how we go about fulfilling the dreams of *all* our stakeholders.

As the information in an annual report is explained, HDI is used as an example.

ANNUAL REPORT'S FIRST SECTION—LETTER TO SHAREHOLDERS, PRETTY PICTURES, AND FINANCIAL HIGHLIGHTS

The first section usually includes the letter from the chairman, pictorial review of products or services, descriptions of specific business segments and their performance, and graphic presentation of recent sales, profits, dividends, market share, and return on investment. Rising stock price comparisons is a favorite, especially if the stock has done very well. Graphic highlighting is most prevalent when the graph depicts excellent managerial performance. Important information about the company can be found in the presentation of its products and services.

The theme of inspiring, experiencing, and sharing the "dream" of owning a Harley is the focus of the first part of the HDI annual report. Right after the letter to shareholders, HDI reviews its overall financial results in a table. The financial highlights include a stripped-down income statement with net sales, income before provision for income tax, net income, basic and weighted earnings per share, recap of the balance sheet with assets and equity, low and high market price per share by quarter, and number of shareholders of record. The table lists this information for 1999, 1998, and 1997. Photos of motorcycles and riders are next. As an illustration of the latest products and motorcycle technology, the new "Twin Cam 88B" engine is featured. The Twin Cam 88B offers more horsepower, better acceleration, and reduced vibration. A review of the Genuine Parts & Accessories and General Merchandise business unit follows, with a graph outlining revenue growth of Parts and Merchandise from 1990 to 1999. A discussion of the all-important Harley Davidson dealer network is marked, along with its Customer and Dealer Financial Services program. Marketshare gains in the United States and abroad are highlighted next, with a short paragraph about its newly opened limited assembly plant in Brazil. This plant allows for limited value-added production in that country, which generally reduces import tariffs and product costs, creating a more competitive market price. Harley riders, their riding clubs, and company-sponsored events are important enough for the company to devote several pages of pictures and captions. The next few pages thank the employees, suppliers, and investors for their work and patience. The last page of the first part of the Harley Davidson annual report is a photograph of a gentleman sitting at the foot of a large oak tree, with his red and chrome Harley in the background. The gentleman seems to be closer to 60 years of age than 20 and appears to be gazing off in the distance through a pair of traditional aviator-type sunglasses. The caption reads, "When Harley Davidson made its initial public offering back in 1986, Leonard Holt called his stockbroker. 'I told him to buy all I could afford, which wasn't a lot at the time, but it grew considerably,' says Holt, who has ridden Harley Davidson motorcycles since 1956. 'Its been a great ride!'"

Harley Davidson's presentation in the first part of its annual report superbly outlines the focus and the strength of the company, its new products, and its customers' loyalty. Subtly presented is the reward to long-term investors.

ANNUAL REPORT'S SECOND SECTION— MANAGEMENT'S DISCUSSIONS AND CASH FLOW

After reviewing the pretty pictures of products and employees hard at work, an investor gets to the meat of all annual reports: tables of financial numbers and management's discussions of its financial performance. No pretty pictures, just a bunch of tables and small print. Here, however, is where investors can find the results of management's ability to increase the value of shareholders' capital. Usually included in this part of the report are tables with a 5-year history of selected financial data. These may include net sales, cost of goods sold, gross profit, operating income, selling, general, and administrative expenses (SG&A), income from discontinuing operations, basic and diluted number of shares, dividends paid, and shareholders' equity.

Compare upward trends in revenue, profit growth, and expenses. Focus on data from continuing operations. Discontinued operations are the result of businesses the company has decided to exit and probably will not have an impact on future performance. Basic shares are the number of shares currently outstanding, whereas diluted shares are the number of shares that would be outstanding if all stock options were exercised. With a higher number of shares outstanding after including options, earnings per diluted share are usually a bit lower than earnings per basic shares. Table

TABLE 5-2

Selected Financial Data from 1995 to 1999, Harley Davidson in Millions, Except Share Data

	1999	1998	1997	1996	1995
Net sales	$2,452	$2,063	$1,762	$1,531	$1,350
Gross profit	835	690	586	490	411
Operating income from financial services	27	20	12	7	3
SG&A	(447)	(377)	(328)	(269)	(180)
Net income	$267	$213	$174	$177	$112
Number of basic shares	152 million	152 million	151 million	150 million	149 million
Earnings per share	$1.75	$1.40	$1.15	$0.95	$0.74
Dividends per share	$0.175	$0.155	$0.135	$0.11	$0.09
Shareholders' equity	$1,161	$1,029	$869	$662	$494

Source: Harley Davidson 1999 Annual Report.

5–2 lists select financial data for HDI from 1995 to 1999, in millions, except for per-share data.

Sales and Profits

Look for positive trends in revenue and net income growth. HDI's sales increased from $1.350 billion in 1995 to $2.452 billion in 1999, for a total 5-year revenue growth of 81.6 percent or by an annual average of 16.3 percent. Net income grew during the same time period by 138.4 percent or by an annual average of 27.6 percent. Investors should be seeking companies with net income that is growing faster than net revenues. HDI's management produced $0.083 of net income per dollar of revenue in 1995, and increased net income to $0.108 per dollar of revenue in 1999.

Overhead, SG&A and R&D

Overhead expenses and general and administrative (SG&A) expenses are categorized as required to operate the business. These include salaries for salespeople and management, the cost of running the company offices, and other nonproduction expenses. These days, companies are trying desperately to reduce the SG&A expenses and become more efficient. Reductions in the SG&A translate to direct improvements of the company net profit. The company's goal is to reduce administrative costs for each dollar of revenues, thus improving profits. A reduction in SG&A expenses with improving revenues is considered very good. Harley Davidson's SG&A (including engineering or R&D) increased by 89.7 percent over the 5-year period, or an annual average of 17.9 percent. This is slightly more than revenue growth of 16 percent, but far below net income growth of 27 percent. It is preferred for expenses to increase no faster than the rate of net income growth.

Research & Development/
Capital Expenditures

Research and development (R&D) expenses are vital for a company to continually introduce new products. Without new products, a company's profits will usually begin to stagnate. Investors like to see a consistent or rising R&D expense to overall revenues and net income. Companies need to continually update and expand their facilities, be it office space for service companies or equipment for manufacturers. Companies with declining R&D/capital expenditures trends may have difficulty maintaining their competitive advantage. Although some companies report specific R&D budgets, Harley Davidson incorporates these expenses into overall corporate SG&A.

Weighted Basic Average Shares

The number of shares outstanding indicates how many shares the company has issued to investors, with and without consideration for pending management options and adjusted for stock splits. The most commonly used number for the shares outstanding is the basic, or noninclusive, number. Investors should be aware of the possibility of substantial dilution from future stock options given to management. Investors should desire steady numbers of shares outstanding, both basic and diluted. With the popularity of company mergers using stock as the currency, many companies will dramatically increase the number of shares outstanding. However, increases in revenue and net income from the merger should, if successful, offset investor dilution caused by the additional shares. Review earnings per share both with basic and diluted for stock options. If there is a large difference, investors should question the commitment of management to its current shareholders. Many times a company will buy back shares, reducing the number outstanding. If a company believes its stock price is undervalued and finds itself with extra cash flow, management may decide to reduce the outstanding shares. As the number of shares decreases, net income per share generally increases. Hopefully, the stock price will respond accordingly. Harley Davidson's number of basic shares have barely budged over the past 5 years, rising from 149.9 million in 1995 to 152.3 million in 1999, adjusted for stock splits. Diluted shares also increased slightly from 151.9 million to 154.8 million.

Dividends

Many investors prefer companies with rising dividends. Dividends per share should be on an upward trend over the 5-year history. HDI's dividend has almost doubled in the past 5 years. Although not a big cash dividend payer, management has demonstrated a willingness to substantially increase shareholder payout over time.

Shareholders' Equity

Shareholders' equity is the value of the company after repayment of debt—similar to a person's net worth. Equity is calculated by adding together all the company's assets, from cash in the bank to real estate and inventory. Deduct from the assets the corporate liabilities, such as long-term debt and accounts payable. What remains is corporate equity. Corporate equity belongs to the common stock shareholders and represents the assets that support the stock certificates. The best-managed companies increase net income and shareholders' equity at a greater rate than revenue gains. Harley Davidson's shareholders' equity has risen from $494 million in 1995 to $1.161 billion in 1999. This represents a 135.0 percent increase over the past 5 years. HDI's management achieved an average increase in direct shareholder value of 27 percent annually since 1995 on revenues that increased by 16 percent annually over the same period.

Management's Discussion and Analysis of Financial Conditions and Results of Operations

Management has the opportunity to discuss specific financial results in this part of the annual report. Revenue, net income, and earnings per share growth are usually addressed. Specific manufacturing facilities or business units that provided unusually high or low contributions to net income may be discussed. Overall market challenges or opportunities may be explained in more detail. Prior-year comparisons are highlighted. Other financial matters, such as accounting changes, environmental matters, corporate liquidity, and capital resources, and discussion of overall business market risk are presented.

For nonmanufacturing companies, such as a savings and loan, the topics covered in this part are a bit different. Reviewing the 1999 annual report for HomePort Bancorp, the topics discussed in their management's discussion include results of operations, noninterest income, noninterest expense, income taxes, assets and liabilities analysis, loans, borrowed funds, and nonperforming assets. Management's discussion of the annual progress of the business is usually duller, drier, and substantially more boring than even this book. There are lots of numbers, comparisons, percentage increases and decreases, and technical currency conversion rate discussions. It is important for investors to read this part of every annual report of every company they either own or are considering owning.

It's in this part that Harley Davidson discusses its market size, market share, and gross margins. During 1999, the worldwide market for 650cc motorcycles increased by 14 percent, whereas Harley's retail registration increased by 20 percent. This reflects a larger worldwide market share of 26.7 percent, up from 25.2 percent in 1998. Gross profit margin expanded from 33.5 percent to 34.1 percent. Production increased from 157,000 motorcycles in 1998 to 184,000 in 1999. International revenues represented about 23 percent of the total, down from 25 percent in 1998, mainly due to heavy US demand. Management expects the Parts and Accessories business to continue growing faster than overall motorcycle sales, while General Merchandise (Harley Davidson trademarked clothing, etc.) is expected to expand at a slower pace. Income from Financial Services was up 37 percent in 1999, reflecting strong demand for retail installment financing of their motorcycles.

Liquidity, Capital Resources, and Cash Flow

Most annual reports should include discussion of the company's cash position. This should encompass operating cash flow as the major source of corporate liquidity. This part also discusses the corporate credit line at various banks, capital expenditures, additions to long-term debt, and any repurchase or secondary offering of stock. If a company is losing money on an earnings per share basis, it may or may not have negative operating cash flow. Cash is the corporate engine that pulls any company up the track to success. Without cash, companies shrivel up and die. Always look at management's review of cash flow. Cash flow tables may only tabulate the past 3 years, whereas other financial tables may list a 5-year history.

As the heart of any corporation, investors should be sure to review and understand the cash flow statement. Cash flow is divided into several categories: cash flow generated from operating the company, cash generated from investing activities, and cash generated from financing activities. Net cash flow from operations is the net earnings of the company plus all the noncash expenses subtracted to reach net earnings. For example, net earnings include deductions for equipment depreciation and goodwill amortization, which are noncash expenses. Potential credit losses and long-term benefits for employees are deducted from earnings, but are not current cash expenses. Cash from operations is the cash produced by operating the business, not cash generated by borrowing from the bank, liquidating assets, or selling more stock to investors. Cash flow from investing activities is the amount of cash used or generated from investing by the business. These items include purchases or sales of capital equipment, investments in other companies, proceeds from the sales of businesses or assets, and long-term financing and repayment of product sales. Cash flow from financing activities is the corporate cash used or generated from financing by the company. This includes any issuance or repayment of debt, dividends paid, and stock purchased or issued by the company. Some companies with high international revenues will find that fluctuating currency exchange rates will add or reduce their cash flow and will include a specific line item to their statement of cash flow detailing this fluctuation.

Excellently managed companies should always have positive operating cash flow. Sometimes earnings per share may be greatly reduced or even negative due to merger expense or possibly a shift in profitable markets. Excellently managed companies will always find ways to generate cash by operating their businesses. Cash used by investing activities are investments that should improve the value of the business, either by investing in additional plants and equipment or investing in other businesses. Sometimes a company with weak operating cash flow will sell assets or investments to compensate. Cash flow from financing activities usually includes corporate debt and buying back or issuance of shares. Cash generated by adding debt or issuing shares may also mask poor operating cash flow results.

Whenever there is an opportunity to analyze numbers, like earnings or cash flow, always concentrate on those reported for ongoing operational businesses. Sometimes companies sell or discon-

TABLE 5-3

Selected Cash Flow Data from 1997 to 1999, Harley Davidson, in Thousands

	1999	1998	1997
Cash flows from operating activities:			
Cash flow from operating activities	$267,201	213,500	174,070
Adjustments (depreciation, provision for credit losses, deferred income tax, etc.)	148,937	104,562	135,665
Net cash flow from operating activities	$416,138	$318,062	$309,735
Cash flow from investing activities:			
Net capital expenditures	$(165,786)	$(182,770)	$(186,171)
Finance receivable originated	(3,321,382)	(2,722,768)	(1,618,307)
Finance receivable collected	2,616,857	2,105,684	1,107,157
Finance receivable sold	574,997	469,563	300,000
Other, net	(4,308)	(9,952)	(9,189)
Net cash flow from investing activities	$(299,622)	$(340,153)	$(406,510)
Cash flow from financing activities:			
Net decrease in notes payable	$0	$(773)	$(2,580)
Net increase in finance debt	34,421	56,104	112,573
Dividends paid	(26,996)	(24,153)	(21,028)
Purchase of common stock	(130,284)	(15,175)	0
Issuance of stock to employees	24,588	23,786	12,793
Net cash (used) provided by financing activities	$(98,271)	$39,799	$101,758
Net increase in cash:	$18,245	$17,708	$4,983
Cash at the beginning of year	$165,170	$147,462	$142,479
Cash at the end of year	$183,415	$165,170	$147,462

Source: Harley Davidson 1999 Annual Report.

tinue businesses and the earnings attributed to those facilities are separated as *discontinued operations*. Investors should seek companies with strong and growing operating cash flow, which can fund a reduction in debt and shares outstanding and increase investing activities. Harley Davidson's selected consolidated statement of cash flow for 1999 was reported as shown in Table 5–3.

Harley Davidson's 3-year history demonstrates very strong cash management. HDI generated over $400 million in 1999 from operating its business, up over 50 percent from 1997. Much of this cash has been used in either capital expenditures for new plants and equipment ($165 million), net increase in long-term financing for product sales ($135 million), along with dividend payments and stock repurchase programs ($156 million). From a stockholder viewpoint, HDI not only generated ample operating cash flow, but also rewarded investors by increasing their dividend, buying back shares, and reinvesting in their business. At the end of the year, HDI's cash in the bank, or its equivalents, increased in 1999 by $18 million to $183 million.

Consolidated Balance Sheets

A balance sheet is a statement of corporate assets and liabilities. Assets include cash in the bank, accounts receivable, inventory, and prepaid expenses. The original cost of corporate property and equipment—after annual depreciation allowances—is also listed with assets. Liabilities comprise all money owed by the corporation, including accounts payable and short- or long-term debt owed either to banks or investors. Shareholders' equity is the balance between a corporation's assets and its liabilities. Equity includes paid-in-capital from the sale of stock and retained earnings. Retained earnings are the cumulative amount of net income retained by the corporation and not paid to shareholders. Asset and liability data are usually provided for the past 2 or 3 years. Table 5–4 shows selected items from Harley Davidson's December 31, 1999 balance sheet.

The single largest category of HDI's assets is related to financing product purchases to dealers and motorcyclists. Finance receivables due in the next year ($440 million) and those with longer than 1-year maturity ($354 million) represent $794 million, or 37 percent of all assets. Plant and equipment assets of $681 million are next, followed by cash on hand and inventory. HDI has total liabilities associated with product financing of $461 million. Long-term debt is quite small at $65 million. HDI's management has been paying down long-term debt, as seen by the $2 million reduction in 1999.

Equity represents the value of the company if it were sold and

TABLE 5-4

Selected Balance Sheet Data from 1998 to 1999, Harley Davidson, in Thousands, Except Share Data

	1999	*1998*
Assets		
Current assets		
Cash	$183,415	$165,170
Accounts receivable	101,708	113,417
Current portion of finance receivable	440,951	360,341
Inventory	168,616	155,616
Other	55,000	50,000
Total current assets	$948,994	$844,963
Finance receivable, net	$354,888	$319,427
Property, plant and equipment, net	681,741	627,759
Other assets	126,000	126,000
Total assets:	$2,112,077	$1,920,209
Liabilities		
Current liabilities		
Accounts payable	$137,660	$122,722
Accrued and other liabilities	199,331	199,051
Current portion of finance debt	181,163	146,742
Total current liabilities	$518,154	$468,515
Finance debt	$280,000	$280,000
Long-term debt	65,093	67,376
Postretirement health care costs	75,719	72,083
Deferred income taxes	12,031	2,324

Source: Harley Davidson 1999 Annual Report.

all debt repaid, and it should be the amount of proceeds available to shareholders. However, many times the assets on the books do not accurately reflect real-life valuations. Equipment value may be higher than its depreciated book value. Corporate land bought decades ago would be worth many times its value on the balance sheet. Likewise, the value of in-process inventory or specialty raw material would be considered much lower than its value on the

TABLE 5-5

Selected Shareholders' Equity Data from 1998 to 1999, Harley Davidson, in Thousands

	1999	1998
Shareholders' Equity		
Common stock	$1,592	$1,584
Additional paid-in-capital	236,540	211,960
Retained earnings	1,113,376	873,171
Other income (loss)	(2,067)	1,128
Less treasury stock and unearned compensation	(188,400)	(57,933)
Total shareholders' equity	$1,161,080	$1,029,911

Source: Harley Davidson 1999 Annual Report.

books. More important than the actual book value per share, the trend of consistently increasing shareholders' equity should be a focus of investors. Table 5–5 lists the 1999 Shareholders' Equity for Harley Davidson.

Over its corporate history, Harley Davidson has retained $1.1 billion earned on behalf of its shareholders, up from $873 million in 1998. Before a 2 for 1 stock split in April 2000, HDI had 159 million shares outstanding. Shareholders' equity, also known as the book value, at the end of 1999 was $7.30 a share, up from $6.47 in 1998 or an increase of 12.8 percent.

Notes to Financial Statements and Additional Information

Following the consolidated statements of cash flow and the balance sheet is the obligatory footnotes explaining in detail how some of the financial numbers are calculated. Just as important as the fine print of any personal contract, the notes are an integral part of the financial statements. For example, in the Notes, HDI reveals that of the almost $102 million in accounts receivable, $89 million is from foreign customers. Some investors may find this high percentage of foreign account receivable a bit discomforting due to the inherent risks of overseas collections in potentially hard economic times.

Capital Stock or Stock Option Plans

Stock incentive plans for management are an important method of ensuring that employees and management are working for the same goal—increasing shareholder value. If the company gives employees, both at the top and on the assembly line, the opportunity to become company owners, a portion of their personal wealth is now pegged to their performance on the job. When their company succeeds, the value of their ownership interest increases. Long-term stock options and stock purchase plans can be used as a means to unify all employees toward one common goal—increasing company profits and share prices for the long term. Starting in 1996, due to the huge amount of stock options given to employees, companies are now required to explain in detail their plans and their impact on current earnings per share and shares outstanding. In one high-tech company, management had been given so many stock options that the company had to repurchase large amounts of shares in the open market to prevent diluting ownership by current shareholders. This company is rumored to have spent almost 75 percent of its annual operating cash flow to repurchase stock to satisfy the stock options. That is very excessive and not very investor-friendly. Investors should look for moderate stock ownership by management using stock options. In the case of Harley Davidson, at the end of 1999, there were 5.7 million shares, or about 3.5 percent of all shares outstanding, available to employees through a stock option plan.

ANNUAL REPORT'S THIRD SECTION—REPORT OF INDEPENDENT AUDITORS AND BOARD OF DIRECTORS

As shareholders, investors have the right to approve the selection of outside auditors to review the company's books every year. In the annual report, the auditor certifies the financial numbers were reviewed and validated. Typically, the auditors will report a clean or "unqualified" opinion. The auditor may report that, "in our opinion, the financial statements referred to above present fairly, in all

material respects, the consolidated financial position of the company as of Dec 31, 1999." In a rare instance, the auditor may find problems with the company's bookkeeping and will issue a "qualified"
statement, which may read "except for" and then state the problem.
Investors should review all annual reports for a "clean" opinion
from the outside auditor. At the end of every annual report is a list-
ing of the board of directors. Usually management is represented
with several positions on the board including its chairman. Review
the outside directors and their listed professions. As investors' representatives, outside directors should be looking out for the best interests of the shareholders. For example, HDI has nine board members, two of whom are either current or retired HDI employees. The
other members include executives from SBC Communications,
General Motors, Motorola, a Harley Dealer, and a corporate lawyer.

PROXY STATEMENT AND NOTICE
OF ANNUAL MEETING

Included in every annual report is an announcement of votable issues that will be decided at the next annual meeting of the board of
directors. As a holder of voting shares in the company, stockholders
have the right to cast a vote for specific decisions. These may include
increasing the board of directors, authorizing and increasing shares
outstanding to accommodate a stock split, or approving a merger
with another company. Shareholders also have the right to vote for
their representative on the board of directors and select the company's outside auditors. Sometimes investors will place specific initi-
ates to be voted on by all shareholders. If shareholders are unable to
attend the annual meeting to cast their vote in person, the company
will allow for a response by proxy and vote by absentee ballot.

Proxy statements include interesting bits of information about
your company. For instance, it will outline the stock holdings of all
current board members. Usually investors like to have their representatives on the board, the outside directors, to also be shareholders. Because it is the job of outside directors to look out for the
interests of shareholders, by holding shares themselves, their decisions will impact them equally. The proxy will disclose all investors
holding more than 5 percent of the outstanding shares. This information will allow investors to know who are the majority share-

holders. There is detailed information concerning compensation for the top executives along with the current status of their stock options and corporate pension plans. Included in all proxy statements will be a 5-year history of the performance of their common stock compared to the S&P 500 and a peer group.

Harley Davidson's 1999 proxy statement allowed shareholders to vote for members of the board of directors and an outside auditor. The annual meeting of shareholders was held in Milwaukee, Wisconsin, on April 29, 2000, and was open to all shareholders. The proxy statement revealed that in 1999 the CEO of the company received a salary of $653,000, a bonus of $1.3 million, and stock options for 55,000 shares of HDI stock at a pre-2000 stock split cost of $51.59 a share. The board of directors, as a group, owns 2.6 percent of outstanding shares, and the largest shareholders are The Equitable Companies with 6.3 percent and Ruane, Cuff & Co with 5.4 percent. The statement also disclosed that top management received 20 percent of all stock options granted in 1999, with the balance going to other employees. HDI stock has outperformed both the S&P 500 Index and the S&P Mid Cap 400. Further, $100 invested in HDI stock on December 31, 1994, would be worth $469.09 on December 31, 1999. The same $100 invested in the S&P 500 would be worth $351.11. If invested in the S&P Mid Cap Index, it would have grown to $282.01.

As management grew revenues, profits, and returns on investors' capital, share prices have responded by climbing from a low in 1997, adjusted for stock splits, of $16 a share to a high in 1999 of $64 a share. For those long-term DRIP investors with the foresight to invest in HDI, their stock could have been bought for $0.65 a share at the end of 1986, adjusted for stock splits through December 1999, $2.41 in 1990, or $14.30 in 1995. In April 2000, HDI split its stock again 2 for 1 after reaching an all-time high of over $80 a share.

Investors should take reading annual reports seriously. Because corporate earnings and interest rates are the primary movers of stock prices (except for this.com company or that.com company), it is vital to understand the quality of a company's earnings. In the eyes of management, the goal of an annual report is to tell investors all the good things about their company. It is not usually in the best interest of management to tell their shareholders that the competitors are eating their lunch or that the next-generation product has just been introduced by someone else, making their products completely antiquated. The reports are usually filled with pretty graphs comparing such things as earnings or dividends or return on assets, and they are filled with colorful pictures of factories, employees, products, or all three. The graphs and pictures are designed to elicit the reply, "Man, is this company cool!" In addition to these graphs and pictures, the annual reports are filled with lots of small printed, unfriendly text and an array of financial tables. Much of this information is never read.

Look for a few specific numbers or sections in management's discussion to aid in getting past all the PR and hype typical in annual reports. Going past the pretty pictures and graphs reveals interesting information on the past and potential future performance of any company. Although it seems by design to be difficult and uninviting to read, management's discussions of the consolidated financial statements and footnotes to the consolidated financial statements are critical sections of all annual reports.

There are some red flags that may appear hidden to a casual review of an annual report, but an astute reader can easily find them. Listed next are a few of the danger signs.

Exploding Inventory Levels—If inventory levels (found in the asset side of the balance sheet tables) are growing faster than sales, it may infer several possibilities. Maybe the quality of the product is in trouble or the competition is taking a larger market share and manufacturing has not responded accordingly. Maybe customers have become financially strapped and are canceling orders. On the positive side, increasing inventories may be from a new plant or process and sales have yet to catch up with production. However, keep in mind that the specific industry has a great impact on the meaning of exploding inventories. For example, in a high-tech industry where product improvements are quick, rising inventories represent a potentially worse situation than commodity products such as lumber or plywood. In these product lines, obsolete and old inventory is not as great a financial threat.

Accounts Receivables Rising Faster Than Sales—Accounts receivable is the amount owed to the company by its customers, and it is also found on the asset side of the balance sheet. Customers owing more money may indicate a slow-down in their business, indicating a possible slowdown in overall sales. Trial or consignment orders will increase accounts receivables, as will end-of-the-quarter or end-of-the-year discounting to generate immediate revenue increases.

Extraordinary Expenses—These are usually a sign of management's recognition of festering problems. Sometimes management "restructures" due to sudden recognition of problems in its business. Is the company trying to reduce overhead costs by laying off employees or closing factories? Is it writing off obsolete inventory or cutting overlapping responsibilities after a merger?

Assets Sales—Sales of company assets are sometimes used to inflate earnings. As one-time gains, asset sales will not contribute to future earnings unless the proceeds are reinvested in the business.

Research and Development/Capital Spending—Both are vital for the longevity of a company. Without a steadily growing R&D program, along with consistent updating of facilities, many companies are putting the last nail in their own coffins. A trend of lower R&D and capital spending without adequate explanation should be a serious red flag to the long-term investor.

Currency Transactions—This seems to be a huge black hole on a company's earnings statement. If your company has extensive overseas business, changes between the value of the US dollar and the local currency where the company does business can have a positive or negative impact on earnings. A rising value of the US dollar in international currency markets usually hurts companies converting overseas profits to US dollars, whereas a falling value usually helps profitability.

Operating Cash Flow—This table will tell you exactly how much cash profit was generated by operating your company. Cash flow is an excellent indicator of the long-term financial health of your investment.

Don't forget to read the enclosed proxy statement. It not only invites shareholders to attend the annual meeting, but also provides investors with interesting bits of information, like how much you are paying management to run your company. The proxy statement is also a great place to review the 5-year performance of the company's stock. The SEC requires all proxy statements to include a comparison of a $100 investment in the S&P 500 Index, a peer group, and the company. Hidden on the last few pages of the proxy statement is the single most important bit of information—how your investment has performed over the past 5 years.

CHAPTER 6

How to Research Stocks, Part III: Third-Party Resources, the Internet, and Market Timing

Key Concepts
- Value Line Investment Survey
- Standard and Poors' Stock Reports
- *Forbes, Fortune,* and Industry Publications
- Company Updates
- How to Research Stocks Using the Internet
- Market Timing

Company and stock research information is available from third-party sources, such as Value Line investment survey and Standard and Poors' stock reports. These third-party resources make a profit by selling their services to individual and institutional investors, rather than soliciting business from the companies they follow. In theory, these third-party resources are more objective and have fewer potential conflicts of interest than brokerage firms. Most top business magazines offer their "Best" ratings of companies, such as the Best 100 Managed Companies published annually by *Forbes* and *Fortune,* and these could be resources for investment ideas.

The local library usually has a Business or Investing Resource section where Value Line and Standard and Poors' reports, among others, can be found. The circulation or periodicals section of the library should also have the latest business magazines.

Expanding investors' knowledge about a company and their future prospects is quite easy using the Internet. It furnishes investors with access to broker research and individual company financial results. Keeping up with the latest in company news and economic data used to take hours and required scouring the pages of daily newspapers or periodicals. Company updates are now just a few clicks away, and finding key information takes just a few minutes' time.

Many investors try to time their specific stock purchases against the fluid movements of the overall market. With long-term investment horizons and dollar cost averaging, the risks associated with market timing are greatly diminished using DRIPs and direct investing as investment tools.

The investment research focus for DRIPs and direct investing should be to uncover well-managed companies whose stock is trading at reasonable values and then stick with those investments for the long haul. Within that focus, there may be times when an investor's current stock selection may be considered undervalued in price. During those times, a DRIP investor may choose to send additional OCPs, increasing the stock holdings in the DRIP account.

VALUE LINE INVESTMENT SURVEY

Value Line Publishing Inc. develops and distributes stock research on over 1700 companies. For example, 100+ investment research professionals evaluate these companies based on many different criteria, ultimately offering a stock recommendation, called a *timeliness rating,* of between 1 and 5 (1 being a *buy rating,* 3 being a *neutral rating,* and 5 being a *sell rating*). Their rating evaluates probable stock performance relative to the overall market during the next 6 to 12 months. Company investment surveys are updated every 3 months.

Value Line's investment survey begins with a brief description of each company and its business, recent acquisitions, amount of foreign revenues generated, number of employees, amount of stock owned by officers and directors, and major shareholders of more than 5 percent ownership. The company's CEO, street address, phone number, and website are also listed. A 400-word report on recent corporate developments and Value Line's assessment of the company's prospects for the near term follow.

Future stock price targets for the next 3 to 5 years are offered, along with a history of stock splits for the past 12 years. Monthly stock prices for the past 10 years are graphed along with comparison of cash flow per share (reported earnings plus depreciation) and stock price strength relative to overall market.

Many investors believe that Value Line's format and presentation provide easy access to historical company financial data. Value Line also offers various unique information and forecasts, such as anticipated future dividend and cash flow growth, along with respective historical comparisons. Value Line lists quarterly EPS for the last 3 years, along with anticipated quarterly results for this year and next. Quarterly dividends are listed for the current year and the past 4 years. Information for the most recent 15 years is included, such as revenues per share, cash flow per share, EPS and dividends, book value, shares outstanding, average PE ratio, and average dividend yield. Information for the past 10 years includes net revenues, operating and net profit margins, total long-term debt, return on capital and equity, and dividend payout ratios.

More important than their proprietary timeliness ranking, Value Line can become an invaluable asset in locating specific company information. Their dividend growth and cash flow growth forecasts assist investors in better understanding the possible future of specific investment selections. The ability to review management's annual return on capital and return on equity for the past 10 years assists investors to quickly evaluate upward or downward trends. A swift review of specific financial results, such as net profit margins, over the past 10 years may help investors locate upward trends.

Value Line company reviews are grouped by industry. At the beginning of each industry section is a short critique of new industry developments and a commentary about that specific industry's short-term forecast. Because stock selections generally move in price along with the industry, this short analysis should be of interest to readers.

Examples of the type of information available include Interpublic Group (IPG), which is the third largest advertising agency holding company in the world, and Computer Associates (CA), which is the fourth largest US manufacturer of computer software. Value Line estimated IPG should increase cash flow an average of

12.5 percent a year over the next 5 years. This should allow for a regularly increasing dividend, with anticipated growth of 12.5 percent a year. Management has provided shareholders with return of capital around 16 percent to 17 percent over the past 8 years and return on equity in the 23 percent to 28 percent range over the same time period. IPG has been well managed and focused on increasing shareholder returns. Long-term shareholders have been rewarded by stock appreciation of 243 percent from April 1995 to April 2000.

CA is anticipated to grow cash flow by 14.5 percent annually over the next 5 years. CA has extremely low dividend payout ratio of just 7 percent of earnings, allowing for annual dividend increases of as much as 21.5 percent. Over the past 10 years, return on capital and return on equity have been very high, peaking at 30 percent and 64 percent, respectively. Returns have since declined to a more "industry normal" 15.0 percent and 18.5 percent. CA's stock appreciated 95 percent between April 1995 and April 2000.

STANDARD AND POOR'S STOCK REPORTS

Standard and Poor's (S&P), a division of McGraw-Hill (publishers of this book), offers stock analysis on over 1100 companies. Published monthly and updated quarterly, S&P's stock reports also provide investors with easy access to historical information. S&P offers a stock rating system based on a five-star rating, with five being the highest (a buy) and one being the lowest (a sell). S&P offers an equity rating for consistency in earnings and dividend growth, and an evaluation of a "fair market value" for the company's stock. The S&P reports list total dollar cash flow and long-term debt over the past 10 years. S&P's graph is a weekly price chart for the past 3 years and illustrates quarterly earnings per share changes. S&P's commentary is separated into standard categories: "company overview," "valuation," and "business summary." S&P's commentary is more detailed than Value Line's, but does not appear to be as forward thinking.

IPG has earned S&P's highest equity rating (A+) for consistency in earnings and dividend growth. Based on S&P's estimated fair market value for the stock of $45.25, the market price of $41.00 represents a 9.3 percent discount to their valuation model. Cash flow increased from $118 million in 1990 to $512 million in 1999.

Management increased corporate cash flow by an average of 33.3 percent a year. CA is rated B+, or average, for consistency in earnings and dividend growth, and is undervalued by S&P's estimates by as much as 50 percent at its current market price of $53. Cash flow soared from $265 million in 1990 to $1.5 billion in 1998, but fell in 1999 to $951 million.

Both Value Line Investment Surveys and S&P stock reports are available by paid subscription or at the business resource deck of your local public library. These publications offer additional insight into the performance of management and should greatly aid an investor in understanding the company and its business direction, leading to more prudent DRIP stock selections. Value Line is available as an Internet publication for a year 2000 subscription price of $570. For more information, visit *www.valueline.com*.

FORBES, FORTUNE, AND INDUSTRY PUBLICATIONS

Every year, major business publications recognize the best-managed or fastest-growing companies. These lists may provide confirmation of previous evaluations or may be a resource for new investment ideas. It is important to understand the criteria for selection in each publication's list.

For example, *Forbes Magazine* publishes the "Forbes Platinum 400" list. These are the best overall performing companies with annual revenues over $750 million. Companies are ranked based on a high return of capital, along with revenue, net income, and cash flow per share growth for the past 1 and 5 years. Well-known companies with DRIP programs listed in the 2000 Forbes Platinum included #18 Intel (INTC), a large semiconductor manufacturer; #30 Citigroup (C), a bank, insurance, and stock brokerage powerhouse; #40 TYCO Int'l (TYC), a diversified manufacturer; #41 Lucent Technologies (LU); #51 Pfizer (PFE), a large US drug company that recently merged with Warner Lambert; #57 Home Depot (HD); #59 General Electric (GE); #77 Computer Associates (CA); and #86 Interpublic Group (IPG).

Fortune Magazine publishes its annual "Most Admired Companies." The selection process begins with the top 1000 US companies and the top 25 foreign subsidiaries based on revenues. The 10 largest companies in each of 57 separate industry categories are included in *Fortune*'s final list, for a maximum total of 570 companies. Ten thousand executives, directors, and securities analysts are requested to select their top five most admired companies regardless of industry. In addition, these respondents are requested to rank their industry competitors based on eight criteria ranging from long-term investment value to corporate social responsibility, such as environmental issues. The responses are compiled into an overall list and again by industry. The top three overall winners for 2000 were #1 General Electric (GE), #2 Microsoft (MSFT), and #3 Dell Computers (DEL), a manufacturer and direct marketer of personal computers. Companies that are recognized by *Forbes* as industry leaders, are either first or second within their respective industry group, and offer a DRIP program include Intel, Citigroup, Home Depot, General Electric, Lucent Technologies, Computer Associates, and Interpublic Group.

There are many other published lists, such as the Fortune 500, *Smart Money Magazine*'s Top Tech Picks for Year 2000, and *Your Money Magazine*'s 400 Top Mutual Fund Choices. Most industry publications offer a list of the best companies or products in their specific industries. For instance, *Auto Interiors Magazine* awarded Johnson Controls (JCI), a large automotive interior and parts manufacturer, its 1999 Design and Technology Award for JCI's prototype auto interior designs. Investors in JCI should be pleased that their company continues to lead the auto industry in new interior product development. This should translate into continued market leadership, increasing market share, and ultimately increasing revenue and profit growth. As another piece to the investment selection puzzle, information from business publications is often more focused on a specific company and its management.

COMPANY UPDATES

Just as important as finding companies with great management is maintaining a working knowledge of those same companies. Products and markets shift, management changes, and competition mutates. Anticipating how these may affect an investment should be of significant consideration to the astute investor. Reading annual and quarterly reports is an easy and painless means of keeping up with company developments. They will come uninvited and automatically to shareholders' homes. If the company is local, it may be the focus of the local news media, possibly covered by the business editors of the local newspaper. Take an outing to the library on a rainy weekend for a few hours of peace and quiet (especially when your kids are particularly affected by cabin fever). Value Line and S&P stock reports are updated quarterly and may provide new information for investors. Investors connected to the Internet will find the latest corporate news stories are just a click away at sites such as *www.cbs.marketwatch.com*.

For example, Omnicare (OCR) is the leading provider of geriatric pharmaceutical services in the county, with over 635,000 long-term care patients as clients. Omnicare also provides clinical research services to major drug manufacturers and pharmaceutical benefits oversight services for retired employees of major US corporations. During the 1990s, OCR built its business by targeting specific geographic areas and acquiring independent competitors. In early winter 1999, the US government severely adjusted downward their long-standing reimbursement schedule for Medicare patients. This negatively impacted the nursing home industry. OCR not only realized lower revenues per patient, but the long-term care admittance rate of Medicare patients was greatly reduced. OCR's management restructured. It consolidated facilities and evaluated the profitability of all existing contracts. In the first 9 months after the Medicare changes, OCR canceled several unprofitable contracts and readjusted pricing on others. Even with this realignment of clients, OCR realized a net increase in internal sales growth. Management also began to refocus its efforts on expanding its market base. The company's overall emphasis is to reduce pharmaceutical costs for the elderly in long-term care facilities, and it possesses industry-leading expertise concerning geriatric pharmaceuticals. OCR began offering its services to reduce retirement medical benefit costs for large corporations by reviewing each retired employee's current and future prescription drug needs. Their clinical research data have been gathered from years of experience in the drug needs of older patients, in addition to ongoing access to a large patient population. OCR offers its research services to large drug manufacturers seeking information on newly developed products for geriatric diseases. As OCR's management dealt with this dramatic change of corporate direction and opportunity, its earnings stumbled and so did its stock.

After rising from a stock split adjusted price of $1 in May 1990 to over $41 in July 1998, OCR saw its stock plummet to $7 a share by March 2000. In the spring of 2000, investors became more confident with management's reaction to the new Medicare realities and with the new change of business direction. Investors began to believe the worst was behind the company and started buying the stock again. By June 2000, the stock had rebounded to $18 a share and has been consolidating these gains. Investors who bought the stock at around $32 in January 1999, just prior to the Medicare fiasco and who evenly dollar cost averaged through the use of a monthly OCP, would have been buying their shares down to the low of $7. As a result, their average cost per share could have shrunk to below $20 a share from over $30, or just a bit above the price as of June 2000. As management regains its momentum and if earnings again reach $1.07 a share in 2002, with a 17 percent to 20 percent future earnings growth rate, OCR's share price should continue to appreciate. Investors who had been keeping up with the events of the company and its management would have realized at below $10 a share the stock was far undervalued, and they would have been buyers. Current investors who had spent the time to understand OCR's marketplace transition would have been dollar cost averaging their investment either via the dividends or their optional cash payments.

HOW TO RESEARCH STOCKS USING THE INTERNET

Much of the financial information discussed so far is available over the Internet. Personal finance advice is of huge interest to web surfers, and the Internet has become a direct investor's best friend. It gives individuals substantially easier access to more information and opinions than does conventional print media. Buying long-term stock positions on-line, enrolling in DRIP programs effortlessly, and researching potential investments make it easy for web surfers to invest wisely.

A lot of content on the Internet is hype and public relations, designed to feed one's emotions. Investing tips from Internet chat rooms are the equivalent of a local town crier standing on his soapbox in the middle of the town square. There are many, many stock advisors hawking their services, claiming to have the latest high-return, low-risk investment. Investors are better off reviewing the commentary posted on well-known and heavily trafficked sites, such as *cbs.marketwatch.com* or *netstockdirect.com*. Investors should be more attuned to reviews posted on *cnnfn.com* versus the hottest mini-micro-tech stock touted in an anonymous and unsolicited e-mail. Much like all other media, the big names will carry the most clout and should offer the best, most logical commentary.

Because the Internet is expanding very rapidly, new websites with more information and better presentations are being introduced every day. Many magazines and newspapers list their "Best of the Web." Nearly all the major business and investing publications, such as *Forbes* or *Fortune*, offer up-to-date listings that are available either at their respective websites or in print. These lists are worth reviewing. For example, *Your Money* magazine, a *Consumer Digest* publication focused on personal investing, suggests several investment research sites in their April/May 2000 issue entitled "Online Investing Guide." They include Morningstar at *morningstar.net*, CNET at *nordby.com*, the SEC at *edgar-online.com*, and The Motley Fool at *fool.com*. We do not try to offer the ultimate guide to surfing the web for investing information, but rather overview where certain information important to knowledgeable DRIP investing may easily be found.

Many websites offer visitors a free service called a Personal Portfolio Tracker. This service allows web surfers to upload different stock holdings, either actual or theoretical, and then track their performance as the market fluctuates. Each stock in the portfolio should be linked to recent company news articles, historical price charts with moving averages, earnings estimates, and financial data. Most sites provide the opportunity to track more than one portfolio. Portfolio tracker services substantially reduce the time required to look up each stock price and then calculate its worth. Portfolio tracking services are a great idea, but investors should choose the provider after careful comparison. Investors will return to this site most often. As a free service to the investor, the site in return receives another loyal and repetitive client for its advertising.

Suggested Internet Websites

Company Websites

These are the first places a potential investor visits. Product information, investor information, and corporate history should be available at company websites. It should be easy to obtain an understanding of what the company does by its product or services presentation. Investor relations information should include annual reports going back 3 years, along with the most recent quarterly results. News articles and press releases about the company are usually available, along with the corporate mission statement. Many companies provide the most recent stock price, sometimes with a graph of stock price history. To locate a company website, use a major search engine like Yahoo! or Northern Lights. *netstockdirect.com* offers an easy direct link to each of the companies listed on its site.

netstockdirect.com

NetStock Corporation operates the leading Internet DRIP resource website with a wide range of services available free to DRIP investors. *netstockdirect.com* is impressive both with the quality of company management and the quality of services to its clients. *netstockdirect.com* allows investors to review DRIP program details of over 1600 companies. By searching the database using its Stock-Finder search engine, investors can find specific DRIP fees, minimum direct investment if allowed, minimum and maximum OCPs, and a brief description of the company all on one page. The same page lists the DRIP plan administrator, also known as the *transfer agent,* and there is a direct link to the company website. Further down the page are direct links to various stock research sites such as *zacks.com, multexinvestor.com,* and *wallstreetresearch net.* These allow investors direct links to research for the specific company. Linked to the company page are historic price charts along with the most recent stock quote.

Some companies allow for direct investing through *netstockdirect.com.* Investors may have the choice to establish an account on-line, complete with scheduled automatic bank withdrawals, also known as *ACH transfers.* The initial direct investment may be transacted using an ACH. Some companies allow *netstockdirect.com* clients to complete enrollment forms on-line. The investor then prints the form and mails it to the company along with a check for the initial investment. Either method of enrolling in a specific company's DRIP program with a direct investing option is easy, fast, and almost effortless.

All DRIP investors who have access to and regularly visit the Internet should visit *netstockdirect.com*. There are several sites that offer slimmed down versions of NetStock Direct's service, such as *stockpower.com* and *buyandhold.com*, but none has the depth of companies, variety of commentary, or ease of use offered by *netstockdirect.com*. Commenting on its leading position with the on-line DRIP and direct investor, Mr. Jeff Seely, CEO of NetStock Investment Corporation, parent of Netstockdirect and Sharebuilder, said, "Our corporate goal is to provide the best database available for DRIPs and direct stock plans, and to provide editorial focused around those as well." So far, *www.netstockdirect.com* has succeeded in achieving this goal.

cbs.marketwatch.com

This site is a joint venture between CBS (the media giant) and Marketwatch Inc. It provides a complete personal financial website. It is a leading site for the latest in business and company news, offering commentary from some of the best on Wall Street. *cbs.marketwatch.com* provides site areas devoted to specific financial interests, such as IPOs and technology and mutual funds. There is commentary on basic tax issues and assistance in understanding real estate. *cbs.marketwatch.com* offers a personal portfolio tracking service that investors can upload and then track the value of various stock portfolios. The site allows for advanced graphing of historical stock price quotes, provides market capitalization and 200-day moving stock price averages, along with recent financial numbers such as the latest 3 years' income, balance, and cash flow statements. Access to the latest SEC filings has become a fairly standard offering from personal financial websites and is available through *cbs.marketwatch.com*. Anticipated earnings estimates and median broker recommendations are available through a link with *zacks.com*. There are also links to *hoovers.com* and *multexinvestor.com* for basic company descriptions.

zacks.com and firstcall.com

zacks.com collects and distributes the weekly stock brokerage recommendations on over 1300 companies. *zacks.com* publishes a broker consensus for market timeliness, anticipated earnings per share,
and long-term earnings growth. EPS estimates for the next two
quarters, and annual estimates for the current year and next year are
published and updated weekly. The number of brokers following a
company and earnings estimate changes over the past 90 days are
also available. Anticipated earnings growth rates over the next 5
years are presented as a median number along with the corresponding high and low estimates. The detailed business description
presentation of *zacks.com* is more concise and complete than that of
its competitor, *firstcall.com*.

multexinvestor.com and hoovers.com

These sites offer basic company descriptions along with recent financial data. *multexinvestor.com* sells stockbroker company reports
and investment recommendations for specific companies. For example, through *multexinvestor.com,* an investor can purchase the latest Merrill Lynch or Solomon Smith Barney report for literally thousands of companies. *multexinvestor.com* offers a portfolio tracker,
market commentary, and a "What's Hot" list in its research section.
What's Hot lists industries that are of the most interest to site visitors, along with companies within the industry that are the most
popular for investor research.

quicken.com

Much like *cbs.marketwatch.com, quicken.com* is a full-service financial
website. Its company research information, however, is among the
most comprehensive and user-friendly on the Internet. *quicken.com*
provides the same links to *zacks.com, multexinvestor.com,* and SEC filings. Management's buying or selling of company stock is listed on
the insider trading page. On the financial results section, site visitors will find easy links to management's discussions, as filed with
the SEC, of the most recent quarterly and annual reports. The information provided by *zacks.com* for earnings estimates is cleanly and
graphically presented. Their stock evaluator is worthy of review. It
graphically illustrates growth rates for earnings, cash flow, long-
term debt, and ROE for the past 10 years while providing industry

comparisons for the same. Stock value assessment tools such as PE, price to sales, and PEG are presented in easy-to-read tables. Of most interest should be the intrinsic value calculation. Based on the sum of future earnings and using a mathematical discount model, an estimated stock value for each company is determined. This calculation may provide investors with an added benchmark to determine current stock valuations.

yahoo.com

Also a full-service financial website, *finance.yahoo.com* provides company news, price charts, and a portfolio tracker, along with links to *zacks.com*. Its industry research section can be a valuable tool for investors in the beginning phase of their stock selection. *finance.yahoo.com* allows investors to search for companies by industrial sector and then by industry group. For instance, an investor may want to research companies in the water services business. Under the heading Utilities, Water, there are 13 companies listed. There are 240 companies listed under the heading Computer, Software. After the name of each company within the industry group are several additional options for further research. These offer *zacks.com* company estimates and *multexinvestor.com* links. Market Guide, a service of *multexinvestor.com*, provides the company description and industry financial ratio comparisons. Market Guide's presentations have always been easy to read and understand.

smartmoney.com

As an extension of *Smart Money Magazine*, a *Wall Street Journal* publication for personal finance, *smartmoney.com* is both comprehensive and easy to use. This site offers stock and market commentary, stock quotes, historical charting, portfolio tracking, company and business news, company financials, and stock research. For investors researching specific stocks, *smartmoney.com* offers a unique graphic of major competitors within the company's industry group. As the investor moves from one page of information to another, similar graphic comparisons are available. For example, as an investor investigates stock valuations, dividends, and dividend payouts, a graph of the selected stock's performance versus its peers is quickly displayed. The next section investigated may be financials with comparisons for return on equity ratios, 5-year EPS growth rates, and net profit margins. Again, a peer group graph appears. *smartmoney.com*'s presentation makes comparing a wide variety of financial and management performance criteria for specific stock selection leisurely, understandable, and fast. *University.smartmoney.com* provides an informal education on the basics of investing and stock selection; it should be a great reference resource for novice investors. More experienced investors may find the information a great refresher course.

 smartmoney.com recently introduced the next wave in personal investment graphics—a monthly fee-based three-dimensional graphic software to assist in analyzing companies and market trends. The program, called MapStation, allows subscribers to review a specific portfolio or an entire industry and its performance using three-dimensional graphics. As an offshoot of its award-winning SmartMoney Map of the Market, MapStation will not be the last to offer fancy computer-generated graphics.

America Online

While trying hard to improve their personal finance site, AOL's business and market news is not as complete as some other sites. AOL offers portfolio tracking, quotes, and historical charts. However, the ability to adequately customize historic stock price charts is sorely lacking at AOL. Its stock screening program is of minor interest, and it is cumbersome. Market Guide, along with *hoovers.com*, provides company descriptions, financial data, and industry comparative information. There are links to Market Guide's basic information about the company's DRIP program if available.

 Investors should use the Internet as a tool to gather the information needed to make wise and intelligent DRIP and direct investing decisions. With the wealth of data and information available, Internet surfers should be fairly focused on the specific information desired. Market commentary and editorials are most likely evenly weighted between those with a perennial downbeat theme and those with the perennial upbeat theme. Market timing commentary will run the gamut from "now is the best time to sell all stocks" to "now is the best time to buy all stocks." These commentaries should be taken with a grain of salt, but may include bits of interesting and possibly revealing information. Reading specific stock reviews posted at major websites should offer potential investors new ideas, which either support or contradict the investor's current predictions.

Above all, Internet investment commentaries, much like their printed cousins, should be entertaining, easy to read, and informative for the reader.

MARKET TIMING

Joe Ricketts, founder of Ameritrade, is quoted as saying, "Trading often and heavy is not something that makes you a lot of money. That's contrary to my own interests, but it is the truth."[1]

Market timing calls for marked changes in an investor's stock/bond/cash mix based on expected near-term market prospects. Within an investor's stock portfolio, market timing calls for trading positions based on a belief that the overall market will move short-term one way or the other. By definition, market timing advocates precarious risk exposure. Many investors believe they can increase their returns by timing stock market swings either up or down. There will always be investors who believe the market is too expensive, whereas there will be those who believe the market is too cheap. Because the market is fluid and thrives on the dichotomy of opinions between buyers and sellers, there will always be those who expound on the benefits of buying only at the bottom and selling only at the top. Investors should love that theory. It is most difficult, however, to actually achieve.

The concept of market timing is quite different from determining that a specific stock is undervalued. Market timing is an attempt by the investor to buy stocks during times of overall rising markets, selling when the markets reach a short-term peak, and then being on the sidelines during times of declining markets. When the market reaches a short-term bottom, the investor begins the cycle again. According to the *Hubert Financial Digest*, which tracks investment newsletter performance, only 2 out of 65 market timing–oriented newsletters beat the Wilshire 5000 Index during the 1980s.[2]

Consider the following studies comparing investments when trying to time the market versus a long-term invest-and-hold strategy or investing in treasury bills.

Worth Magazine

Over the long term, securities prices have increased. The market has concluded business down in only 9 of the last 40 years. This means that if you did nothing but hold, you would have been right 3 years out of 4. Selling at the wrong time—trying to time the market, in other words—could have been disastrous. For instance, $1000 invested in stocks over the past 40 years would have grown to $86,550, contrasted to only $8670 if the money had been kept in treasury bills. If you had missed the 34 best months for stocks, however, your $1000 investment would have amounted to only $4492; even t-bills would have been better, according to Ibbotson Associates.[3]

DRIP Investor

I came across the following study in *Investor's Business Daily* recently that provides an interesting angle on the notion of timing the market. The study looked at the difference in investment returns achieved by an individual who invested $1000 in the Dow Jones Industrials at the market high each of the past 20 years versus an individual who invested $1000 in the Dow at the market low every year over the same period. What the study found was that if you would have invested at the market high every year, you would have earned roughly 80 percent of what you would have had with perfect timing (buying at the low every year). Thus, the reward for perfect market timing every year for 20 years was just 20 percent. The study concluded, "The biggest mistake would have been not to invest at all." Unfortunately, being out of the market is usually what happens when investors sell stocks in hopes of buying them back at market lows.[4]

Associated Press

Ibbotson Associates tracks the market's performance in intricate detail, and its findings are often used to support the invest-and-hold school. Ibbotson shows that just $1.00 invested in large-company stocks at the end of 1925 would have grown in value to $1371 by the end of 1996. But had that investment missed the 35 best months over that 71-year period, the total value would have been $12.50. The lesson should be obvious. Out of 852 months over seven decades, a period encompassing the Great Depression of the 1930s, who could have foreseen the 35 months in which the stock market spurted to its greatest gains?[5]

Charles Schwab

According to the University of Michigan, in a study commissioned by Towneley Capital Management, researchers examined monthly returns for the three major US markets (the NYSE, the AMEX, and the NASDAQ) from 1963 to 1993. They found that $1.00 invested in this hypothetical portfolio in 1963 would have grown to $24.30 by 1993. But if you were out of the stock market during the best 90 days—just 90 days randomly scattered over 31 years—you would have missed 95 percent of the market's gains. Your $1.00 would have grown to just $2.10—less than you would have earned investing in t-bills. Conversely, if you'd been on the sidelines during the market's worst 90 days, your $1.00 would have grown to $326.40. If you think you can pluck those days out of a 31-year period, I'd say you've been spending too much time in the sun.[6]

Paul Ferrell, writer for *cbs.marketwatch.com,* published a great review of the pitfalls relating to market timing. In his article, "Market-Timing Is Bad for Your Health," dated May 15, 2000, Ferrell proclaimed,

> Short-term traders have an inherent "faith" in market timing, you might even call irrational exuberance. Traders believe deep in their soul that market timing is a tool that is guaranteed to help them *beat the market*. In fact, they need to prove they are winners, to build their egos, to enhance their sense of self-worth. On the other hand, long-term investors react quite the opposite. Investors have an inherent emotional "fear" of market timing. They believe that the markets are capricious and unpredictable. Therefore, inherently, they just do not trust market timing. This fear is, in part, why less than half of all Americans own securities and two-thirds are saving far too little for retirement. Their fear of making mistakes in the market results in inaction.

Ferrell used a study by Professors Terry Odean and Brad Barber from the University of California School of Management. They interviewed over 66,400 investors and found

> transaction costs and lousy stock picking seriously eroded investor returns. Specifically, between 1991 and 1997, the most active traders earned 5 percent points a year less than the average traders and 7 percent points less annually than invest-and-hold investors. Here are their reported results:

Most active trader	258% portfolio turnover	11.4% annual return
Average trader	76% portfolio turnover	16.4% annual return
Least active trader	2% portfolio turnover	18.5% annual return

Get it? The more you trade, the less you earn.[7]

DRIPs and direct investing are great tools for the individual who believes in investing in common stocks for the long term, regardless of market action, and then reinvesting the dividends. The dollar cost averaging strategy associated with DRIPs buys shares when the market falls, and some purchases will be made at the very bottom of every market cycle.

Every market timer dreams about buying at the bottom and selling at the top. One-half of that dream comes true automatically with regular DRIP investing—the half that wants to buy at the absolute market bottom.

CHAPTER 7

Investment Risk

Key Concepts

- ◆ Risk Comes from Many Directions
- ◆ Risk versus Returns
- ◆ Time Mitigates Risk
- ◆ Evaluating Personal Risk
- ◆ Beta Ratios, Standard Deviation, and Market Risk
- ◆ How to Minimize Investment Risk

What is the likelihood of realizing a gain from a particular investment selection? What is the chance a specific investment may outperform similar investments? What is the possibility of losing money on a specific stock purchase?

The basic concepts of investment risk can be summarized with these simple questions. As much as all investors try otherwise, whenever capital is put to work generating capital gains, dividends, or interest, there is always the risk that the capital may be lost. A key ingredient in any investment strategy is the trade-off between the level of risk accepted and the level of returns realized. Stashing personal savings in your mattress or in your personal safe is about as risk-free as one can get (unless you get robbed or your house burns down). There is no future, however, in replacing bedding with dollar bills.

Investment risk is a very important attribute of investing and is often overlooked by investors, novice or otherwise. Risk is the one four-letter word that most investors fear to utter, but its importance cannot be understated. Everyone is risk averse, and it is human nature to desire huge gains on our investments without accepting any risk. But the investing game does not work that way. In many cases, the fear of investment risk is merely a fear of the unknown. The best way to overcome fear of investment risk is to understand what it is, how it may affect you, and how to evaluate you own personal comfort level with the amount of risk each investment offers.

The mission of all investing strategies should be to earn the highest possible rate of return without placing hard-earned capital at more risk than is bearable. Although a reluctance to accept greater levels of risk limits overall returns, investors should never accept greater risk than they can afford. Generally speaking, the higher the risk of losing all or some investment capital, the higher the potential return. If investors desire to reduce their investment risk, they should expect a reduction in their rate of return as well. Investments that are the least likely to lose invested capital will almost always lose ground to inflation over time. Investors need to determine their own personal comfort level for the amount of risk they are willing to accept. It is important to realize that investors cannot eliminate all types of risk, and that any form of investing will have some level of risk, including the risk of not keeping up with inflation.

The most popular financial investments fall into three categories: cash (certificates of deposits, money market, savings, and checking accounts), bonds, and stocks. Cash is, by nature, the safest investment. Corporate bonds expose investors to a medium amount of risk, and stock the greatest risk. In the world of investing, US government bonds are considered to be "risk-free" and are used as the benchmark for determining a base level of risk to reward. It is assumed that the US government is financially secure and will have the ability to repay outstanding bond principal as it comes due.

RISK COMES FROM MANY DIRECTIONS

In all aspects of daily life, there are risks. For example, what is the chance of our getting run over by a truck today? It is pretty small depending on your eyesight. What is the chance of a gambler winning by placing the entire bet on the double zeros in roulette? Probably a bit better than a fully sighted person in the previous question depending on the honesty of the casino. When investing in stocks, the risk to an investor's capital comes from many different places. Understanding where risk comes from is the first step in adequately evaluating not only your personal risk tolerance, but the risk involved with a specific stock selection. There is overall market and business risk, interest rate risk, inflation risk, currency risk, political risk, investor behavior risk, and excessive speculation theory risk. The following are brief descriptions of various types of investment risk.

Overall Market and Business Risk

During the last 50 years, the market trend has been up, and an investor with a 20-year investing horizon has never lost money buying the S&P 500 Index. However, within that trend, there have been down years and up years. In the short term, the market may do a header and drop by 20 percent or so, but if you are a long-term thinker, history is on your side and markets will climb back up. Remember, on average, the stock market rises 6 out of every 7 years. So if you invest in that 1 year when the markets fall, you may experience short-term losses.

Where does market risk come from? A declining market may be caused by a slowing of corporate earnings associated with a slowing of the economy. If investors believe that company earnings will grow at a slower pace or even decline, due to a recession or changing business environments, they may not be willing to pay as high a premium for stocks. As corporate earnings decline, the PE (price-to-earnings) ratio investors are willing to pay usually declines, which is a double whammy for investors: lower earnings and a lower PE ratio. Within a rising market, specific companies may have unforeseen short-term problems with their business, which affects revenues and profitability.

Interest Rate Risk

As stocks compete with bonds for investors' money, rising interest rates translate to higher bond yields and may make bonds more at-

tractive than stocks, causing an overall stock market decline. Investors may reallocate their portfolios to include more bonds and
fewer stocks. With rising interest rates, corporate profits tend to fall
as the debt load carried by companies becomes more expensive to
service and corporate interest expense increases. In addition, it is
more expensive for clients to finance purchases, and revenue slows.
Interest rates and stock prices historically move in opposite directions. Some companies are more susceptible to rising interest rates.
Financial companies, for instance, profit from the spread between
what money costs to acquire (mainly from the interest they pay to
depositors) and what they realize from lending to borrowers. When
rates rise, financial companies experience shrinking spreads and
lower profitability.

Inflation Risk

Inflation risk comes from two directions. Inflation impacts corporate profitability and overall investment returns. In inflationary
times, product costs increase, and the company may or may not be
able to pass on these increases to its customers. If not, profits suffer.
Also in inflationary times, investments must provide a higher return just to maintain purchasing parity. For example, if domestic inflation rate equals 4 percent, a 6 percent investment return yields
only 2 percent after inflation considerations.

Currency Risk

Companies with substantial business overseas will have exposure
to changes in currency exchange rates. Prior to the economic crisis
of 1997 in Thailand, for example, the value of the local currency, the
Baht, was pretty stable. For years, the exchange rate did not fluctuate much above or below 25 Baht to 1 US dollar. However, in July
1997, the country went into a deep economic and financial crisis,
and the Baht quickly fell to an exchange rate of 40 to 1. Almost
overnight, imported products became 60 percent more expensive.
US exporters found it increasingly difficult to compete with the locally manufactured products. In addition, US multinational businesses that accepted the local Thai currency for their products or services suddenly received substantially fewer dollars for the same
amount of Baht, adversely affecting their profitability. The other

side of the currency risk coin is US multinational companies realize a gain in their profitability when the local currency rises in relation to the US dollar.

Political Risk

Political risks, both foreign and domestic, come in many forms. It is difficult to analyze the political risks of foreign governments to multinational corporations. One of the most recent dramatic examples of political risk is the takeover of South Vietnam by the communist regime of North Vietnam in the mid-1970s. All American business interests were immediately confiscated and companies lost their investments, along with any sales and profits generated.

It is also difficult to assess the risk that our own Congress will change the rules for business. If the government decides to reduce its reimbursements for Medicare patients in nursing homes, those companies that service that market will be adversely affected. In early 1999, the government did, in fact, reduce payments for Medicare. Companies servicing that market have seen revenues and profits decline, along with their stock prices. Likewise, if the government decides we all need to insulate our homes to reduce energy consumption and offers additional tax incentives to do so, businesses serving this market should expect improving sales and profits. This happened during the oil crisis of the early 1970s.

Investor Behavior Risk

Investors, much like wild dogs, tend to move in packs. Too many investors and mutual fund managers love stocks that are trendy and are believed to be a hot investment. These stocks usually garner greater publicity than those involved in more mundane businesses. Stock prices in these hot companies may explode to unrealistic heights, creating greater risk to investors. This speculative buying trend has been seen several times over the decades, with oil stocks in the 1970s, biotech stocks in the 1980s, and again in the late 1990s. Recently, the wild dogs' mentality returned with the new economy and Internet stocks.

DRIP investing, by nature, uses a dollar cost averaging strategy and assists investors to build long-term positions in volatile stocks. By averaging an investor's cost, short-term price dips in these stocks are used to purchase more shares, reducing the overall cost per share of the position.

Excessive Speculation Risk

Too often investors buy a stock based solely on the hopes that someone else will pay a higher price. Many times there is no fundamental reason for an investor to buy a specific stock at a specific price except that the stock value is "sure" to go higher. The "stock tip" could have come from a gathering at the water cooler or from chatting with a neighbor over the back fence. When investors finally wake up to the real valuation of their investment selections (as they eventually always do), these overpriced stocks usually fall faster than the New Year's Eve ball in Times Square.

DRIPs are an especially poor means of accumulating short-term positions in hot or trendy stocks. DRIPs do not usually allow for the precise market timing needed to succeed when implementing an excessive speculation investment strategy. In addition, many fad stocks neither pay dividends nor offer a direct investing option.

RISK VERSES RETURNS

Most investors like certainty. The more certain a return, the lower the return is likely to be. The more uncertain the return, the higher the return is likely to be. Investors in US government bonds, for example, have a high level of certainty that they will receive their next interest payment. Investors in a highly leveraged and struggling company probably do not have a high level of certainty concerning the future of their investment. Although bonds may return 6 percent to 7 percent annually long term, stocks in struggling companies may return 10 to 100 times that amount based on management's ability to turn the company around. The trade-off between risk and certainty is fundamental to all DRIP investment decisions.

TIME MITIGATES RISK

Figure 7–1 provides a telling story of real investment returns after inflation for 1-year, 5-year, 10-year, 15-year, 20-year, and 25-year holding periods since 1900 for stocks, bonds, and short-term t-bills.

The longer the holding period of all investments, the lower the

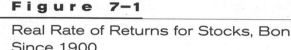

Real Rate of Returns for Stocks, Bonds, and T-Bills Since 1900

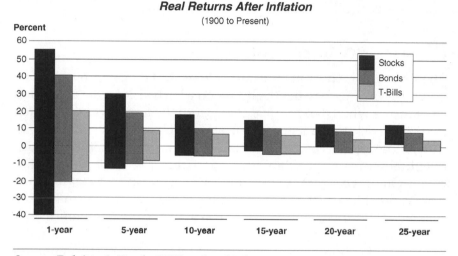

Source: *Deloitte & Touche LLP, updated July 1996.*

risk of losing money. Although historic performance is never a guarantee of future returns, a 100-year history should provide skittish potential investors with a comfort level going forward. The chart provides a comparison of inflation-adjusted returns for each asset category based on the investment holding period. Short, 1-year horizons for stocks can be very painful, with a high risk of losing substantial amounts. The risk diminishes as the holding period lengthens. Stocks have outperformed both bonds and t-bills in longer than 10-year investment horizons.

The holding period for an investment is the single greatest factor in all portfolios. Based on the specific investing goal and time frame, investors can mitigate their risk by carefully choosing their desired return. For example, based on the chart in Figure 7–1, a stock investor with a 1-year time frame has as much chance, historically, of gaining 55 percent as losing 40 percent. The bond investor with the same 1-year time frame has about as much chance of making 40 percent as losing 20 percent, whereas the investor who maintains a cash or t-bill position has as much chance of making 20 percent as losing 12 percent. Longer term, the risk of investing in stocks greatly diminishes. Stock investors with a 10-year horizon have as much chance of gaining around 18 percent annually as losing around 4 percent. Investments with higher risk may not be appropriate for portfolios with shorter term horizons.

EVALUATING PERSONAL RISK

The first basic instinct of investors is to protect their capital. The second basic instinct is to bet the house on a high-risk venture. Finding a balance is where the *personal* comes into the term *personal investor.* Investors' risk tolerance, or their ability to watch as some investments lose money or tread water while waiting for their stocks' eventual return to profitability, varies from one individual to another. One investor may feel comfortable buying stocks in small companies that are currently out of favor and wait for a turnaround, whereas other investors may prefer to invest in big companies with more consistent earnings.

Consider how you would react to a 25 percent decline in an overall stock portfolio, with losses on individual companies of over 40 percent. In the worst down market since World War II (January 1973–October 1974), the S&P 500 Index declined by 48 percent. If this keeps you up at night glued to your computer screen, a more conservative investing plan may be appropriate. However, over the long term, more conservative portfolios provide lower real rate of returns. People who are afraid to cross the street will never leave their block. Generally speaking, the older an investor is and the shorter the investment holding period, the more conservative the portfolio should be.

Because the usual DRIP investment horizon is a minimum of 3 years, investors with shorter term goals should probably look elsewhere for lower risk, but also lower return, investments.

BETA RATIOS, STANDARD DEVIATION, AND MARKET RISK

Beta

A stock's price performance verses a specific index is considered by some investors as an excellent means of determining risk. As one measure of past risk, the beta usually compares a specific stock's volatility to the S&P 500 Index over the past 60 months. If the stock's price performance tracks the S&P 500, the beta is considered to be 1.00. Stocks that outperform the S&P Index by 10 percent have a beta of 1.10 and may be considered more volatile and risky. Those that have underperformed carry a beta less than 1.00 and may be considered less risky, but also less rewarding.

One problem with evaluating investments by respective beta ratios is that the calculations are based solely on stock price performance. A company may expand long-term earnings faster than the underlying index, causing investors to bid up the price of the stock faster than the index. When comparing beta ratios, keep in mind that changes in company fundamentals can affect stock prices.

In down markets, stocks with a beta of more than 1.00 are expected to drop in price more than the S&P Index, whereas those with a beta of less than 1.00 are expected to decline less than the Index. It is important to judge the potential downside a stock may offer. Be sure to review each investment's price performance during the most recent down markets of July 16 to October 11, 1990, and July 17 to October 31, 1998.

For example, the S&P 500 Index averaged a 12 percent price gain over a 5-year holding period. If a specific stock also returned 12 percent annually, its beta would be 1.00, whereas a stock that gained 19 percent annually would have a beta of 1.58 and a stock that gained an average of 7 percent annually would have a beta of 0.58. In a down market, the stock with a beta of 1.58 is anticipated to decline 15.8 percent for every 10 percent decline in the Index. Also in a down market, the stock with a beta of 0.58 would be expected to decline 5.8 percent for every 10 percent decline in the S&P 500 Index. To review, Table 7–1 is a list of the current betas as reported by Market Guide as of June 2000 for some of the companies previously discussed.

Betas for specific stocks are available in the Value Line investment survey and various places on the Internet, such as *market-guide.com.* Investors need to calculate their own beta for an entire portfolio if interested. Because a good long-term portfolio will have many investment components, an overall portfolio's beta may be much different from any individual component.

Beta ratios relate to a stock's price movements only and do not reflect an overall return of capital. When dividend yield is factored

TABLE 7-1

Beta for Selected Stocks, June 2000

Company	Beta	Company	Beta
Philadelphia Suburban	0.24	Johnson Controls	0.89
Intimate Brands	1.21	Apache Corp	0.52
Sears, Roebuck	0.83	SunTrust Bank	1.31
Chicago Bridge & Iron	0.60	Home Depot	1.21
Hawaiian Electric	0.15	GATX Corp	0.88
Merck	0.77	Wal-Mart	1.18
Pitney Bowes	0.41	HomePort Bancorp	0.34
PepsiCo	1.28	Coca-Cola	0.94
Tecumseh Products	0.32	Briggs & Stratton	0.65
Wells Fargo Bank	1.20	Lucent Technologies	1.65
Federal Signal	0.60	Harley Davidson	1.23
Interpublic Group	1.01	Computer Associates	1.28
Omnicare	1.14		

Source: www.marketguide.com.

in, a low-beta stock may provide acceptable overall returns. For example, Hawaiian Electric (HE) has a beta of 0.15. HE's stock should offer a 1.5 percent gain for every 10 percent gain in the market while declining only 1.5 percent in value with an overall market decline of 10 percent. An investor who bought HE in March 2000 at a price of $28 and an annual dividend of $2.48 would have an annual dividend return of 8.8 percent. With a stock price increasing 1.5 percent in a 10 percent market up cycle, the investor would realize a total return of 10.3 percent (8.8 percent from the dividend plus 1.5 percent capital gain), thus almost matching the overall return of the Index. Compounding returns offered by low-beta and high-yielding stocks is facilitated by enrolling in DRIP programs.

Standard Deviation

Stock price volatility will affect an overall portfolio's return. For instance, suppose an investor buys two stocks. Both stocks return an average of 8 percent a year for 20 years. The first investment gyrates wildly: Year 1 returning 13 percent; Year 2, 3 percent; Year 3, 13 percent; Year 4, 3 percent; and so on, averaging 8 percent a year. The second investment returns exactly 8 percent a year, just like clockwork. At the end of 20 years, the stock with the steady return would be worth $1000 more than the stock with the gyrating returns. This demonstrates the statistical concept of standard deviation.

Being a more complex mathematical formula, standard deviation calculations are not as popular as the beta ratio for evaluating investment risk. *Standard deviation* is defined as the historical annual performance above and below the average annual return. In the previous example, the stock that provided a steady return did not deviate from its 8 percent return. Its standard deviation would be 0. The investment that fluctuated five percentage points above and below its 8 percent return (13 − 8 = 5 and 3 − 8 = −5) has a standard deviation calculated at 5. In other words, the steady investment had a 20-year average annual return of 8 percent plus or minus 0 percent for any given year. The gyrating investment had a 20-year average annual return of 8 percent plus or minus 5 percent for any given year. The higher the standard deviation, the more risky the investment due to higher volatility of annual returns. With a standard deviation of 5, the volatile investment was riskier than the steady investment with a standard deviation of 0. Some investors have categorized standard deviations ranging from 0 to 3 as *almost no risk* (such as cash), 3 to 11 as *low risk* (such as bonds), 11 to 15 as *medium risk* (such as big-cap stocks), and 15 to 23 as *higher risk* (medium- and small-cap stocks). Standard deviations over 23 indicate extremely volatile investments. Some very conservative investors may desire deviations of a maximum of 9.

Standard deviations can be used to forecast potential future risk. The standard deviation theory statistically projects that 68 percent of the time (or almost 7 out of the next 10 years), future annual returns will be within one deviation of the anticipated return rate. Going forward, there is a 68 percent chance that stocks will continue to provide real 10-year returns in the −4 percent to +18 percent range.

For the average DRIP and direct investor, however, there is no easy place to find a specific stock's standard deviation, and it must be individually calculated. Although the standard deviation can be used as a tool to determine the likely minimum and maximum rewards of a specific investment, the calculations are done manually. Standard deviation calculations for entire portfolios may be available soon at financial websites. As part of an on-line portfolio tracking service, evaluating a specific portfolio's standard deviation would assist individual investors to better manage their risk.

HOW TO MINIMIZE INVESTMENT RISK

Investors can protect themselves against undue investment risk with intelligent stock selections. History is no guarantee of the future. However, companies that are led by management focused on increasing shareholder value, recognized as industry leaders, and have provided a 10-year history of increasing earnings and dividends probably have the best chance of doing so in the future.

Within an investor's overall financial portfolio, asset diversification and allocation are logical methods of managing investment risk. This means spreading investment capital over the spectrum of different industrial sectors and asset categories. Diversification is discussed in greater detail in an upcoming chapter.

DRIP and direct investing assist long-term investors to build stock assets in a variety of companies carrying a variety of risks. Dollar cost averaging a higher risk, higher beta stock protects an investor against miscalculated market timing. If the market should fall and the high-beta stock falls at a greater percentage, the dollar cost averaging investor will be buying more shares at the lower price and will be better poised when the stock rebounds at a greater pace than the overall market.

CHAPTER 8

How to Buy Stocks Using DRIPs and Direct Investing

Key Concepts

- ◆ Direct Investing
- ◆ DRIP Programs with Existing Registered Shareholder Requirement
- ◆ Stockbrokers
- ◆ Synthetic DRIPs
- ◆ On-line Synthetic DRIPs

Once a specific stock investment is selected to be purchased, an investor has several options to accomplish that seemingly simple task. If the company has a direct investing plan, the investor should be able to send in a check directly to the company or its transfer agent. Possibly a full-service broker would be more suitable if the investment is to be made in a tax-deferred account, such as an IRA. Many brokers offer free dividend reinvestment services, also known as synthetic DRIPs. Depending on the company's DRIP details, an investor may need to purchase the initial shares from a broker, have the certificate delivered, and then enroll in the DRIP. The expansion of financial services on the Internet is legendary, ranging from day-trading firms to full-service brokers with Internet access for their clients. A new hybrid of on-line synthetic DRIPs provides investors the easiest method of developing a "personal mutual fund," one weekly or monthly payment at a time.

DIRECT INVESTING

The list of companies offering direct investing options is growing.
Companies in every industrial sector and of all sizes offer direct investing. *netstockdirect.com* currently lists over 600 US companies and
more than 280 foreign companies that allow stock purchases directly from them or their transfer agents. Investing with companies offering direct investing options is easy.

For non-Internet users, contact the company's Investor Relations Department and request direct investing enrollment forms.
Company addresses and phones numbers are available in both Value Line and S&P stock reports. The company may refer you to the
transfer agent for the appropriate forms. When they arrive in the
mail, complete the forms and return them along with a check for
the initial investment. The company or its agent usually mails a confirmation of the investment. DRIP transaction statements are sent to
all program participants showing purchases and sales at least for the
most recent quarter and most likely year to date.

For Internet users, *netstockdirect.com* offers the best overall
DRIP enrollment service. Their site allows for on-line electronic enrollment and automatic bank transfers (ACH) for the initial investment based on individual plan details. If the investor prefers and
the plan details allow, enrollment forms can be downloaded and
printed; these are then mailed to the company along with a check
for the initial investment.

Each company sets its own minimum initial investment, which
may range from $20 to $1500. For example, a few of the companies
requiring between $1000 and $1500 initial investment include:

AFLAC (AFL)
American Express (AXP)
Bank America (BAC)
Bell Atlantic (BEL)
Federal Express (FDX)
Ford (F)
Gillette (G)
Regions Financial (RGBK)
Walt Disney (DIS)

Some of the companies requiring a minimum investment of $500 include:

Air Products & Chemicals (APD)
American States Water (AWR)
Equifax (EFX)
IBM (IBM)
Intimate Brands (IBI)
Mattel (MAT)
Motorola (MOT)
Pfizer (PFE)
SBC Communications (SBC)
Sears (S)

Companies with $250 minimum investment include:

American Electric Power (AEP)
Becton, Dickinson (BDX)
Chevron (CHV)
Enron (ENE)
ExxonMobil (XOM)
Home Depot (HD)
Lowes (LOW)
Proctor & Gamble (PG)
Wal-Mart (WMT)
Yahoo! (YHOO)

Some companies that offer initial direct investments options of $100 or less include:

Bob Evan's Farms (BOBE)
Connecticut Water Services (CTWS)
Johnson Controls (JCI)
Libbey (LBY)
Montana Power (MTP)
Southwest Gas (SWX)
Walgreens (WAG)

Whenever possible, direct investing should be the preferred method of purchasing common stock. Due to lower transaction costs and, in some cases, no cost at all, direct investing permits most investors to put larger amounts of capital to work.

All direct investing programs have maximum investment limits. Many investors have the misconception that DRIPs and direct investing programs are tailored to the needs of just the small investor. This is not true. Many companies have high maximum investment limitations. Examples of a few direct investing maximum investment limits are:

Home Depot	up to a single investment of $100,000 or $100,000 annually
AFLAC	up to a single investment of $120,000 or $120,000 annually
Sears	up to a single investment of $150,000 or $150,000 annually
American States Water	up to a single investment of $20,000 or $240,000 annually
Intimate Brands	up to a single investment of $250,000 or $250,000 annually
Chicago Bridge and Iron	up to a single investment of $250,000 or $13 million annually

It is quite feasible for an investor, who happens to realize a one-time windfall of $1 million from Great Uncle Louie or from a winning number at MegaLotto, to develop a very diversified portfolio of top-rated companies with sizable dollar initial investments in each without going through a stockbroker.

DRIP PROGRAMS WITH EXISTING REGISTERED SHAREHOLDER REQUIREMENT

Many companies require investors to be shareholders of record prior to enrolling in their DRIP. This requirement forces investors to purchase a minimum number of shares from a third party, such as a broker, and have the stock certificate issued in the investors' names; then the investors are eligible to enroll in the DRIP. For example, the following companies require DRIP participants to be initially a registered shareholder of the indicated number of shares:

Abbott Labs (ABT)	1 share
Apache Corp (APA)	1 share
Boeing (BA)	50 shares
Coca-Cola (KO)	1 share
Intel (INTC)	1 share
The Limited (LTD)	1 share
PepsiCo (PEP)	5 shares
State Street Bank (STT)	10 shares

When investing in these types of DRIPs, investors need to be aware of brokerage fee charges for the delivery of certificates. These may range from $25 to $75 per stock certificate and will increase the initial costs to enroll. For example, Apache Corp (APA), the large independent oil and natural gas producer, requires investors to own a minimum of one share prior to enrolling in its DRIP. If an investor had an existing account with an on-line broker, the fees may include $20 commission to purchase the share and another $25 for certificate delivery—for a total fee of $45. With the stock trading at $50 a share, an investor may pay $95, including fees, for the initial share required to be eligible for APA's DRIP. When considering enrolling in DRIPs that do not offer the option for direct investing of the initial investment, investors should strongly consider purchasing sufficient shares to reduce the transaction and delivery fees per share.

Regardless of the fees associated with these programs, it is imperative that investors get in the investing game and that they do not let the task of buying just one share stop them from beginning a DRIP. Most serious DRIP investors have a brokerage account that can provide access to companies requiring a minimum number of shares prior to enrollment.

Once the stock certificate is issued and investors become shareholders of record, they are eligible to enroll in the company DRIP. Contact the company or its transfer agent and request DRIP enrollment forms. Most DRIPs allow shareholders to send the original stock certificate along with the completed forms for credit to their account. Once enrolled, DRIP investors can send in optional cash payments (OCP) as desired and allowed by plan details.

STOCKBROKERS

On the other side of the spectrum from direct investing is buying common stocks through a brokerage firm. As previously outlined, when investing in tax-deferred accounts, it may be preferred to hold those assets at a broker. Due to tax regulation and requirements concerning contributions, recordkeeping, and disbursements, brokers can provide valuable services. In addition, having all tax-deferred account assets at one location should reduce annual IRA fees. However, these services do not come free of charge. There are usually minimum account balances, transaction commissions, and sometimes account service fees. Using the full-service broker Solomon Smith Barney as an example, for an IRA account, the minimum investment to open is $500. If an investor funds an IRA account using an annual contribution of $2000 and buys shares in one company, a commission of $50 to $65 may be deducted. For trades of $10,000, the investor should expect to pay approximately $110 in broker commissions. Annual IRA account fees are $50.

With the advent of discount and on-line brokers, transaction commissions have been reduced. Charles Schwab, the large discount broker, charges a minimum commission of $39 for broker-assisted trades and $30 commission for on-line trades. Minimum account balances at Schwab range from $500 for custodian and educational IRA accounts to $1000 for traditional IRA accounts to $5000 for a regular brokerage account. Schwab charges $25 for each share certificate delivery. Internet brokers advertise stock trades as low as $7 per transaction, but many have high account minimums ranging from $2000 to $3000 all the way up to a minimum of $10,000 for each account.

All full-service brokerage firms offer their full array of retail investment research to all their clients, regardless of type of account. An IRA account holder at Solomon Smith Barney, for instance, has access to its stock research either using access over the Internet or by requesting information from his or her broker. Deeply discounted on-line brokers do not usually offer much specific advice and should be used mainly as a stock-purchasing tool. Many discount brokers are mainly interested in selling mutual funds. However, mutual funds may not be as advantageous to an investor's portfolio.

Smart Money's Money Basic educational section of their website offers an interesting review of the decision process concerning full-service, discounted, or on-line brokers. The main advantage of full-service brokers, according to Smart Money, is their top-notch advice on a wide variety of economic topics. It is far easier to generate capital gains during an overall up market, and the advice of a seasoned pro at a broker may assist investors in better stock selections in down markets. "During periods of unpredictability, the do-it-yourself investors are left hanging in the wind with no one to turn to but themselves and the Internet chat columns. Clients of full-service firms benefit from those firms' strategies."[1] Some investors may desire the time savings offered by listening to the advice of a well-educated and trusted broker and still utilize the advantages of dollar cost averaging dividend reinvestments. The downside to full-service brokers is that they usually cost more, either charging per-transaction commissions or an overall asset value percentage fee. It is important for investors to select a specific broker whom they can trust and who is not overly interested in churning the account for added commissions nor stuffing a portfolio with higher commission investment products.

For investors who are interested in making their own decisions, discount and on-line brokers offer less expensive transaction costs, but many lack both investment advice and, in many cases, the personal touch needed to resolve problems. With the merging of discount brokers and Internet access, clients can still deal with their neighborhood broker and review their assets on-line. For example, Edward Jones, Inc., offers broker-assisted trades and on-line review with no account minimums and stock trade fees beginning at $50 with no certificate delivery fee. IRA fees range between $15 and $30 a year.

The cheap on-line trades advertised at $7 come with no frills, and there is no option to visit a nearby office to speak with someone face to face. Communications with low-cost on-line trading firms is limited to telephone contact and e-mail.

> While trading online can be cheap, it can also be a horror show. During times of high volume in the market, servers can clog up and create extensive trading delays. You can call customer service to complain, but in some cases you'll wait as long as an hour. Checks get lost in the mail, orders go unfilled,—you name it. Unless you trade a lot,

you should avoid the deep discounters. They aren't reliable enough yet.[2]

SYNTHETIC DRIPs

For years, many full-service brokers have offered their clients the service of reinvesting dividends. Although the actual certificates still remain in the broker's name, also known as the *street name*, cash dividends received in the account are used to purchase additional shares. Like company DRIPs, brokers record fractional share ownership and purchase less than full shares with the dividend received. Broker DRIPs are also know as *synthetic DRIPs*. The major drawback to synthetic DRIPs is that additional investments beyond the actual cash dividend are subject to the firm's usual brokerage commission. Synthetic DRIP services should be used with all long-term accounts at third-party brokers.

ON-LINE SYNTHETIC BROKERS

The most exciting development in the world of DRIPs and direct investing since the whole concept was first introduced 50 years ago is the latest offering of on-line synthetic DRIP services. *Sharebuilder.com* is a sister site to *netstockdirect.com;* both are subsidiaries of Net Stock Investment Corporation. Sharebuilder allows investors to purchase shares using regularly scheduled, predetermined dollar amounts in as many as 4000 publicly traded companies and index securities. Through electronic transfer from an investor's bank account, Sharebuilder buys stock on a weekly basis, usually on Tuesdays. Investors can choose between weekly or monthly purchasing cycles, with one-time trades also available. Sharebuilder buys fractional shares in dollar-based amounts. Sharebuilder costs $3.00 per trade, $2.00 for custodian accounts. There is no minimum account balance or minimum purchase amounts for Sharebuilder accounts. Dividends are reinvested at no charge.

Sharebuilder is an ideal tool for novice investors wanting to get started or as a supplement to existing brokerage and company or bank-sponsored DRIP accounts. For example, a smaller investor may decide to buy $1200 each in stock of three different companies over the next 12 months. Sharebuilder will accept a $300 monthly investment transfer and invest $100 in each of the three companies, for a $3 per transaction fee. Larger investors have used Sharebuilder to invest $10,000 to $20,000 a week for several months running, and these investment dollars are usually split among several stock issues. Sharebuilder offers investors the opportunity to easily and cost-effectively dollar cost average a stock position. If an investor wants a position in a specific stock that is offered at the Sharebuilder site and is tenuous about miscalculating market timing, dollar cost averaging monthly or weekly purchases would be a perfect solution.

The advantages of an on-line synthetic DRIP service are many. Sharebuilder offers a consolidated monthly statement of all DRIP transactions, including purchases using additional capital and reinvestment of dividends. Unlike some brokerage firms that may offer as short as a 45- to 90-day transaction history, Sharebuilder stores account transaction history for as long as the account is open. Account history is crucial for many DRIP investors who are less than diligent at their own recordkeeping. Years from now, determining a cost basis for DRIP shares can be problematic without proper records. Sharebuilder charges a flat fee per transaction, which is less than some DRIPs charge for an optional cash payment.

There are many stocks available through the dollar cost averaging services of Sharebuilder that do not offer DRIPs or direct investing plans of their own. For example, an investor can dollar cost average a position in Qualcomm (QCOM) or in the Unit Trusts Index funds, such as the NADASQ 100 or the S&P Select Spiders. According to Jeff Seely, CEO of NetStock Investment Corporation, the profile of the typical Sharebuilder client is a monthly investor averaging $100 to $200 investments in two to three different securities. The average investment selection leans heavily to well-known, large-capitalization, high-tech, and blue chip stocks, along with a few Index securities. On-line synthetic brokers allow for flexibility within regular investment schedules. With a click of a mouse, investments can be suspended or resumed. Within a predetermined dollar investment schedule, investors can easily shift their investment focus, changing the dollar amount to be invested in each security.

Seen as an additional valuable tool for long-term investors, Sharebuilder is beginning to co-brand their services with banks, credit unions, and insurance companies. Wells Fargo Bank (WFC) offers the Wells Fargo Sharebuilder services right next to its on-line Wells Fargo stock brokerage services. There are other on-line synthetic DRIP brokers, such as *buyandhold.com;* but compared with Sharebuilder, their securities selection is inferior and their fees are higher. Sharebuilder was named as one of the top-10 broker services site by *Forbes Magazine* in their May 2000 issue of "The Best of the Web." *Forbes'* review of the Sharebuilder concept stated:

> After a while, online brokers begin to look alike. Not Sharebuilder. It specializes in automatic investment accounts for small investors who want to invest directly in stocks. It is an outgrowth of Net Stock Direct, which specializes in DRIPs and Direct Stock Plans for the 1500 or so companies that offer them. Popular stocks such as Cisco and Microsoft don't have direct plans, so Sharebuilder creates its own direct stock plan for these companies and charges $3 per trade. Great for systematic savers. BEST: Start your child's stock investing here and consolidate all your DRIPs and DSPs. WORST: Just stocks. No mutual funds.[3]

CHAPTER 9

Asset Allocation and Portfolio Diversification

Key Concepts

- Asset Allocation
- Asset Allocation Changes Based on Investors' Age and Investment Time Frame
- Asset Allocation for Retirement Accounts
- Stock Portfolio Diversification
- How to Build a Diversified DRIP Portfolio
- Rebalancing a Diversified Portfolio

A popular television commercial for a well-known brokerage firm depicts an aging rock band in a love song writing session; the writer is trying to rhyme a verse that ends in *elation*. He asks for help, and the camera pans to Ringo Starr saying, "Dividend reinvestment participation, asset allocation, portfolio diversification." It seems everyone is taking about allocation and diversification. In the rush to market catchy phrases, the real meanings of *allocation* and *diversification* are bound to get lost. In reality, every investor utilizes these concepts every time an investment is made, even in money market accounts. Investors must decide whether investment allocation and diversification is being done by default or by design.

ASSET ALLOCATION

Asset allocation is a practiced investment strategy. According to Ibbotson Research, "A prominent magazine in 1926 recommended that a portfolio contain 25% sound bonds, 25% sound preferred stocks, 25% sound common stocks and 25% speculative securities. This may not be an entirely appropriate portfolio for today, but the importance of asset allocation remains."[1]

Asset allocation is the investment strategy of separating financial investments into the basic categories of cash (or short-term notes), bonds, and stocks. The combination offers the minimal risk and principal-preserving attributes of cash, the income generation, and the relative stability of bonds, along with the growth potential of stocks. Cash and short-term notes have little risk, but also subpar returns. Stocks have a much higher risk than cash, but also have the potential for much higher returns. High-quality bonds lie between cash and stocks for risk and returns. With each additional investment, the asset allocation ratio among cash, stock, and bonds changes either by design or by default. Over time, even a balanced asset allocation may become unbalanced.

Asset allocation is an evolving concept. Because stock positions usually increase in value faster over time than bonds or cash, the asset allocation for stocks will creep higher within a particular investor's portfolio. For example, Ivan the Investor begins the year with $30,000 in long-term investments. He has allocated 33 percent in cash, 33 percent in bonds, and 33 percent in stocks, or $10,000 in each asset category. Ivan realizes a 4 percent annual return on the cash investments, 7 percent return on the bond investments, and 12 percent return on the stock investments. At the end of the first year, Ivan owns $10,400 in cash, $10,700 in bonds, and $11,200 in stocks. At the end of the second year, Ivan owns $10,816 in cash, $11,449 in bonds, and $12,544 in stocks. By the fifth year, Ivan owns $12,166 in cash, $14,025 in bonds, and $17,623 in stocks, for a total portfolio worth $43,814. Ivan has earned an average annual portfolio return of 9.2 percent. Ivan's balanced portfolio began with 33 percent in each asset category; after 5 years, cash represented 27.7 percent, bonds 32.0 percent, and stocks 40.3 percent. Due to higher investment returns of stocks over cash in the 5-year time frame, stocks have crept up to a higher allocation than originally planned.

Every specific investment purchased, or even assets held for the long term, is preceded by an allocation decision either by design or by default. During the investment-selection process, an investor is actively implementing an asset allocation strategy. The initial decision of the asset category to be purchased invokes the theory of allocation. An investor deciding to take funds out of a savings plan (cash) and invest in stocks is increasing the stock allocation and reducing the cash allocation of the portfolio.

Stocks and bonds rise and fall at different times, and not always together. For example, in times of rising interest rates, bonds may outperform stocks, whereas in times of stable rates, the opposite may be true. A portfolio that invests in both may outperform in times of declining stock prices, but may underperform in times of rising stock prices. A balanced asset allocation will reduce overall portfolio risk. Although it is fair to predict that assets will appreciate in value over time, it is impossible to accurately predict which assets will outperform others in the future. An investor can hedge this uncertainty by maintaining investments in each asset category.

Asset allocation has greater impact on overall investment returns than any other factor in long-term investing. According to a study published by Ibbotson Research, the allocation of assets is responsible for 91.5 percent of the performance of a specific portfolio. Actual stock selection was responsible for only 4.6 percent of the overall portfolio's performance, 1.8 percent on market timing, and 2.1 percent on other factors.[2] An individual portfolio's performance is determined much more by deciding whether to buy stocks as a diversified asset category, rather than making a specific stock selection. For instance, an investor may decide to buy Briggs & Stratton as an investment over Tecumseh Products while another remains in larger cash position. The precise allocation of investments in each of the three categories will vary based on the investors' age, the time frame of the investment, and the overall risk tolerance of the investors.

ASSET ALLOCATION CHANGES BASED ON INVESTORS' AGE AND INVESTMENT TIME FRAME

The amount invested in cash, bonds, and stocks should be based on how soon the funds are needed. A financial goal is achieved after the portfolio goes through three phases: accumulation, consolidation, and spending (or disbursement). Reaching a financial goal begins with the accumulation of assets, usually by savings from earned income. Being long-term in nature, most portfolios can assume greater risk. If there is a declining period in the investment's value, there is plenty of time for the portfolio to recuperate. During the consolidation phase, the annual contribution as a percentage of the overall value begins to decrease. The financial goal should be relatively far off, but within sight. Investment risk should be reduced to enable greater capital preservation.

In the spending phase, the funds are withdrawn for the expenses associated with that specific financial need. With the financial need at hand, it may not be a great idea to invest in high-risk investments due to the consequences of a decline in value.

For example, a young couple wants to save for their newborn daughter's college education in 20 years and plans to invest $2000 a year to reach that goal. In the early years, they accept a higher degree of risk and invest mainly in stocks. As the years progress, the actual need to spend the funds becomes closer and their tolerance for risk decreases. The cash and bond allocation of the portfolio grows and reflects this more conservative, risk-adverse approach. The young couple may have chosen the asset allocation in Table 9–1 based on the 20-year investment time frame.

Years 1 to 10 would be considered the accumulation phase, Years 11 to 20 the consolidation phase, and Years 20+ as the spending phase.

If the young couple invested $2000 annually on January 1 and maintained an asset allocation as outlined in the table, their portfolio value may resemble Table 9–2. The annual return on the cash as-

TABLE 9–1

Asset Allocation Based on 20-Year Financial Goal

Asset	Years 1–5	Years 6–10	Years 11–15	Years 16–20	Years 20 +
Cash	0%	0%	0%	0%	20%
Bonds	15%	15%	25%	50%	50%
Stocks	85%	85%	75%	50%	30%

TABLE 9-2

$2,000 Annual Investment in a Conservative Portfolio
with a 20-Year Investment Time Frame

Year	Jan 1 Account Balance	Cash Assets	Bond Assets	Stock Assets	3.50% Cash Return	6.00% Bond Return	12.00% Stock Return	Account Balance Year End
1	$2,000	$0.00	$300	$1,700	$0.00	$18	$204	$2,222
2	4,222	0.00	633	3,588	0.00	38	430	4,690
3	6,690	0.00	1,003	5,687	0.00	60	682	7,433
4	9,433	0.00	1,415	8,018	0.00	84	962	10,480
5	12,480	0.00	1,872	10,608	0.00	112	1,273	13,865
6	15,865	0.00	2,379	13,485	0.00	142	1,618	17,626
7	19,626	0.00	2,944	16,682	0.00	176	2,001	21,805
8	23,805	0.00	3,570	20,234	0.00	214	2,428	26,447
9	28,447	0.00	4,267	24,180	0.00	256	2,901	31,605
10	33,605	0.00	5,040	28,564	0.00	302	3,427	37,335
11	39,335	0.00	9,833	29,501	0.00	590	3,540	43,465
12	45,465	0.00	11,366	34,099	0.00	681	4,091	50,239
13	52,239	0.00	13,059	39,179	0.00	783	4,701	57,725
14	59,725	0.00	14,931	44,793	0.00	895	5,375	65,996
15	67,996	0.00	16,999	50,997	0.00	1,019	6,119	75,135
16	77,135	0.00	38,567	38,567	0.00	2,314	4,628	84,078
17	86,078	0.00	43,039	43,039	0.00	2,582	5,164	93,825
18	95,825	0.00	47,912	47,912	0.00	2,874	5,749	104,449
19	106,441	0.00	53,224	53,224	0.00	3,193	6,386	116,029
20	118,029	0.00	59,014	59,014	0.00	3,540	7,081	128,652
21	93,652	18,730	46,826	28,095	655	2,809	3,371	100,489
22	65,489	13,097	32,744	19,646	458	1,964	2,357	70,269
23	35,269	7,053	17,634	10,580	246	1,058	1,269	37,844
24	2,844	568	1,422	853	19	85	102	3,052

sets is calculated at 3.5 percent, bonds at 6.0 percent, and stocks at 12 percent. At the end of 20 years, their account would have a balance of $128,000. Starting in Year 21, the couple withdraws $35,000 a year for 4 years to pay the anticipated college expenses.

ASSET ALLOCATION FOR RETIREMENT ACCOUNTS

The same asset allocation approached used by the young couple to save for future college expenses can be used for retirement accounts. During our younger years, IRA accounts should include both stocks and bonds, with the majority of the funds invested in stocks. At age 40, we begin to enter the consolidation phase, where capital preservation becomes more important; thus, the portfolio should begin to reflect a more conservative approach. Our earned income during the consolidation phase may be considered by some to be at its prime. Around age 65, we begin to enter the spending phase, and earned income tapers off. We begin to rely on our IRA or other retirement accounts as a financial resource. Capital preservation and adversity to excessive risk should be paramount as we age. There is probably not as much time to recoup from a bad investment when we are 75 years old.

DRIP and direct investing are available to both stock and US Treasury bond holders. DRIPs are a proven means of acquiring stock and bond assets over the long term; they provide an easy method for investing smaller amounts of money especially during the accumulating phase.

STOCK PORTFOLIO DIVERSIFICATION

The old adage "don't put all your eggs in one basket" applies to portfolio diversification. The concept of diversification is simple: Owning a little bit of stock in a lot of different companies is preferred to owning a lot of stock in only two or three companies. A diversified portfolio is usually associated with lower overall investment risk and usually will perform better in volatile or down markets. In strong up markets, as we experienced in the late 1990s, a diversified portfolio of stocks may underperform a higher risk, more focused, and less diverse portfolio.

With a large and growing number of companies offering DRIP and direct investing options, it is becoming easier to develop a diversified portfolio without going through a broker or buying a mutual fund. Seasoned DRIP investors may have 20 or more DRIP accounts in different sectors of the economy and will add to their investments in whichever company they believe offers the best value in the current market. One constant reality of investing is that there will always be industries or sectors of the economy that lag others. What is good for energy companies (high oil prices) is not good for transportation companies (higher fuel costs). DRIP investors, using the OCP feature, can easily increase long-term stock positions in either sectors that are in favor or those not currently popular.

As asset allocation divides investments by major category, diversification furthers divides assets by type. Within the asset category of stocks, for instance, there are many different selections from which to choose. Stocks are divided by both industrial classification (industrial, cyclical, consumer) and their historic investment characteristic (growth, income, value, speculative). Issuer (US Treasury, municipalities, and corporations) divides bonds by maturity (5 year, 10 year, and 30 year), by federal tax status (taxable or tax-free), and by yield. An investor holding several different industrial classifications and investment characteristic stocks is said to have a diversified portfolio of stocks. Likewise, an investor with several different maturities and yields is said to have a diversified bond portfolio.

Just as default or design accomplishes asset allocation, so does portfolio diversification. Every stock purchase and sale alters the composition of the portfolio and potentially changes its diversification. Even mutual fund selections should be analyzed for their top-20 holdings, and especially their top-5 stock positions, to ensure an individual's overall account diversification. Owning five mutual funds, each with a substantial position in Intel, and then buying Intel as a DRIP may not accomplish further portfolio diversification.

Every company operates its business within a specific industry or industries. These industries are classified by type, and industry competitors are usually grouped together. As with different companies, different industrial sectors expand at different rates. For instance, technology companies are usually associated with high earnings growth, whereas utilities are well known for more stable earnings. Generally speaking, a competitive group and most companies within an industrial sector will move together in the stock market, rotating from being liked by investors to being out of favor. S&P offers an industrial classification by both major industrial and subsectors. There are eight S&P major industrial sectors: Industrial, Cyclical, Noncyclical, Basic Materials, Technology, Utilities, Financial, and Energy. Listed next is a brief explanation of each category:

Industrial—These are usually manufacturing companies or firms providing services to manufacturers. These companies usually expand with a growing economy. Companies in this sector include Honeywell, TYCO Int'l, Federal Signal, and Caterpillar.

Cyclical—These are companies whose businesses are directly tied to the ups and downs of the economy, such as retailers, paper manufacturers, and automakers. Cyclical stocks can have sizable fluctuations in both earnings and stock prices. Companies in this sector include Home Depot, Sears, Kimberly Clark, and Johnson Controls.

Noncyclical—These are companies whose businesses are not as directly tied to the swings in the economy, such as food, household items, and medical companies. Noncyclicals are usually the slow, steady growth companies. Companies in this sector include Albertsons, Sara Lee, Johnson & Johnson, and Merck.

Basic Materials—These are companies involved in providing raw materials to manufacturers, such as chemicals, fertilizers, and metals. Basic materials companies' fortunes fluctuate with economic activity and inflation rates. Companies in this sector include Crompton Corp, LESCO, and Dow Chemical.

Technology—This industrial sector is quite broad, ranging from aerospace to computers to office equipment. Tech companies usually have higher earnings growth, but many tech stocks carry a rich price premium. If earnings expectations are not met, high-priced tech stocks have farther to fall, creating greater investment risk. Companies in this sector include Raytheon, Lucent Technologies, Intel, and Pitney Bowes.

Utilities—These companies usually operate in a price-regulated environment, providing electricity, water, and telecommunications services. Many utilities are expanding into nonregulated businesses, such as telecommunications and energy trading. Some utilities are diversified in their regulated business, such as an electricity producer owning a water utility. Utilities offer higher dividend income, greater dividend payout ratios, and much lower earnings growth. Companies in this sector include Hawaiian Electric, Philadelphia Suburban, and SBC Corp.

Financial—These companies are banks, savings and loans, insurance, and financial services firms. Financial companies prosper during times of decreasing or stable interest rates and suffer during times of rising rates. Companies in this sector include SunTrust Bank, Washington Mutual, AFLAC, and Merrill Lynch.

Energy—These companies are involved in the oil and natural gas business. Energy company earnings are directly tied to the commodity price of oil and gas. In times of rising inflation or increasing oil prices, energy stocks can perform very well. However, if oil prices decline, as they did to 20-year lows in late 1998, these companies may struggle. Companies in this sector include Apache Corp, ExxonMobil, and Chevron.

Most every company traded on the various stock exchanges falls within one of these categories. Individual S&P stock reports provide not only the major industrial sector, but the competitive subsector as well.

A well-diversified portfolio should have stock positions in each of these sectors, and an equally weighted portfolio would have 12.5 percent invested in each industrial sector. There is great debate concerning appropriate sector portfolio weightings to minimize investment risk while maximizing returns. A conservative investor may have 35 percent to 40 percent invested in a combination of lower risk utilities and noncyclical stocks, whereas an aggressive investor may have 40 percent or more in higher risk tech stocks.

Within each industrial sector, stocks can be classified by their potential investment charactitics: growth, income, value, and speculative. Growth stocks are bought on the premise that the company will continue to expand earnings at a sustainable above average rate, and higher earnings will cause the stock price to rise over time. Income stocks are bought due to an attractive relative dividend yield and are usually more conservative investments. Value stocks are usually out of favor companies or companies with short-term earnings problems, creating a momentary shortage of investor interest and low stock prices.

A younger investor may focus on growth stocks within the technology and industrial sectors, whereas an older investor may search for higher-yielding value stock within the same industrial sectors. Based on the time frame of the financial goal, stock selection within the perimeters of a diversified portfolio may change. A newly established IRA account may be more heavily weighted to high-tech growth stocks, whereas an IRA account in the spending phase may utilize more high-yielding utility stocks.

HOW TO BUILD A DIVERSIFIED DRIP PORTFOLIO

DRIP and direct investing make it easy for investors to build a diversified portfolio. Much like a mutual fund invests in many different stocks, a DRIP investor can build a portfolio of several different companies without needing a large amount of start-up capital. Within the wide selection of companies offering DRIPs and direct investing programs, investors can find several individual stock choices that may fit their personal investment criteria.

For investors with current holdings of mutual funds or individual stocks, the diversification process is simple. Make a list of all current holdings along with their respective industrial sectors and subgroups and the value of the investment. For mutual funds, list at least the top-10 stock holdings, along with an estimation of the value your investment represents of each. The annual reports and most quarterly reports will notify fund holders of the names and percentage of the fund in each of the top holdings. With this list, investors can rearrange the stock positions by industrial sector and can determine the extent of their current diversification. Investors can clearly evaluate which sectors and specific stocks may be overly weighted and which industrial sectors may not be represented at all. From this list, investors can begin to research specific stock selections to balance the account.

For beginning investors, the field is wide open. First-time investors may want to start with a mix of industrials sectors, such as technology, utilities, and energy, and diversify into the other sectors over time.

Sometimes new investment selections come along that can be added to a portfolio to gain better diversification. The introduction of S&P Sector Selects Unit Trusts shares, also known as Select Spider, has helped investors easily diversify without paying mutual fund management fees. As alternatives to mutual funds, these securities offer excellent avenues for investing potentially small amounts of money in entire industrial sectors. There is more information on the Unit Trusts and Spiders in the chapter concerning mutual funds and alternatives. Most Unit Trusts are not forward thinking enough to offer either a DRIP or direct investing program, but they are suitable for ShareBuilder and broker accounts, with the option of reinvesting all dividends.

REBALANCING A DIVERSIFIED PORTFOLIO

Investing is a fluid process, and it is important to monitor each account and portfolio. Some stocks experience huge capital gains, and what was once a balanced and diversified portfolio may get out of kilter. For example, as technology stocks exploded in the late 1980s and early 1990s, many portfolios became overweighted in tech issues. It was common for even large-cap tech stocks, like Intel or Motorola, to have provided long-term investors with capital gains in the 500 percent to 1000 percent range. However, with these large stock gains, some portfolios have been actually getting riskier as a greater percentage of the total portfolio is represented by very well-performing, but higher risk, technology stocks.

A portfolio can be rebalanced two ways—either by selling a portion of those stocks that have had an excellent run up in price and reallocate the investment dollars into other sectors, or by investing additional dollars into sectors that are underweighted. Whenever a stock is sold for a long-term capital gain in a nontax-deferred account, however, remember the US Government currently takes 20 percent of the profit in capital gains taxes.

Most financial advisors agree that investors should analyze every account portfolio for overall return, asset allocation, and stock diversification at least once a year. Annual visits to these subjects will assist investors in remaining current with their investments and revisiting the reasons the DRIP selection was initially made. In addition, annual visits will remind investors that the clock only moves one way—forward—and that every financial goal has its own day of reckoning.

CHAPTER 10

Bonds

Key Concepts

- Types of Bonds
- Why Invest in Bonds?
- Bonds Offered Through Direct Investing
- Treasury Inflation Protected Securities (TIPS)
- How Do Bonds Fit into a DRIP Strategy?

Investors lend money to companies or various government entities through bonds. Companies or various government entities, such as the federal government, states, towns, cities, or even school districts, can issue bonds. Most bonds are redeemed on a specific date, called the *maturity date,* and pay investors a regular fixed interest payment. For example, an investor may lend the US Treasury $10,000 for 30 years and receive semi-annual interest payments of $300 ($600 a year), for a 6.0 percent yield. At the end of 30 years, the government repays the original $10,000. Due to their relative safety and low risk, along with offering higher cash yields than most stock investments, bonds should be a part of every DRIP investor's overall portfolio.

TYPES OF BONDS

Bonds are categorized by several criteria. The issuer initially classifies bonds. Government bond issuers are usually the federal government, also known as the US Treasury Department. Corporate bonds run the gamut of companies, but usually are issued by large- and medium-cap companies. Loans of 3 years or less are called *notes*, whereas loans of 5 years or longer are called *bonds*. The most common loan durations or maturities are 30-day, 60-day, 90-day, 120-day, 1-year, and 3-year notes; and 5-year, 10-year, and 30-year bonds.

Bonds are then categorized by their tax status. Interest received from US Treasury and corporate bonds are fully taxable under current IRS regulations. Municipal bonds, school district obligations, and similar loans issued by municipal governments are called *muni bonds*. Interest payments to investors of muni bonds are exempt from federal income taxes. Some state tax regulations exempt state bond interest income from state income taxes. For example, the state of Illinois might exempt residents from paying taxes on income generated from owning State of Illinois bonds. Muni bonds are of particular interest to investors with sizable portfolios who also have a higher tax exposure. Historically, the yield from US Treasury bonds is higher than muni bonds on a pretax basis. However, after-tax yields may at times favor muni bonds. Investors should compare the after-tax returns, based on their individual tax situation, for both US Treasury and muni bonds prior to investing in either. Investors should check with their accountant or consult their current state tax code to determine potential state income tax liabilities of muni bond interest.

WHY INVEST IN BONDS?

DRIP investors should include bonds in their asset allocation to achieve two important goals: capital preservation and income generation. The investment risk of bonds is quite simple. Will the government agency or corporation issuing the bond have the financial ability to make the scheduled interest payments and repay the bond on the maturity date? Considered by many to be the benchmark of risk-free investing, US Treasury bonds are considered to be a very secure investment. There are several bond-rating services, such as Moody's and S&P. Bond investors straying from US Treasury notes and bonds should consult these rating services to further understand the investment risk.

Government bonds from some foreign countries, however, may be a different story. With intercountry lending, the threat of default, or not paying principal owed at maturity date, by one country will have a "domino" effect in other countries. For instance, at the height of the 1997 to 1998 Asian financial crisis, Indonesia threatened to default on its government bonds. With this threat of default, the bonds lost their good credit rating and the value of the bonds plummeted. The Korean government owned over $10 billion of Indonesian bonds. Investors became nervous about the financial stability of Korea if Indonesia were to default and sold their holding in Korean bonds, reducing the value of those bonds as well. Japan and Taiwan were also heavy investors in Indonesian bonds, and they suffered similar fates. Russia defaulted on their debt obligations in 1998, causing a similar worldwide financial crisis. When considering corporate and foreign government bonds, investors need to have a high level of confidence that the company and country will continue to be financially viable come maturity date. Higher-risk bond investments are called *junk bonds* mainly because repayment may be in question.

BONDS OFFERED THROUGH DIRECT INVESTING

Currently, only US Treasury notes and bonds are available directly to investors. Muni and corporate bonds require a broker. US Treasury notes and bonds, along with muni and corporate bonds, do not offer the opportunity to reinvest earned interest. For DRIP and direct investors, the best program is offered by the US Treasury—the TreasuryDirect. It is a book entry system and, like DRIPs, no actual certificate is issued. Interest and principal payments are done electronically to a preselected bank account. Principal can be reinvested on maturity by a touch-tone telephone. Bond investors can place orders via the phone or the Internet and buy bonds without a broker. The minimum investments using the TreasuryDirect program are as follows:

* $1000   Inflation Protected Securities, 30-year, 10-year, and 5-year bonds
* $5000   3-year and 2-year notes
* $10,000   Less than 2-year notes

For more information, surf at *www.publicdebt.treas.gov* on the Internet or call 202/874-4000.

TREASURY INFLATION PROTECTED SECURITIES (TIPS)

A few years ago, the US Government introduced a new investment concept called Treasury Inflation Protected Securities (TIPS). One severe drawback to investing in bonds is a low real rate of return after consideration for inflation. As we saw earlier, after adjusting for inflation, bonds historically underperformed stocks and barely maintained purchasing parity over time. Investors attempt to realize a real rate of return by demanding bond interest yield to be higher than their expectations for inflation. For example, currently the 30-year government bond is yielding 6.0 percent while inflation is around 2.5 percent, creating a real rate of return of 3.5 percent. In the mid-1990s, the US Treasury decided to offer securities whose principal increases with the rate of inflation. On maturity, the government will repay the investor the original principal, indexed to inflation. A standard 30-year government bond bought in 1969 would pay the investor $10,000 in 1999. If TIPS had been offered in 1969, a $10,000 30-year TIPS investment would have been redeemed in 1999 for an estimated $46,655 (the value of $10,000 in 1969 increasing at the inflation rate for 30 years). TIPS pay interest semi-annually, but at a lower percentage rate than a standard government bond. TIPS pay a fixed interest rate, however, on the indexed value of the investment. For example, if the benchmark 30-year Treasury bond is yielding 6 percent, the 30-year TIPS may pay 4 percent of the indexed value. As the inflation indexed value of the TIPS increases, so does the cash interest payment.

Although not seeming like much of a return compared with stocks, the US Government is offering investors the opportunity to receive a virtually risk-free 4 percent real rate of return, and the principal is repaid to the investor with pricing parity. For the bond asset allocation of a diversified DRIP and direct investing portfolio, TIPS should be strongly considered.

With TIPS, the US Government has offered all investors an opportunity of a lifetime. The only method the US Government has of getting ahead of bond investors is the ability to repay today's loans with inflated tomorrow dollars. Thus, $10,000 lent to the government in 1969 would be worth $2140 when repaid in 1999, due to inflation. However, with TIPS, the government guarantees purchasing parity of the original $10,000 investment and, had they been available, would have repaid approximately $46,655. In addition, if the $10,000 TIPS had a 4 percent yield in 1969, the first year annual income would have been $400. The annual interest received would have grown to $1822 by 1999 as the indexed value increased with the inflation rate. This is virtually a no-brainer bond investment that should be the core holdings of all nontax-exempt bond assets held to maturity.

For mutual fund lovers, or those who have no other options but mutual funds, TIPS bond funds are starting to be offered. In June 2000, Vanguard opened a bond mutual that invests in TIPS, Vanguard Inflation Protected Securities Fund, and it trades using the symbol VIPSX.

Bonds are sold in denominations of $1000, but are issued, traded, and redeemed in $100 units. A $1000 bond is priced as ten $100 units, whereas a $10,000 bond is priced as one hundred $100 units. Bond prices fluctuate inversely with the rise and fall of overall interest rates. For example, a $1000 bond offers a fixed $60 annual interest payment, yielding 6 percent and trades at $100. If interest rates rise to 8 percent, new $1000 bonds would be offering $80 interest payments. An investor would want to buy the 6 percent–$1000 bond for $750 (yielding 8 percent to the investor) to compete with the current rates of new bonds. The 6 percent bond would be quoted in the market at $75. If interest rates were to drop to 5 percent, an investor would pay $1200 for the 6 percent–$1000 bond (yielding 5 percent to the investor), and the bond would be quoted as $120. Regardless of the market price, on reaching maturity date, the bond issuer will repay the original amount of the bond, be it $1000, $10,000, or $100,000. Bond risk and returns are normally tied to the length of time until maturity. A 30-year bond will usually fluctuate in price greater than a 10-year bond and will generally pay a higher yield.

HOW DO BONDS FIT INTO A DRIP STRATEGY?

Bonds are considered by many investors to be desirable investments due to greater capital preservation characteristics and higher yields than stocks. But most bonds do not allow for reinvestment of interest, and most brokers do not offer synthetic reinvestment programs for bond interest. This provides a quandary for an investor who does not have a broker account. With the exception of US Treasuries, bonds need to be bought and sold by a broker. Opening a broker account for the bond asset allocation of an investor's portfolio may provide interesting opportunities. Like an IRA account, an account used to principally buy bonds opens an investor to other brokerage services as well, such as stock research. Because bond interest is paid in cash, a brokerage account can accumulate cash payments along with regularly scheduled additional contributions until the investor has sufficient cash to purchase additional bonds. It is feasible for an investor to use a brokerage account to electronically purchase and receive interest payments for the TreasuryDirect program.

Bond Funds

Bond mutual funds with interest reinvestment and direct investing options are another avenue to gain bond exposure. However, annual bond mutual fund management fees and undistributed capital gains tax exposures may substantially reduce their attractiveness. Large, conservative bond funds with exposure to many different maturities are considered by many investors to be preferred. Make sure to review the fees and potential tax exposure associated with any bond mutual fund purchase.

A major problem with investing in bond funds is that they have no maturity. Unlike investing in the actual bond, where there is a promise to pay the initial capital at maturity date, bond funds will continue to reinvest interest received and proceeds from bond maturities. If an investor is hugely unlucky and invests in 10-year bonds at the beginning of a very long-term upswing in interest rates, owning the actual bond instrument will secure repayment of capital regardless of market price. A bond fund, however, may not recover, and there is no secure repayment of capital.

Bond Investments Lost Favor in the 1990s

With the stock market boom of the 1990s, many new and seasoned investors failed to maintain a balance between stock and bond investments. Too few investors focused on the concept of asset allocation, and many portfolios lacked any exposure to bonds. According to the American Association of Individual Investors, in April 2000, investors held only 8 percent of their assets in bonds—down from 20 percent in 1987. Cash assets also declined from 35 percent in 1987 to 17 percent in 2000. Stocks, however, increased as an asset allocation, from 45 percent in 1987 to 75 percent in 2000.[1] Some investors have discovered that a great place to reinvest a portion of capital gains realized from stock investments is to buy some bonds. These investors increase their bond assets with profits made in their stock assets. Not only do they protect a portion of their realized profits with the capital preservation features of bonds, but investors find this to be an easy strategy to increase their asset allocation in bonds.

Some stockbrokers and financial planners advocate that investors have a percentage of their nontax-deferred portfolios in tax-free municipal bonds equaling their age. Their advice translates to a newly retired individual investing 65 percent of non-IRA assets in tax-free bonds and increasing the muni bond positions as the investor ages. Restricting the asset allocation, however, to only tax-free municipal bonds seems a bit overly focused and conservative, especially for a newly retired person with 20 or more years to live. For the average investor, a preferred income allocation should include other income-generating investments, such as utility stocks and other types of bonds like TIPS.

For extremely conservative, high-income investors who are most concerned about capital preservation and generating income free of taxes, municipal bonds investments sometimes provide interesting opportunities. Muni bonds, however, do not offer DRIPs and direct investing options and must be bought through a broker. There are muni bond mutual funds that do provide direct investing options, but then investors are exposed to added fund fees and potentially unwanted fund capital gains tax exposure.

Using the TreasuryDirect program to purchase US Treasury bonds augments stock DRIP accounts. It is important that all DRIP and direct investors allocate a portion of their assets to the bond market, and with the TreasuryDirect program, it is easy to accomplish this diversification.

CHAPTER 11

Investors Don't Need Stock Mutual Funds

Key Concepts
- What Are Mutual Funds?
- Mutual Fund Fees
- Mutual Fund "Phantom" Capital Gains Tax Exposure
- Mutual Fund Diversification
- Investment Unit Trusts and Exchange Traded Funds
- What to Do When Mutual Funds Are the Only Choice
- DRIPs As An Alternative to Mutual Funds

Most American investors own at least a few stock mutual funds. Many of us like the comfort of knowing that someone else is making all our investment decisions for us. When we give our money to mutual fund money managers, we make the assumption that they are better than we are at managing our hard-earned money. We also make the assumption that money managers are able to make our capital grow quickly with less risk. Mutual fund investors, however, are paying dearly for the comfort of believing that these "pros" can deliver on our assumptions. Too many mutual fund investors not only fail to fully analyze the holding of each fund owned, but fail to understand the full impact of paying mutual fund fees. There are times and specific accounts, such as in company-sponsored 401(k) accounts, where mutual funds may be the only choice available to investors. In this case, mutual fund investors should know a few simple rules for fund investing.

WHAT ARE MUTUAL FUNDS?

Mutual funds are a very simple concept. Investors pool their money, hire a "professional" to make their investment decisions, and collectively reap the rewards of the investment pro's decisions. The value of the fund per share is known as the net asset value (NAV). Over time, as the NAV of the fund increases, so should the share price and the value of the fund holders' positions. Sometimes a fund may trade at a discount to the NAV. When this occurs, the fund investor is paying less in the open market than the assets of the fund are worth. Sometimes the opposite also happens and the fund may trade at a premium to its NAV. With investors pooling their capital, a fund has the ability to diversify their holdings into many different investments. The fund may have a specific investment strategy, such as focusing on chemical companies or limiting their investments only to bonds. Some funds concentrate on specific overseas markets, whereas others try to replicate overall market indexes like the S&P 500. Some funds are more conservative, such as a fund that specializes in tax-free municipal bonds, whereas some may be very aggressive, such as an Internet IPO fund. Basically mutual funds come in just about all investment flavors and styles, with more being added every day.

Mutual funds are very popular because they are usually easy to invest in and the hard part of profitable investing (finding top-quality companies whose stock is currently trading at reasonable prices) is left up to someone else. Some mutual funds allow for direct investment of the initial shares, offer the option to reinvest all dividends, and will accept small or large amounts of money. Other funds are available only through a broker, which can use the broker's synthetic DRIP services to reinvest dividends.

MUTUAL FUND FEES

It would seem that mutual funds would be the perfect solution to diversifying a portfolio. However, buying funds may not be as simple or easy as investors believe, and it is very profitable for the mutual fund managers. One reason there are over 7000 mutual funds offered to investors is because the money management business is very profitable. According to *Mutual Fund Magazine,* the "average" mutual fund charges 1.5 percent of assets for its services. Depending on the fund's structure, fees are deducted from the cash balance of the fund on a monthly or quarterly basis. Cash is generated by the fund in one of four ways: sales commissions to buy or sell (called *loads*), dividends or interest received on current investments, realized capital gains, and new investment capital. The NAV of the fund is calculated and management deducts its fee, which then reduces the assets of the fund and the corresponding NAV. As the NAV increases over time, so does the real dollar amount paid in annual management fees. Total assets of the funds almost always include investments in cash or short-term securities, partly to ensure the availability of money to pay fund fees. Based on total industry-wide mutual fund assets of over $3 trillion, it could be safe to say that professional money managers, as an industry, reap over $45 billion in annual fees.

Some funds charge a commission to buy or sell their fund shares, and this is known as a *load.* If there is no commission charged to the investor to purchase or dispose of shares, the fund is said to be a *no-load* fund. Some mutual funds impose a sales commission if the shares are not held for a specific amount of time, such as 3 years. Loads cannot exceed 8.5 percent, but some funds may have loads from 3.5 percent to 5.0 percent on both investors' capital and dividends received by the fund. Like a broker's commission, loads reduce the investor's net dollar amount invested.

Mutual fund fees are separated into several categories and may be substantially above or below the average of 1.5 percent. Fees are used to not only provide investment decision services, such as what stocks to buy and sell, but also the fund's cash flow required for day-to-day operations. These expenses include the telephone bill, rental of office space, and salaries for investment advisors to answer your questions. Operating expenses usually range from 0.2 percent to 2.0 percent of the fund's assets. Some funds charge a very controversial "12(b)-1 fee," which is charged to all the fund holders for fund advertising expense, annual reports, prospectuses, and sales literature. If a fund levies a 12(b)-1 fee, current investors are being asked to pay the cost for finding new fund investors. Someone has to pay for expensive prime-time TV advertising, and it's usually current fund investors. 12(b)-1 fees are capped by SEC regulations at 1 percent of the NAV annually. Mutual funds imposing excessive fees reduce investors' profits, which has a negative impact on overall investment returns.

Morningstar, Inc. is an investment advisory service focused on the mutual fund industry; it is available either at the local public library or over the Internet at *www.morningstar.com*. Morningstar offers a historical profile of a fund's return and risk along with a ranking system of 1 to 5 stars (1 being *low*, 3 being *average*, and 5 being *high*). Selected were the following average or low-cost funds with a miminum history of 10 years. Next are their investment objectives, net assets under management as of December 31, 1999, Morningstar ranking, 10-year annual total return, and the growth of $10,000 invested from 1990 to 1999:

> *Alliance Growth and Income A*—objective: growth and income, net assets $1.577 billion, 3 stars, 15.3 percent 10-year total return, $41,597
>
> *Vanguard Growth and Income*—objective: growth and income, net assets $8.816 billion, 4 stars, 17.9 percent 10-year total return, $29,056
>
> *Fidelity Magellan*—objective: growth net assets $105.938 billion, 4 stars, 18.4 percent 10-year total return, $54,510 (Note: the Fidelity Magellan fund is closed to all new investors, and only those with current positions can add to their investment.)
>
> *USAA Aggressive Growth*—objective: aggressive growth, net assets $1.657 billion, 4 stars, 20.9 percent 10-year total return, $67,051
>
> *Dodge and Cox Income*—objective: high-quality corporate bonds, net assets $0.974 billion, 4 stars, 8.3 percent 10-year total return, $22,293
>
> *T. Rowe Price Tax-Free Income*—objective: muni bonds with longer-term maturity, net assets $1.3 billion, 4 stars, 7.36 percent 10-year total return, $19,558

Based on Morningstar's reporting, examples of their fees are listed in Table 11–1, but exclude specific reporting of 12b-1 fees,

TABLE 11-1

Selected Mutual Fund Fees

	Sales Load	Management Fees (Mgt) Distribution Fees (Dist) (%)	Expense Projections 10-yr, $10,000
Alliance Growth and Income A	4.25%	Mgt 0.48, Dist 0.23	$1,519
Vanguard Growth and Income	none	Mgt 0.33, Dist 0	$456
Fidelity Magellan	3.0%	Mgt 0.57, Dist 0	$1,202
USAA Aggressive Growth	none	Mgt 0.38, Dist 0	$894
Dodge & Cox Income	none	Mgt 0.41, Dist 0	$591
T. Rowe Price Tax-Free Income	none	Mgt 0.47, Dist 0	$689

Source: Morningstar.

which could add an additional 1 percent to overall expenses. The fees are split between management fees assessed on the NAV and any fees charged for fund distributions. The SEC mandates that each fund provide in its prospectus to new investors projected expenses for 3-, 5-, and 10-year investment time frames. Calculations are made based on a $10,000 investment, a 5% NAV growth rate, and redemption at the end of the investment period. Expense projections are the total fees investors should expect to pay over the next 10 years. However, if the fund returns greater than 5 percent and/or the fund imposes additional fees, the actual fees paid can be much higher. Table 11-1 also lists the mutual fund fee structure as reported by Morningstar for our selected mutual funds.

Using Morningstar's total cost to investors relative to fund category, Alliance Growth and Income A is considered average in its fees, whereas Fidelity Magellan is below average and Vanguard Growth & Income, USAA Aggressive Growth, Dodge and Cox Income, and T. Rowe Price Tax-Free Income were low in their total cost structures.

Each and every year, mutual funds charge each and every investor asset-based fees. That is a fact of life for mutual fund investors. However, many investors have become lulled into a state of fee complacency. Over the past 15 years, the stock market has done very well, and most stock mutual funds have followed the market, providing investors with double-digit annual gains. A 1.5 percent fee seems small if the value of the fund rises 12.5 percent a year. However, over time, annual mutual fund fees will severely erode the potential value of the fund compared with similar returns with no fees.

In 2000, the US House of Representatives' Subcommittee on Finance and Hazardous Materials began looking into the issue of mutual fund fees and full disclosure (or lack of) of fees to mutual fund investors. The subcommittee is appropriately named to research how mutual funds report the fees charged to their investors. Currently most funds report their fees as a percentage of the NAV, rather than in real dollar terms. For example, an annual statement from a mutual fund might say it is deducting 1.5 percent for its fees. The Subcommittee believes that investors should know that their fund's value of $100,000 will be charged an annual fee of $1500 and a fund account worth $225,000 would be charged an annual fee of $3375.

Companies offering DRIPs and direct investing programs historically have not used an asset-based fee to generate revenues to cover their costs. DRIPs use transaction-based fees, charging only for services to buy or sell shares. There are many companies offering DRIPs and direct investing plans free of fees, which is better for an investor's long-term financial health than asset-based fees.

1.5 Percent Annual Management Fees Add Up

Why should anyone get upset about paying a 1.5 percent annual mutual fund management fee? To any serious DRIP investor, that comment should be like waving a red flag in front of a bull. Over a lifetime, even a seemingly minor 1.5 percent annual fee can add up to huge dollars. According to Morningstar, an investment of $10,000 in a fund growing at 11 percent a year for 25 years would generate over $39,000 in fees. In addition, mutual fund investors lose out on the capital appreciation of fees paid.

For example, a young investor, age 20, starts saving $1000 a year in a money market account. At age 30, the investor buys $10,000 in Fund A and repeats the process at age 40 (Fund B), age 50 (Fund C), and again at age 60 (Fund D). The investor retires at age 60 and discontinues the mutual fund contribution. Because the investor had other retirement investments, the mutual funds were not sold. At age 85, the investor passes away, leaving heirs with a tidy sum of money. Over the lifetime of the investments, the investor realized an average 11 percent annual return, in line with historic returns for the S&P Index. Investing in mutual funds was chosen over direct investing because it seemed easier. Plus, the fund fees were only 1.5 percent a year. When the investor died at the ripe old age of 85, the mutual funds were worth as follows:

Fund A	$1,480,800	Fund B	$606,600
Fund C	$ 248,500	Fund D	$101,700
Total	$2,437,600		

Not bad for $40,000 of principal invested in mutual funds. A 1.5 percent fee sounds like a small price to pay for the honor of owning a specific fund, but it adds up. Had the investor spent the time to research investment choices and had he chosen DRIP companies with no purchase fees, and achieved an annual return of 11 percent a year, the portfolio would look much different.

In our example, the investor would have paid $37,133 in annual fees during just the last year of life. Not only had the investor paid a lifetime total of $427,000 in mutual fund fees, but had lost a lifetime of capital appreciation of those fees. If the investor had chosen a diversified portfolio of no-fee DRIPs with the same 11 percent annual return, the investment would have been worth:

Portfolio A	$3,452,100	Portfolio B	$1,215,700
Portfolio C	$ 428,100	Portfolio D	$ 150,700
Total	$5,246,800		

Table 11–2 outlines the investment value of the example of mutual funds and lifetime to-date amount of annual fees paid versus the value of the diversified portfolio of no-fee DRIPs.

DRIP fees, if any, are charged only for purchase and sale. Some company programs, such as Wal-Mart, charge a $1 DRIP fee if a regular investment schedule is established with automatic transfers

TABLE   11–2

Comparison of Mutual Fund Value and Lifetime To-Date Fees Paid versus Value of No-Fee DRIP Portfolio, at 11% Annual Return

Investor's Age	Mutual Fund Value	Lifetime To-Date Fees Paid	Value of No-Fee DRIPs
30	$10,934	$167	$11,100
40	$38,197	$3143	$42,616
50	$104,343	$12,981	$132,109
60	$265,816	$39,566	$386,214
70	$646,893	$106,867	$1,096,623
80	$1,584,036	$271,158	$3,113,775
85	$2,437,600	$427,673	$5,246,893

from an investor's bank account (ACH or ETF transfers). There are hundreds of companies offering DRIPs and direct investing programs with no purchase fees. These DRIPs allow investors to put every penny of their hard-earned money to work for them.

MUTUAL FUND "PHANTOM" CAPITAL GAINS TAX EXPOSURE

As a mutual fund manager trades stocks and bonds for a profit, each capital gain generates a tax event. Federal tax code requires all mutual fund investors to report their share of the fund's capital gains on their individual income tax return. The fund sends an annual tax statement to both the IRS and the fund holder reporting the dividends paid and the amount of undistributed capital gains. These are the capital gains generated by the fund, but not distributed to its investors, and the investor is liable for the 20 percent federal capital gains tax. The proceeds from these stock sales are usually either reinvested, used for fund fees, or paid to investors seeking to redeem their shares for cash. Although investors may not have sold their shares in the fund, they are liable for the capital gains taxes generated by the fund's trading activities. The phrase "phantom" capital gains tax liability refers to the increased federal and state income taxes paid by mutual fund investors, even if investors do not create the capital gain themselves by selling the fund shares at a profit. The less a fund trades, the less fund holders are exposed to phantom capital gains tax. The latest marketing buzzword in mutual funds is *tax-advantaged funds.* These funds have low portfolio turnover, creating lower phantom capital gains taxes for fund investors.

Many savy mutual fund investors won't buy funds in the fourth quarter of the year. Phantom capital gains are usually calculated in the fourth quarter, and all investors as of that day are subject to a potential tax liability. If a fund is bought in October, the investor is potentially liable for higher taxes in just 2 months. If a fund is bought in January, the investor may have 12 months until he or she is potentially subject to undistributed capital gains tax liability. If an investor insists on investing nontax-deferred capital into mutual funds, he or she should check the date when fund holders become liable for these phantom gains. If mutual funds are held in IRA-type tax-deferred accounts, the capital gains tax exposure is a nonissue.

As mutual funds' unrealized capital gains exploded in the 1990s along with the market, so did the potential for increasing future capital gains exposure. Many funds are currently sitting on huge gains in stocks like Intel or Microsoft. Someday, especially if the market corrects and the funds need to generate additional cash for redemptions, the funds will sell their positions in these winners and pass along the respective large capital gains tax exposure to fund investors.

Table 11–3 is a list of selected mutual funds, the undistributed capital gains per share, and dividends from 1990 to 1999, along with the potential future capital gains tax exposure of unrealized fund gains as a percentage of fund assets, as reported by Morningstar.

With a current long-term capital gains tax rate of 20 percent, funds with undistributed capital gains greater than five times the dividend will actually create a larger tax bill than the cash dividends paid. Because most mutual fund investors reinvest the dividends, investors usually pay any capital gains taxes due from earned income. Using the prior examples, each fund would create the following estimated increase in federal income tax per share for fund investors. The list also illustrates the net difference between the es-

TABLE 11-3

10-Year Combined Dividends Paid Per Share, Undistributed Capital Gains Per Share from 1990 to 1999, Potential Capital Gains Exposure, NAV Range Per Share 1990 to 1999 for Selected Mutual Funds

	Total Dividend Paid 1990–1999	Total Undistributed Capital Gains 1990–1999	Potential Capital Gains Exposure As % of Assets	NAV Price Range 1990–1999
Alliance Growth and Income A	$0.57	$2.39	13%	$2.17–$3.60
Vanguard Growth & Income	$4.06	$11.59	21%	$13.19–$37.08
Fidelity Magellan	$8.60	$65.10	46%	$53.93–$136.63
USAA Aggressive Growth	$0.13	$15.76	77%	$14.23–$55.15
Dodge & Cox Income	$7.70	$0.49	–2%	$10.61–$11.40
T. Rowe Price Tax-Free Income	$5.32	$0.27	0%	$8.91–$9.09

Source: Morningstar.

timated federal income taxes paid (not including state taxes, if any) and the dividend received per share for the 10-year period 1990 to 1999.

	Total Estimated Capital Gains Tax Due Per Share 1990–1999	Total Dividend Minus Total Estimated Tax Due Per Share 1990–1999
Alliance Growth and Income A	$0.48	$0.09
Vanguard Growth & Income	$2.32	$1.74
Fidelity Magellan	$13.02	−$4.42
USAA Aggressive Growth	$3.15	−$3.02
Dodge & Cox Income	$0.10	$7.60
T. Rowe Price Tax-Free Income	$0.05	$5.27

In other words, investors holding positions of Fidelity Magellan Fund in nontax-deferred accounts would have paid more in federal income tax than received in dividends. All mutual fund holders should analyze the portfolio turnover ratio of every fund. The higher the historic turnover ratio, the higher the potential annual capital gains tax bill owed by the fund investors.

There are rumblings within the SEC to require mutual funds to report their performance based on the after-tax returns. By deducting phantom capital gains taxes paid by fund investors, money managers would be more accurate in calculating an investor's total returns. Morningstar calculated after-tax returns for most mutual funds, and the following lists the 10-year pre- and posttax returns for the example funds.

	Pretax Annual Return (%)	Tax-Adjusted Return (%)
Alliance Growth and Income A	15.32	11.64
Vanguard Growth & Income	17.92	14.96
Fidelity Magellan	18.48	15.47
USAA Aggressive Growth	20.96	18.98
Dodge & Cox Income	8.35	5.60
T. Rowe Price Tax-Free Income	6.94	6.85

Source: Morningstar.

The concept of phantom capital gains tax exposure is not just a theoretical problem for mutual fund investors. Warnburg Pincus Japan Small Company Fund (WPJPX), with assets of $290 million, invests in small Japanese companies. In March 1999, WPJPX had a NAV of around $8 a share. The Japanese stock market was very hot from early 1999 to early 2000 as investors were hoping for an improvement in the multiyear recession in the Japanese economy. WPJPX followed the boom, rising to $27 by March 2000. It was a false alarm, however, and the Japanese market quickly cooled. WPJPX sank to an NAV of $6.43 by September 2000. Short-term investors who had bought shares of WPJPX on the way up in 1999 started selling in 2000, either realizing their gain or cutting their losses. The fund was forced to liquidate profitable positions to generate cash for these redemptions. The sale of profitable investments created capital gains tax liability for the fund, which was passed onto fund investors. In August 2000, WPJPX declared a $7.40 per-share short-term undistributed capital gain.

An investor buying $5000 of WPJPX in March 2000 at its peak of $27 would have owned 185 shares. As of September 2000, the 185 shares would have been worth $1190, representing a loss of $3810, and the investor would also report a taxable short-term gain of $1360 ($7.40 times 185 shares). Assuming a tax rate of 33 percent (short-term gains are taxed as earned income), the investor would have to pay an additional $450 in income taxes.

The same $5000 investment in March of 1999 in WPJPX at a pre-boom NAV of $8 a share would have purchased 625 shares. At its peak, the investment would have been worth over $17,700, but would have shrunk to a value of $4050 by September 2000. The investor would also have to report short-term gains of $4620 and pay additional income taxes of $1520.

Unfortunately, a similar story was posted on an Internet chat room by a young investor. It seems the novice investor was trying to diversify a portfolio invested 100 percent in Internet stocks. In March 2000, tech stocks were getting hammered, and the young investor was seeking less risk, but somehow decided to invest in a small high-tech fund focused on Japanese companies. The mutual fund purchased experienced the same fate as WPJPX and the young investor lost even more capital. This young investor is a great example of why stock research, adequate portfolio diversification, and an overall investment game plan are essential prior to investing.

DRIPS and direct investing allow investors to time capital gains tax liabilities to their specific tax situation. With DRIPs, capital gains are only realized when the investor decides to sell shares at a profit. If there is no stock sale, there is no capital gain to report and no current tax is due. DRIP investors may discover their money grows faster without unnecessary mutual fund management fees nor unwanted capital gains tax exposure. DRIP investors, over the long term, should realize the added financial benefit of every dollar not spent on fees or increased taxes compounding into sizable amounts of money.

MUTUAL FUND DIVERSIFICATION

There is a myth that different sounding mutual fund names will have different stocks in their respective portfolios. This is not always the case. Sometimes a family of funds will own the same stock in several different fund portfolios. If investors fail to research the top 10 or 20 stocks held by each fund, they may discover that just a few companies will represent a larger than expected weighting in the total mutual fund portfolio. Listed next are the 10 largest holdings by fund as of June 30, 2000:

> *Alliance Growth and Income A*—United Technologies, Pepsi, Kroger, First Data, Tenet Healthcare, Tyco International, Chase Manhattan, Household International, Bank of America, Schering Plough
>
> *Vanguard Growth & Income*—Microsoft, Cisco Systems, Intel, Pfizer, AT&T, MCI Worldcom, ExxonMobil, Citigroup, Wal-Mart, General Electric
>
> *Fidelity Magellan*—General Electric, Microsoft, Cicso Systems, Home Depot, Intel, Texas Instruments, Citigroup, ExxonMobil, Time Warner, Tyco International
>
> *USAA Aggressive Growth*—Applied Micro Circuits, Metromedia Fiber Net Class A, Network Solutions Class A, SanDisk, JDS Uniphase, Immunex, Medimmune, Transwitch, Harmonic, Genentech

Dodge & Cox Income—Federal Home Loan Mortgage Co bonds, US Treasury bonds, HSBC bonds, Raychem bonds, Seagrams bonds, Lockheed Martin bonds

T. Rowe Price Tax-Free Income—New York, South Carolina, Texas, Washington State, Pennsylvania, Georgia, Alaska State agencies muni bonds

For investors of both the Vanguard Growth & Income Fund and the Fidelity Magellan Fund, there would be overlapping investments in six stocks in the top-10 positions of each fund. Thirty percent of the stock selections are the same in the top-10 holdings of each fund. Ten stocks in the top-15 positions of each fund are duplicates, as are 14 stocks in the top-20 holdings each. Through the use of DRIPs and direct investing, an investor can easily develop a diversified portfolio.

INVESTMENT UNIT TRUSTS AND EXCHANGE TRADED FUNDS

Over the past few years, there have been several hybrid fund-type investments offered to investors. Similar to a mutual fund, Investment Unit Trusts and Exchange Traded Funds invest in a diversified portfolio of stocks or bonds and offer shares to the public. Currently traded on the American Stock Exchange, Unit Trusts are offered with many different investment strategies. For instance, S&P offers an overall S&P 500 Index Unit Trust (SPY), which owns stock in each company comprising the S&P 500 Index. These Units Trusts are also known as *Spiders*. Each Unit Trust share represents one-tenth of the value of the Index. If the S&P 500 Index is trading at 1400, the Unit Trust shares should trade at $140 a share. Management fees for the SPY Unit Trust is 0.65 percent of the NAV, or less than half of the typical mutual fund. Because positions are sold only when a company is dropped from the underlying Index, the Unit Trust should experience a lower portfolio turnover and lower phantom capital gains exposure to investors.

In addition to SPY Unit Trusts, investors can focus on specific industrial sectors by selecting one of several Sector Select Unit Trusts, and these are known as *Sector Spiders*. Sector Spiders invest in specific sectors of the S&P 500 Index, such as just technology stocks. An investor wishing to own a strong portfolio of top-quality companies in a specific industrial sector should find Sector Select Unit Trusts to be of interest. However, Unit Trusts do not currently provide for direct investing, and a broker is required to purchase shares. Unit Trusts are a good alternative investment to mutual funds in accounts held at a stockbroker. Sector Select Unit Trusts are available through *ShareBuilder.com* and other on-line brokers. Because the Unit Trusts do not offer DRIPs, investors need to enroll in the broker's synthetic DRIP.

Traded on the American Stock Exchange, these types of investments are expanding in numbers and are becoming more focused on their strategies. In addition to the S&P Unit Trusts, Exchange Traded Funds are becoming popular investments. Recently, Barclays Global Investors (iShares), Merrill Lynch (HOLDRS), and the NASDAQ 100 (QQQ) Exchange Traded Funds have been receiving more attention as easy tools for portfolio diversification.

WHAT TO DO WHEN MUTUAL FUNDS ARE THE ONLY CHOICE

Many 401(k) or employer-sponsored retirement accounts limit employees to a select number of mutual funds. Many employees do not have the option to invest in specific stocks and are offered various growth funds, growth and income funds, income funds, bond funds, or money market funds. It is just as important to be diversified in a mutual fund portfolio as it is in a stock and bond portfolio. Investors should have their account diversified in several funds with different investment strategies and goals. Investors should ask for information concerning each fund's stock positions and review the information to make sure there is diversification in the overall fund selections. Because these are tax-advantaged accounts, the phantom capital gains tax issue is not a consideration.

DRIPS AS AN ALTERNATIVE TO MUTUAL FUNDS

Using the power of DRIPs and direct investing, an investor can build a diversified portfolio of stocks and bonds. With over 700 companies offering direct investing and an additional 900 offering DRIPs, an investor can easily build a portfolio of top-quality companies. If an investor is drawn to the performance of a specific fund, researching the top holdings for companies with DRIPs and direct investing plans may allow for duplication of the fund's portfolio without the cost of a broker. An investor who wants to buy a series of mutual funds with a focus on growth and income may be better off investing directly in those stocks that are the most duplicated in the combined portfolio.

How to Build a Personal Mutual Fund

Key Concepts
- Building a Personal Mutual Fund
- Stock Certificate Registration
- ACH and EFT Transfers
- Affinity Groups
- Value DRIP Investing
- When to Sell
- Building a Broker-less Portfolio
- Building an *Almost* Broker-less Portfolio
- Selected Companies Offering Direct Investing Plans

With several hundred companies offering DRIPs and direct investing options, it is simple to develop and maintain a diversified portfolio of stocks and bonds without paying annual management and advertising fees. Reasonable financial goals, realistic investment returns, and comfortable investment risks are all integral parts of developing an overall portfolio strategy. As an investor ages and the need to use investments for college tuition or retirement living expenses (or even that new '38 Catboat) grows closer, asset allocation and portfolio diversification should shift its focus to capital preservation and income over higher risk capital gains. Investing is a fluid process: Some stock selections will not perform as well as the overall market and others will far exceed investor expectations.

CHAPTER 12

BUILDING A PERSONAL MUTUAL FUND

A truly diversified portfolio will have exposure in all eight industrial sectors. Within these industrial sectors, there are some companies that have a higher risk factor and would be more appropriate for younger investors. Older investors, or those with financial goals close at hand, should select less risky investments within each industrial sector. In the utility sector, for example, a 25- to 30-year-old may chose Progress Energy (PGN) due to its higher than industry average revenue and profit growth potential. A 65-year-old investor may prefer the higher yield of companies such as Hawaiian Electric. Bond weightings should also increase as the investor ages.

All 401(k), IRA, and educational IRA accounts should be funded to the maximum prior to establishing and contributing to a non-tax-advantaged account. If a new parent wants to begin saving for educational expenses, first fund an educational IRA to its maximum annual limit of $500. Additional funds can be invested in custodian accounts. If an employer offers matching retirement account contributions, always accept as much as available. For example, an employer may offer to equally match the first 3 percent of annual wages contributed to a retirement account. Employees who enroll with contributions of 3 percent of income will receive the full benefit of the dollar-matching program. If an employer offers an employee stock purchase plan, review the program details because many plans include a long-term fixed price or a specific discount to market price. Most companies offer a simple payroll deduction plan for these investments, and employees should strive to live within the means of a slightly reduced paycheck to invest for the future. Matching retirement contributions and long-term employee stock purchase plans are great ways to build personal wealth at a reduced cost.

When developing a diversified portfolio, always consider assets owned in tax-advantaged accounts and employee stock purchase plans. For example, an investor may be underweighted in technology issues in a 401(k) account, or an employee stock purchase plan may be overweighted in a portfolio to one specific industry (their employers).

For an under-30 investor, the following are a few stocks and bonds that might fit into a conservative to average risk portfolio category. With many years until the funds are actually needed, an under-30 investor can afford to take higher risks and may select both more stable large-cap stocks and higher risk mid- and small-cap stocks. For the most part, technology stocks are higher risk than other industrial sectors, but also may offer larger returns than other sectors. The young investor should have little cash and short-term investments.

Technology	35%	Computer Associates, National Data Corp, Pitney Bowes
Basic Materials	5%	Crompton Corp, RPM
Cyclical	10%	Home Depot, Intimate Brands, Chicago Bridge & Iron
Noncyclical	10%	Newell, Omnicare, PepsiCo, Medtronics
Utilities	5%	Progress Energy, SBC Corp, Century Telephone
Energy	5%	Apache Corp, Enron
Financial	10%	SunTrust Banks, Morgan Stanley Dean Witter, Franklin Resources
Industrial	5%	Federal Signal, Pentair, Kenametals
Bonds	15%	30-year Treasury Inflation Protection Securities (TIPS)
Cash	0%	

For investors ages 30 to 45, a portfolio could include some of the following stocks. Technology weighting may be reduced, lowering the overall risk exposure. Other industrial sectors are weighted more heavily.

Technology	30%	Lucent Technologies, Textron, Hewlett-Packard
Basic Materials	5%	Air Products, Dow Chemical
Cyclical	10%	Clayton Mobile Home, Harley Davidson, Johnson Controls
Noncyclical	10%	Merck, Coca-Cola, Colgate Palmolive, InterPublic Group
Utilities	5%	Verizon, Philadelphia Suburban, DQE Corp
Energy	10%	ExxonMobil, Chevron
Financial	10%	5th Third Bank, Wells Fargo, AFLAC, Jefferson Pilot
Industrial	5%	TYCO Int'l, GATX Corp, Paychex
Bonds	15%	30-year TIPS, 20-year TIPS
Cash	0%	

For investors ages 45 to 65, a diversified portfolio may be weighted more heavily toward lower-risk stock selections. Large-cap stocks should comprise the majority of each industrial sector. Utilities, with their historically increasing and relatively safe dividends, should continue to be a growing part of the portfolio. A conservative portfolio may include some of the following.

Technology	25%	Crane Co, Intel
Basic Materials	5%	DuPont
Cyclical	10%	Lowes, Target, Wal-Mart
Noncyclical	10%	Johnson & Johnson, Pfizer, Proctor & Gamble, Lancaster Corp
Utilities	10%	Hawaiian Electric, American Water Works
Energy	10%	ExxonMobil, Chevron
Financial	10%	Federal Home Loan, Aon Corp, State Street Bank
Industrial	5%	Illinois Tool Works, Sherwin Williams, General Electric
Bonds	15%	30-year TIPS, 20-year TIPS, 10-year Bonds
Cash	0%	

For investors ages 65 and older, a conservative portfolio should focus on income and capital preservation. Technology issues should represent about 10 percent of the portfolio, with the majority of investments in utilities, bonds, and cash. A portfolio for an active retired investor seeking regular disbursements may include some of the following.

Technology	10%	Motorola, Nokia
Basic Materials	5%	Air Products
Cyclical	5%	Sears, Walgreens
Noncyclical	5%	Gillette, Schering Plough, ServiceMaster, Abbott Labs
Utilities	20%	California Water Services, Duke Energy
Energy	5%	ExxonMobil, Chevron
Financial	5%	Comerica, KeyCorp, Washington Mutual
Industrial	5%	Emerson, Donaldson Inc, EDS
Bonds	25%	20-year TIPS, 10-year TIPS, 10-, 7-, 5-year Treasury bonds
Cash	15%	Money Market, 6-month, 12-month Treasury notes

STOCK CERTIFICATE REGISTRATION

When a stock is purchased, the buyer is registered with the company or recorded in the permanent corporate books, as a registered shareholder and a stock certificate is issued. *Shareholder of record* refers to the name on the stock certificate and indicates who has been identified to the company as the shareholder. The certificate is proof of ownership of a specific number of shares. Registered share-owners receive all corporate communications, dividends, and proxy material directly from the company.

When buying from a stockbroker, share certificates are not usually issued to the shareholder. The brokerage firm keeps the stock certificate in its corporate or *street* name and, through a monthly statement, informs each client of his or her exact positions. Because the investor is not the shareholder of record, all investor communications are forwarded to the investor through the brokerage firm. Because DRIPs require a participant to be the stockholder of record, it is important to have share certificates delivered from the broker, which transfer legal ownership from the broker to the investor.

There are several choices in the legal form of stock ownership. The basic registration options are:

1. *Individual*—The stock is owned by just one person.
2. *Joint Account Registration*—With a joint account, an investor has several options:
   - *Joint Tenants with Rights of Survivorship (JTWROS):* If an investor wishes to share ownership, joint tenancy is one method. On the death of one of the joint tenants, the surviving tenant acquires sole title to the shares. Acquiring sole title does not usually require probate of a will. It is possible for parents, grandparents, and/or any other nonrelative to establish a JTWROS account. Be aware, however, that this account establishes immediate rights for both joint tenants, and these rights cannot be severed in the future without the consent of the other tenant. It is not necessary for married couples to establish a JTWROS account, although in most cases it is the most convenient.
   - *Tenants by Entirety:* In some states, when establishing an account for a married couple, the account is designated *tenants by entirety*, but has the same characteristics as the standard JTWROS account.
   - *Tenants in Common:* Tenants in common registration makes tenants equal owners unless they otherwise

agree, and it allows the right to transfer ownership while living or at death. This allows persons who wish to maintain their own legal interest in the shares, but also to share the acquisition and cost of maintenance with another person.

◆ *Community Property:* Nine states—Arizona, California, Idaho, Louisiana, Nevada, New Mexico, Texas, Washington, and Wisconsin—use the community property system to determine the interest of a husband and wife in property acquired during a marriage. If an investor now lives or previously lived in one of these states, he or she should be aware that some special rules apply to community property. Any property acquired while living in one of these nine states is probably community property even today. Under the community property system, the general rule is that all property acquired during the marriage is community property, owned one-half by each spouse. Property received by inheritance or gift and property owned before marriage are separate property, however.

3. *Trust Account Registration*—A trust is a legal device by which a trustee holds shares for the benefit of another. It is a useful tool in the following situations: (a) when the trustee is seeking to protect the beneficiary from his or her own financial irresponsibility, from creditors of the beneficiary, or from marital claims on the beneficiary; (b) when the beneficiary is unable to manage his or her own financial affairs; (c) when the trustee wishes to provide income to the beneficiary, but does not wish to allow the beneficiary access to the principal of the trust; and (d) when the trustee desires to remove the shares from his or her estate. A living trust allows an individual to establish a trust for his or her own benefit for life, and provides for the distribution of shares on his or her death.

4. *Uniform Gifts to Minors Act (UGMA)* and *Transfers to Minors Act (UTMA)*—With a UGMA account, the parent generally maintains control over the investment until the child reaches the age of majority (18 or 21, depending on the state). Once the child reaches the age of majority, the par-

ent no longer has control over the account. UTMA accounts work in the same way as UGMA accounts, except that UTMA accounts let the parent maintain control over the account for a longer period of time, such as when the child finishes college. Although UGMA money is available to the child at the age of majority, UTMA accounts permit postponing distributions until age 18, 21, or 25, depending on the state.

5. *Partnerships*—Investment clubs are an example of a partnership owning shares.

ACH AND ETF TRANSFERS

All companies have minimum investments required to enroll in either their DRIPs or directing investing plans. The minimum for a DRIP is usually 1 share, but there are companies that require up to 50 shares to participate. Direct investing plans usually have minimums of $250 to $500, but some plans require as little as $20 and others as much as $1500.

Some companies with relatively high minimum direct investing requirements offer the option to waive the minimum through ACH transfers, also known as electronic funds transfers (EFTs). ACH transfers are regularly scheduled electronic transfers of funds from an investor's bank account for the purpose of investing in a DRIP. Investors who enroll in ACH transfers invest a minimum amount per month. For example, Air Product Corp (APD), a basic materials manufacturer, offers a direct investing program with a minimum investment of $500 and a minimum OCP of $100. If an investor enrolls for an automatic ACH transfer of a minimum investment of $100 a month for 5 months, APD will waive its $500 minimum to participate. Focused on the small investor wanting to develop a diversified portfolio of stocks, waiving the minimum investment through ACH transfers is a great option that should be duplicated by more programs.

AFFINITY GROUPS

Some companies offer direct investing options that are more lenient for customers or residents of a particular state. These are called *affin-*

ity groups. For example, Progress Energy (PGN) offers a $20 minimum direct investing option for investors who are also customers. If an investor is not a customer, the DRIP requires a minimum of one share registered in the shareholder's name. In other words, PGN offers a direct investing option for customers only. Check program details to verify whether an affinity group preference is offered and to verify whether you qualify.

VALUE DRIP INVESTING

Many DRIP investors have a predetermined dollar amount to be invested on a regular basis. An investor may have $300 a month ACH established with three different DRIP programs, investing $100 a month in each. Once a predetermined goal of a specific number of shares or market value is reached (200 shares or $5000), additional DRIPs can be established. The monthly ACH of $300 may be reallocated to these new DRIPs.

An alternative to this rigid approach is to establish a series of DRIPs. Rather than have a prearranged investment, a value DRIP investor can choose which companies are trading at the most advantageous long-term price. Those stocks are then bought with the investor's monthly OCPs.

For example, in times of peaking interest rates, an investor may decide to contribute more to higher yielding utility stocks. Historically, utility stocks move opposite of interest rates. When rates go up, utility stock prices usually decline, increasing the dividend yield. As interest rates peak and begin to decline, utility stock prices usually increase. However, these interest rate peaks and valleys usually occur over a several-year time frame. Thus, when an interest rate peak develops, DRIP utility investors may want to increase their OCP more than usual. Utility stocks experienced this situation from March to June 2000, as interest rates began to peak after the Federal Reserve Board raised the prime rate six times in less than 18 months. DRIP investors who increased their OCPs early in 2000 would have been buying most share prices at multiple-year lows and very high historic yields.

Sometimes a stock will sell off for a few quarters as traders take profits after an unusually large run up in stock price. This pause in the stock's long-term upward progression provides a buying opportunity. Sometimes a stock will fall out of favor with investors due to short-term earnings disappointments, potentially sending a stock's price to undervalued levels, which also provides a buying opportunity for long-term value DRIP investors.

Rather than having a predetermined regular OCP investment in specific DRIP stocks, value DRIP investing allows the flexibility to alter an OCP contribution based on a short-term pricing advantage for long-term investors. Value DRIP investing is slightly more sophisticated and requires more discipline. The investor should stick with the strategy and spend a bit more time researching and keeping up to date on current business events. Value DRIP investing should not be confused with an attempt to time the market. The goal is to increase long-term capital gains by increasing OCPs during opportune times when a stock price is undervalued.

WHEN TO SELL

Most investors believe the most important question is, When is the best time to buy? However, they should be asking just the opposite question: When is the best time to sell? Stocks should be sold both when they have performed poorly and when they have done extremely well.

Properly researched, stocks are bought and held based on an investor's belief that excellent management and timely products will produce increasing earnings and dividends over the long term. However, the world is not perfect, and not all business plans are successfully executed. DRIP and direct investing strategies should have a minimum of a 3- to 5-year investment horizon. Within that time frame, investors should be looking for trends showing signs of trouble, such as declining cash flow, declining research and development budgets, changing company management, or decreasing product or service market share. When these signs occur, investors should review the reasons for owning stock in that company. Keep in mind that stocks usually move as a group. If a specific stock selection has not only underperformed the investor's expectations, but also substantially fallen short of a competitor's performance, the company may be a good candidate for replacement.

In addition to selling a stock when there is a dramatic change of events for the worse, some investors sell when there has been a dramatic turn of the better. It may seem a bit counterproductive, but consider selling half an original position when a stock doubles in price. Investors should have a goal of how much money is invested in a specific stock or industrial sector. Some investors set a goal of $7000 to $10,000 per stock as a minimum long-term position and may continue to invest optional cash payments until that goal is met. If the stock doubles in price, the position would be worth $14,000 to $20,000. By selling half the original position, the investor is able to further diversify the overall portfolio, and what remains invested in the position is profit. The best source for an increasing dollar allocation to bonds and utilities is from realized capital gains in other stocks and sector investments.

Investors should be evaluating asset allocation and portfolio diversification at least once per year. Each investment should be reviewed for not only its 12-month return, but also its performance against its peers and the overall market. Investments should be analyzed for future earnings and dividend growth. Does this company have an equal or better chance of expanding profits over the next 3 to 5 years as when it was added to the portfolio?

A truly diversified portfolio will contain some poor performing stocks. In any given year, at least two out of five stocks will underperform, and the trick to successful investing is to maximize the three winners while minimizing the two underperformers. With diversified, long-term stock investments, the risk of the two underperformers in any given year substantially impacting the overall portfolio is reduced. Everyone loves to talk about their stock winners at the office water cooler or at cocktail parties. The few winners everyone has in their portfolio are not what really matters, but how the total package is doing.

DRIPs and direct investing accounts are easy to open, and it is just as easy to close them or sell a portion of a position. Every quarterly statement comes with a form to be completed and returned to the transfer agent authorizing a sale. Proceeds are then mailed to the investor and can be easily reinvested in other companies.

BUILDING A BROKER-LESS PORTFOLIO

It is feasible for an investor to develop a very diversified portfolio of stocks and bonds without using any brokerage services. NetStock

Direct lists over 328 US companies offering direct investing options. The S&P 2000 Directory of Reinvestment Plans catalogues over 150 companies with direct investing options. A partial list of the most popular and well-known US companies is listed at the end of this chapter, along with the stock symbol and the minimum direct investment as of August 2000.

If connected to the Internet, search NetStock Direct's database for companies in each of the eight S&P industrial sectors to develop a diverse portfolio of stocks. If not, a trip to the local library to review the S&P Directory would be helpful. Listed next are several diversified portfolio examples based on the minimum investment required by each.

Very Low Minimum Initial Investment—less than $200

Industrials	Johnson Controls $50
Financial	Interchange Financial Services $100, Tomkins Trustco $100
Noncyclical	LIbby Foods $100, Walgreens $50, Bristol Meyers Squib $50
Utilities	Connecticut Water Services $105, Progress Energy $20 if a customer, DQE Inc. $105, Montana Power $100, Puget Sound Energy $20

Low Minimum Initial Investment—$250

Cyclical	Home Depot, Westvaco
Energy	ExxonMobil, Texaco
Financial	Investors Financial Services, Pacific Century Financial, Wells Fargo
Industrial	General Electric
Noncyclical	Proctor & Gamble, Merck ($350)
Technology	Compaq
Utilities	Hawaiian Electric, Enron, Southern Company

Average Minimum Initial Investment—$500

Basic Materials	USX Corp/US Steel, Air Products
Cyclical	Target Corp, International Paper, Intimate Brands
Energy	Petroleum Resources (exchange traded fund)
Financial	AXA Financial, Lehman Bros, McGraw-Hill Publishers
Industrial	Caterpillar, Deere & Co.
Noncyclical	Pfizer
Technology	Motorola, IBM, Tektronix
Utilities	Philadelphia Suburban, SBC Corp

High Minimum Initial Investment—$1000

Basic Materials	Phelps Dodge
Cyclical	Ford

Energy	Anadarko Petroleum
Financial	Bank America, Morgan Stanley Dean Witter
Industrial	Timken
Noncyclical	Pharmacia, Gillette
Technology	Lucent Technologies, Verizon Communications
Utilities	Entergy

Source: *netstockdirect.com.*

For as little as $170 in total capital, an investor can enroll in four DRIPs (Johnson Controls, Tomkins Trustco, Walgreens, and Progress Energy, if a customer), offering exposure to the industrial, financial, cyclical, and electric utility sectors. Selecting DRIPs with direct investing options and a $250 minimum investment, an investor can develop a balanced diversified portfolio for a total investment of $2000 in eight DRIPs. For investors with over $10,000 to invest in direct investing plans, the choice of companies is extensive.

Keep in mind that the higher minimum investment does not equate to a more desirable investment. Just because Ford Motor requires a $1000 minimum investment, it does not mean the company is better than Home Depot, which requires a minimum of $250. Unlike most things in life, a more expensive direct investing requirement does not automatically translate into higher quality.

More information can be found in the S&P Directory of Dividend Reinvestment Plans at the local library or on-line at *netstockdirect.com.*

BUILDING AN ALMOST BROKER-LESS PORTFOLIO

The introduction of on-line synthetic brokers, such as *sharebuilder.com,* has greatly reduced transaction costs. For purchases as low as $3 a trade ($2 for custodian accounts), ShareBuilder allows DRIP and direct investors to accumulate shares in companies that do not offer a direct investing option. Using their synthetic DRIP service, sites like ShareBuilder allow for easy implementation of a DRIP strategy for all positions. ShareBuilder's strength lies in the low cost to purchase the minimum number of shares required to enroll in many DRIP programs. It costs $3 for a one-time scheduled investment or $15 for a real-time trade, and a $25 share certificate delivery fee. Using ShareBuilder, individuals can satisfy those DRIP plans that require investors to be registered shareholders prior to enrollment. ShareBuilder is an excellent tool to accumulate shares of stocks in many companies without a DRIP program, such as Microsoft. On-line synthetic brokers also provide access to Unit Investment Trusts, such as the S&P Spiders, NASDAQ 100, and Dow Jones Industrials.

An Example of a Diversified DRIP Portfolio with Direct Investing Options

Listed next is an example of a diversified stock portfolio of companies offering direct investing options. Each company is listed with the S&P equity rating for consistency in 10-year earnings and dividend growth, minimum direct investment required, current annual dividend, yield, and a brief description of the company.

Basic Materials/Industrial
Air Products & Chemicals (APD), S&P Rating A, Minimum Initial Investment $500, Dividend $0.72, Yield 1.7 percent. APD is a leading manufacturer of industrial gases and industrial processing equipment. APD is aggressively expanding overseas and has acquired a joint venture partner in Korea. APD is also expanding its medical products, such as its cryogenic service and maintenance business for MRI equipment. ADP currently services over 40 percent of the 7200 worldwide medical locations with an MRI, providing the latest in cryogenic technology.

Cyclical/Construction
Chicago Bridge and Iron (CBI), S&P Rating NR, Minimum Initial Investment $200, Dividend $0.18, Yield 1.4 percent. CBI designs, fabricates, and repairs bulk liquid storage tanks, pressure tanks, and low-temperature and cryogenic facilities. CBI's main business centers around oil-related infrastructure. With the ongoing strength of the oil markets and a recovering Asia consuming more oil, CBI will benefit as additional terminals are built and existing ones are updated. CBI has been expanding by acquiring companies specializing in the ultrapure water needs of high-tech and biotech manufacturers. CBI is headquartered in the Netherlands and is not a US company.

Energy/Oil & Natural Gas
Enron (ENE), S&P Rating A-, Minimum Initial Investment $250, Dividend $0.50, 2–1 Stock Split April 1999, Yield 1.3 percent. ENE is

engaged in exploration, production, and transportation of oil and natural gas. In addition, ENE has recently diversified into owning electrical utilities and wholesaling of electric power along with operating water utilities. With the deregulation of most utility markets, ENE has been aggressive in expanding its services and now offers national contracts to large commercial businesses for a bundling of all their utility needs. ENE is moving into trading access to high broadband networks and is a proponent of structuring a liquid high bandwidth reserves market similar to the electricity market, where time and transmission on the grid is marketed as a commodity.

Financial/Bank

Wells Fargo Bank (WFC), S&P Rating A, Minimum Investment $250, Dividend $0.80, Yield 2.0 percent. WFC is a holding company formed from the merger of Wells Fargo Bank and Norwest Bank. WFC is currently expanding into Alaska for the first time, buying the National Bank of Alaska. WFC will be aggressively cross-marketing more banking services to its new clients, which has been the long-term business strength of the premerger Norwest management team.

Financial/Insurance

AFLAC (AFL), S&P Rating A+, Minimum Initial Investment $1000, Dividend $0.30, Yield 0.6 percent. AFL offers supplemental insurance to the workplace, mainly in Japan and the United States. AFL insures over 40 million employees worldwide through 140,000 payroll accounts. Many employers offer both company paid insurance plans and the option for employees to buy supplemental insurance. Eighty percent of 1998 revenues and 66 percent of 1998 operating profits were generated in Japan. InformationWeek named AFL to its Top 100 E-Businesses for the company's superb Internet communications with its agents and clients.

Industrial/Heavy Machinery

Caterpillar (CAT), S&P Rating B, Minimum Initial Investment $500, Dividend $1.30, Yield 2.8 percent. CAT designs, manufactures, and markets agricultural, earth moving, construction, and materials handling equipment. CAT also provides financing for its products. With the rebound of the Asian economies and the lower value of the

US dollar, CAT should benefit with higher overseas volumes. 1999 revenue and profits were very weak, allowing for improved year-to-year comparison in 2000 and 2001. Few fickle mutual fund money managers like CAT stock, and any modest earnings surprises this year should push their stock back to its highs as money managers scramble to rebuy their positions.

Noncyclical/Medical

Merck (MRK), S&P Rating A, Minimum Initial Investment $350, Dividend $1.16, 2–1 Stock Split Feb 1999, Yield 1.7 percent. MRK is a US leader in the pharmaceutical industry. MRK's Merck-Medco subsidiary, is the leading provider of pharmaceutical managed care and provides mail order services for maintenance prescriptions. Even after the recent wave of mergers, MRK should remain one of the world's largest drug companies, with 1999 pharmaceutical revenues of $16.9 billion.

Noncyclical/Consumer

Gillette (G), S&P Rating A, Minimum Initial Investment $1000, Dividend $0.58, Yield 1.4 percent. G develops, manufactures, and distributes razors and blades, toiletries, electric shavers, small household appliances, oral products, and alkaline batteries. Recently, G has been adversely affected by very slow growth in Asia, a strong US dollar, and extreme competition in the battery business, but these problems should be subsiding. However, these problems hammered the stock to multiple-year lows. Earnings growth going forward should improve as G continues to build on its global brand name. G might be considered a defensive investment, as consumers will continue to buy household products in stable quantities regardless of increasing or decreasing personal earnings. Institutional investors and mutual funds hold 59 percent of outstanding shares, less than many big-cap companies. Improving earnings may bring more institutional buying.

Technology/Telecommunications

Nokia (NOK), S&P Rating NR, Minimum Initial Investment $250, Dividend $0.87, 2–1 Stock Split April 1999, 4–1 Stock Split April 2000, Yield 0.5 percent. NOK is a leader in mobile phone equipment, including handsets and networking systems. With the worldwide explosion of mobile phone use, NOK has experienced huge growth in all aspects of its communications business. The company has estimated that worldwide mobile phone use will double in the next 24 to 36 months, along with increased use of wireless Internet connections. In the face of stiff price competition, NOK should stabilize its margins by manufacturing more components in-house and by moving buyers up to higher margin phones with more features, such as Internet access. As with all high-tech communications-oriented companies, NOK trades at a premium price. However, long-term investors should be well rewarded. NOK is headquartered in Finland and is not a US company.

Technology/Telecommunications
Lucent Technologies (LU), S&P Rating NR, Minimum Initial Investment $1000, Dividend $0.08, 2–1 Stock Split April 1999, Yield 0.1 percent. LU is the leader in telecommunications components. LU provides both hardware and software that enable network operators to provide both wire and wireless access for voice, data, and video transmissions. Capital spending by Sprint PCS, AT&T Wireless, Bell Atlantic, and other wireless providers should continue to increase, driving LU's revenues and profits higher. LU should provide solid return to long-term investors based on its leadership in the rapidly growing communications market.

Utilities/Water
American Water Works (AWR), S&P Rating A, Minimum Initial Investment $500, Dividend $1.28, Yield 3.5 percent. AWR distributes water and electricity in California. AWR provides water to 1 in 30 Californians and services 75 communities in northern, coastal, and southern California. AWR recently acquired Peerless Water and its 1900 customers in LA County. The State of California is encouraging smaller water districts to merge to keep up with more stringent water regulations and to capture cost savings that accompany economies of scale. AWR has increased its dividend every year since 1953, and it may be a merger candidate as the water industry continues its consolidation nationwide.

Utilities/Electric
Hawaiian Electric (HE), S&P Rating B+, Minimum Initial Investment $250, Dividend $2.48, Yield 8.7 percent. HE is a holding com-

pany doing business in Hawaii. HE generates and distributes electricity, develops real estate, and provides banking services through its savings and loan subsidiary. With lower levels of Asian tourism during the past few years, the Hawaiian economy has been left out of the current economic boom. However, due to its geographic location, there is little chance of strong competition developing to challenge HE's monopoly in the wake of industrywide deregulation. Earnings have been hurt due to higher than expected maintenance expense items. To expand revenues and profits off the islands, HE formed the HE Power subsidiary to invest in overseas projects and currently operates a power plant in Guam. In 2000 HE experienced difficulty in these overseas ventures, which adversely affected their stock price. Dividends have been paid consistently since 1901, and HE offers a hefty dividend at its current price.

SELECTED COMPANIES OFFERING DIRECT INVESTING PLANS

The number of companies offering direct investing options is growing, with more being offered each week. Using either the S&P directory of dividend reinvestment plans or *netstockdirect.com*, investors can easily locate potential investment possibilities. Table 12–1 (pages 204–205) is a sample of the companies offering direct investing options.

TABLE 12–1

Selected Companies Offering Direct Investing Options and Minimum Direct Investment, as of September 2000

Company	Abbreviation	Minimum Investment	Company	Abbreviation	Minimum Investment
AXA Financial	AXF	$500	ADVANTA Financial	ADVNA	$1500
Aetna	AET	$500	AFLAC	AFL	$1000
Air Products	APD	$500	Amer. Electric Power	AEP	$250
American States Water	AWR	$500	Bank America	BAC	$1000
BellSouth	BLS	$500	Cascade Natural Gas	CNG	$250
Chase Corp	CCF	$250	Chevron	CHV	$250
Coastal Corp	CGP	$250	Compaq Computer	CPQ	$250
Connecticut Water	CTWS	$100	Conoco	COC.B	$250
DaimlerChrysler	DCX	$1000	Deere & Co	DE	$500
Dow Jones & Co	DJ	$1000	Duke Energy	DUK	$250
DQE Inc	DQE	$105	Enron	ENE	$250
Equifax	EFX	$500	ExxonMobil	XOM	$250
EDS	EDS	$250	Fannie Mae	FNM	$250
FedEx	FDX	$1000	Ford Motor	F	$1000
Freddie Mac	FRE	$250	General Electric	GE	$250
Gillette	G	$1000	Goodyear Tire	GT	$250
Hawaiian Electric	HE	$250	Hillenbrand	HB	$250
Home Depot	HD	$250	IBM	IBM	$500
International Paper	IP	$500	Intimate Brands	IBI	$500
Investors Financial	IFIN	$250	Johnson Controls	JCI	$500

Company	Ticker	Amount		Ticker	Company	Amount
Lehman Bros	LEH	$500		LU	Lucent Technologies	$1000
Marriott A	MAR	$350		MAT	Mattel	$500
McCormack	MKC	$250		MCD	McDonalds	$500
McGraw-Hill	MHP	$500		MEL	Mellon Bank	$500
Merck & Co.	MRK	$350		MTP	Montana Power	$100
Morgan Stanley	MWD	$1000		MOT	Motorola	$500
National Service Ind.	NSI	$600		NFS	Nationwide Financial	$250
NE Business Services	NEB	$250		NNS	Newport News Ship	$500
Pacific Century Finan.	BOH	$250		PEO	Petroleum & Resources	$500
Pfizer	PFE	$500		PHA	Pharmacia	$1000
Phil. Suburban	PSC	$500		P	Phillips Petroleum	$500
PPG Industries	PG	$250		PG	Proctor & Gamble	$250
Radio Shack	RSH	$250		RGBK	Regions Financial	$1000
Roadway	ROAD	$250		ROK	Rockwell Int'l	$1000
SBC Communications	SBC	$500		S	Sears, Roebuck	$500
Sonoco Products	SON	$250		SOU	Southern Company	$250
Target Corp	TGT	$500		TEK	Tektronix	$500
Tenneco Automotive	TEN	$250		TX	Texaco	$250
Timken Co	TKR	$1000		TRB	Tribune Co	$500
Tyson Foods	TSN	$250		UAL	UAL Corp	$250
USG Corp	USG	$500		X	USX — US Steel	$500
Utilicorp	UCU	$250		VZ	Verizon Communic.	$1000
Wal-Mart	WMT	$250		WAG	Walgreens	$50
Walt Disney	DIS	$1000		WFC	Wells Fargo & Co	$250
Whirlpool	WHR	$1000				

Source: *netstockdirect.com*.

CHAPTER 13

Life After DRIPs

DRIPs and direct investing should be one tool used by investors to build a diversified financial foundation. As a replacement for mutual fund investments, DRIP programs should allow investors to build assets quicker without paying unnecessary management fees or unwanted capital gains taxes. DRIP investors can construct a balanced portfolio without using a stockbroker and time their investments by increasing their OCPs when a stock is temporarily undervalued.

As investors grow more comfortable in handling their own investments, and as common stock and US Treasury Bond allocations are reached, there may be other investment options to explore. These may include publicly traded real estate investment trusts (REITs), master limited partnerships (MLPs), preferred stocks, or stocks that do not offer DRIPs. Corporate and municipal bonds may be appropriate investments. Usually restricted to sales through brokers, these investment instruments can further diversify an investor's assets. Many of these investments may be eligible in the broker's synthetic DRIP program.

With a broker account for tax-deferred assets, DRIP investors should have access to a stockbroker for a list of suggested non-DRIP investments. As with stock purchases, investors should research all recommendations before investing and should fully understand any potential investment risks.

Real estate is another investment option. Usually real estate requires a substantial capital investment, the possibility of carrying a large debt load, and federal tax implications. Investing in real estate requires plenty of research. There are many reputable resources to assist investors looking to diversify into real estate, such as our sister book, *All About Real Estate Investing.*

For all investors, especially young investors or those who are just starting out, the most important investment concept is "Get in the Game." Being shy at a high school dance, hanging out on the edge of the dance floor, and watching all the action may be acceptable for some, but that is no way to get ahead in the investing and personal finance game. Money market accounts are great places to put limited amounts of cash for unforeseen short-term events, but are poor places to build financial assets for the future. Investors should take as much risk as they can stand, within the confines of their age, a diversified portfolio, and the specific investment time frame.

For over 50 years, DRIPs and direct investing have provided excellent tools for building personal wealth, one dividend check and OCP at a time. Remember that every $25 invested in a tax-deferred account has the potential to grow into $1000 over time.

DRIP and Direct Investing Companies: The Best of the Best

The following is a list of the companies that could be considered the Best of the Best. To be included, a company had to be rated A+ by S&P, have a 10-year average annual return to shareholders of 20 percent or greater, and have increased dividends every year for the past 10 years.

Best of the Best

Home Depot	44% return	Schering Plough	25% return
Paychex	44% return	State Street Bank	24% return
Pfizer	30% return	Franklin Resources	22% return
Wal-Mart	29% return	Johnson & Johnson	22% return
5th Third Bank	28% return	Jefferson Pilot	22% return
General Electric	28% return	SunTrust Bank	22% return
InterPublic Group	27% return	Illinois Tool Works	21% return
Walgreens	27% return	Merck	20% return

DRIP and Direct Investing Companies, S&P Rated A+

The following is a list of companies that offer DRIPs and direct investing programs. They were selected based on the S&P rating for consistency in earnings and dividends growth from 1989 to 1999. The companies are grouped by S&P rating and represent just a sampling of all companies offering DRIPs. More information on all DRIP companies can be found at the local library in the Business or Investment Resource section. All DRIP companies are listed on the Internet at various websites, such as *netstockdirect.com.* The list includes stock symbol, industrial sector, and a company profile.

Listed are the company's top competitors, company revenues for calendar year 1999 or fiscal year 2000 (through June 2000), and the company's ranking in the Fortune 500 companies (if applicable). It is noted whether the company is a component of a major index.

Included is the minimum number of shares required to enroll in the company DRIP program or the minimum dollar amount for enrollment. It is noted when the minimum direct investment is waived for monthly ACH investments. Minimum additional OCP is provided. Phone numbers to request DRIP enrollment forms are provided. Keep in mind that phone numbers change; if the number listed is incorrect, there are several other resources such as the public library or the Internet. S&P Directory of Dividend Reinvestment Plans, 17th Edition, has calculated the average 10-year annual return ending December 31, 1999, for each company and it is listed as well. If the company increased dividends every year from 1989 to 1999, it is also noted.

S&P rates the following companies A+ for 10-year consistency in earnings and dividend growth. Company information is listed alphabetically.

5TH THIRD BANK (FITB)—FINANCIAL—BANK—REGIONAL

FITB is a regional bank–holding company with about $33 billion in assets. It operates 500 full-service banking offices in Ohio, Indiana, Kentucky, Arizona, Florida, and Michigan. FITB is one of the most consistently efficient banks in the United States, with a 1998 efficiency ratio of 48 percent. This means that 48 percent of revenues go for noninterest-related operating expenses, whereas many other banks hover around 55 percent to 60 percent. This ratio makes FITB more profitable on the same dollar revenue than other banks. FITB's loans consist of about 43 percent commercial and 57 percent consumer, and their loan quality is considered to be excellent.

> Top competitors: Bank One, Huntington Bancshares, PNC Financial
>
> Revenues: $3.6 billion—S&P 500
>
> Minimum DRIP number of shares or minimum direct investiment: $500
>
> Minimum OCP: $50
>
> Phone #: 800/837-2755
>
> Purchase, ACH, or initial setup fee: yes
>
> 10-year annual return: 28 percent

AFLAC (AFL)—FINANCIAL—INSURANCE—LIFE AND HEALTH

AFL offers supplemental cancer and individual health insurance mainly through employer-sponsored benefit packages. More than two-thirds of operating profits originate in Japan, where supplemental insurance is more widely utilized. AFL dominates the Japanese market, and 96 percent of companies listed on the Tokyo Exchange offer AFL products to their employees. In the United States, AFL has expanded beyond cancer insurance and is the leading provider of supplemental health and accident insurance. An aggressive share repurchase plan by the company will continue to aid the upward trend in earnings.

Top competitors: AIG, Conseco, UNUM Provident

Revenues: $8.6 billion—#205 Fortune 500, S&P 500

Minimum DRIP number of shares or minimum direct investment: $1000

Minimum OCP: $50

Phone #: 800/235-2667

Purchase, ACH, or initial setup fee: none

10-year annual return: 27 percent

ABBOTT LABS (ABT)–NONCYCLICAL–HEALTH CARE–DIVERSIFIED

ABT is a leading manufacturer of pharmaceuticals, nutritional products, and hospital and lab products. ABT has become one of the leading producers of testing equipment and diagnostic systems for blood-related care. ABT services fast-growing markets in the health care field and is well diversified in its product offering. ABT has offered long-term investors outstanding sales and profit growth, and should continue to do so in the future. Revenues consist of diagnostics 24 percent, pharmaceuticals 19 percent, hospital products 17 percent, and nutrients 15 percent. International business represented 25 percent of revenues.

Top competitors: Aventis, Merck, Roche

Revenues: $13.1 billion—#135 Fortune 500, S&P 500

Minimum DRIP number of shares or minimum direct investment: 1 share

Minimum OCP: $10

Phone #: 888/332-2268

Purchase, ACH, or initial setup fee: yes

10-year annual return: 18 percent

Increased dividends every year 1989–1999: yes

ALBERTSON'S (ABS)—NONCYCLICAL—RETAIL— FOOD CHAIN

ABS is the second largest operator of supermarkets and combination drug–food stores with almost 2500 stores in 38 states, 780 of which are stand-alone drug stores. Store brand names include Albertson's, Seessel's, Lucky Stores, Jewel, Acme, Osco, Sav-On, and Max Foods. Recently, ABS acquired American Stores and is currently restructuring after the merger. In the short term, ABS will take charges against earnings to close overlapping or underperforming stores. Investors are anticipating merger-related cost savings and a reduction in debt to drive earnings higher.

> Top competitors: Kroger, Safeway, Walgreens
>
> Revenues: $37.4 billion—#24 Fortune 500, S&P 500
>
> Minimum DRIP number of shares or minimum direct investment: 15 shares
>
> Minimum OCP: $30
>
> Phone #: 800/552-6645
>
> Purchase, ACH, or initial setup fee: yes
>
> 10-year annual return: 10 percent

DONALDSON CO (DCI)—INDUSTRIAL— MANUFACTURING—SPECIALIZED

DCI produces air cleaning and air purifying systems, include air cleaners, filters, and mufflers for combustion engines and industrial dust-collection systems. Clients include OEM accounts in construction, industrial, and mining industries. DCI also specializes in air quality systems for industrial manufacturers. DCI operates 24 plants and four joint ventures worldwide. Although headquartered in the United States, 70 percent of revenues are generated in the UK and Europe, with only 16 percent generated in North America. DCI has sustained a high operating profit margin of 32 percent.

> Top competitors: Cummins Engines, MFRI, Pall
>
> Revenues: $944 million—S&P 400
>
> Minimum DRIP number of shares or minimum direct investment: 1 share
>
> Minimum OCP: $10

Phone #: 800/468-9716

Purchase, ACH, or initial setup fee: yes

10-year annual return: 22 percent

EMERSON ELECTRIC (EMR)–INDUSTRIAL– ELECTRICAL EQUIPMENT

EMR is a diversified manufacturer of electronic and electrical equipment, including tools, motors, and controls. EMR has increased revenues, earnings, and dividends every year since 1956—a feat equaled by very few companies. An aggressive R&D program fuels its growth. New products and services generated 33 percent of 1998 revenues, and the company's stated goal is to expand this percentage to over 40 percent. Long-term return on equity has exceeded 20 percent annually. In response to a changing marketplace, EMR is changing its product mix. Recently, EMR has been acquiring companies in the electronics and telecommunications equipment fields. EMR is also aggressively moving onto the Internet, with e-business accounting for 10 percent of revenues in early 2000.

Top competitors: ABB, GE, Hitachi

Revenues: $14.2 billion—#121 Fortune 500, S&P 500

Minimum DRIP number of shares or minimum direct investment: 1 share

Minimum OCP: $50

Phone #: 888/213-0970

Purchase, ACH, or initial setup fee: none

10-year annual return: 14 percent

FEDERAL HOME LOAN MORTGAGE (FRE)– FINANCIAL–DIVERSIFIED

FRE, also known as Freddie Mac, is a federally sponsored enterprise offering home mortgage financing. Similar to a savings and loan, FRE focuses on home lending. Unlike an S&L, FRE uses borrowings rather than retail deposits to finance mortgages. Also, FRE buys mortgages from other financial institutions rather than issuing the mortgage directly to the homeowner.

Top competitors: Citigroup, Countrywide Credit, Fannie Mae

Revenues: $24.2 billion—$62 Fortune 500, S&P 500

Minimum DRIP number of shares or minimum direct investment: $250

Minimum OCP: $25

Phone #: 888 / 279-4029

Purchase, ACH, or initial setup fee: yes

10-year annual return: 25 percent

FEDERAL SIGNAL (FSS)—INDUSTRIAL—MANUFACTURING—SPECIALIZED

FSS is a manufacturer of fire trucks, ambulances, street sweepers, and other specialty purpose vehicles. FSS focuses on niche markets it can dominate through superior technology and acquisitions. Long-term debt is quite low. FSS is jettisoning its Sign Group, which manufactured neon signs, to focus on its core business. Production delays caused by outside vendors slowed production and earnings in 1999, but the company seems to be back on track.

Top competitors: GE, Oshkosh Truck, Vallen

Revenues: $1.0 billion—S&P 400

Minimum DRIP number of shares or minimum direct investment: 50 shares

Minimum OCP: $100

Phone #: 800 / 446-2617

Purchase, ACH, or initial setup fee: yes

10-year annual return: 11 percent

FRANKLIN RESOURCES (BEN)—FINANCIAL—INVESTMENT MANAGEMENT

BEN provides financial services to individual investors and corporate pension plans. BEN's money managers managed over $218 billion in 1999 and earned a tidy 0.62 percent fee. BEN operates the Franklin, Templeton, and Mutual series of mutual funds, which are mainly sold through brokers. Mutual fund investors may find it useful to also own shares in the company that manages their money. If you trust your mutual fund to make the right investing decisions, wouldn't you trust them to increase shareholder value for their own investors?

> Top competitors: FMR, Merrill Lynch, Vanguard Group
> Revenues: $2.2 billion—S&P 500
> Minimum DRIP number of shares or minimum direct investment: 1 share
> Minimum OCP: $100
> Phone #: 800/524-4458
> Purchase, ACH, or initial setup fee: none
> 10-year annual return: 22 percent
> Increased dividends every year 1989–1999: yes

GENERAL ELECTRIC (GE)—INDUSTRIAL— ELECTRICAL EQUIPMENT

GE is a leading manufacturer of jet engines, electric generating equipment, and medical supplies. GE is also a leader in financing and insurance. GE is the parent company of NBC television. Under the superb management and leadership of Jack Welsh, GE has transformed itself from just a manufacturer of industrial equipment to a provider of consumer and commercial financial services, which now generates 75 percent of total operating profits. In 1980, manufacturing generated 85 percent of profits. The key to GE's success has been the basic requirement that each specific business is either #1 or #2 in market share or it is discarded. Jack Welsh has announced his retirement, and the new management team is expected to follow in his footsteps. GE's stock has been a stellar performer mainly due to a history of excellent management.

> Top competitors: Matsushita, Rolls Royce, Siemans
> Revenues: $110.8 billion—#5 Fortune 500, S&P 500, DJIA
> Minimum DRIP number of shares or minimum direct investment: $250
> Minimum OCP: $10
> Phone #: 800/786-2543

Purchase, ACH, or initial setup fee: yes

10-year annual return: 28 percent

Increased dividends every year 1989–1999: yes

GENUINE PARTS (GPC)–CYCLICAL–AUTO PARTS & ACCESSORIES

GPC is the leading wholesale distributor of automotive replacement parts, industrial parts, and office supplies. GPC operates 62 NAPA warehouses, 750 company-owned stores, and several auto parts rebuilding centers. Earnings have been growing at a slowing pace over the past few years. The company has strong cash flow and low debt, however, which adds to its flexibility to expand aggressively. With the strength of new autos, most auto parts companies have been feeling the pinch as older cars are traded in rather than being repaired. If the economy slows down, look for consumers to own their autos a bit longer, rewarding auto parts companies.

Top competitors: Autozone, General Motors, General Parts

Revenues: $7.9 billion—#222 Fortune 500, S&P 500

Minimum DRIP number of shares or minimum direct investment: 1 share

Minimum OCP: $10

Phone #: 800/568-3476

Purchase, ACH, or initial setup fee: yes

10-year annual return: 6 percent

Increased dividends every year 1989–1999: yes

HOME DEPOT (HD)–CYCLICAL–RETAIL– BUILDING PRODUCTS

HD operates a chain of more than 900 retail stores selling a wide variety of home improvements and building products. HD is the world's largest retail building materials company; it has built a network of stores that currently services an estimated 14 percent of the domestic market. The company expects to expand to over 1200 stores by the end of 2001. Revenues continue to grow at a 20 percent + rate fueled by a 22 percent long-term growth rate in store count. Expanding into other specialty retail areas, HD is growing its Expo Store concept of offering more complete home improvement packages and projects. HD is expanding internationally with new stores in Chile, Canada, and Argentina.

Top competitors: Lowe's, Menards, Sears

Revenues: $39.4 billion—#21 Fortune 500, S&P 500, DJIA

Minimum DRIP number of shares or minimum direct investment: $250

Minimum OCP: $25

Phone #: 877/HD-SHARES

Purchase, ACH, or initial setup fee: yes

10-year annual return: 44 percent

Increased dividends every year 1989–1999: yes

ILLINOIS TOOL WORKS (ITW)–INDUSTRIAL–MANUFACTURING–DIVERSIFIED

ITW manufactures fasteners, components, and industrial assemblies. ITW is very unique because its over 500 small industrial businesses are managed in a highly decentralized structure. This facilitates the development of new products and motivates even the lowest level managers to increase profits. It is like a bunch of small, agile businesses lumped together with all the financial advantages of being a big company. ITW has been successful in growing EPS by marketing new products and acquiring small to medium-size businesses. Twenty-five percent of revenues and 35 percent of profits are generated overseas.

Top competitors: Cooper Industries, GE, Nordson

Revenues: $9.3 billion—#181 Fortune 500, S&P 500

Minimum DRIP number of shares or minimum direct investment: 1 share

Minimum OCP: $25

Phone #: 312/360-5155

Purchase, ACH, or initial setup fee: none

10-year annual return: 21 percent

Increased dividends every year 1989–1999: yes

INTERPUBLIC GROUPS (IPG)–
NONCYCLICAL–ADVERTISING

IPG is one of the world's largest advertising agency holding company and marketing communications companies. It is the creator of such slogans as, "Pardon me, would you have any Gray Poupon?" and "It takes a tough man to make a tender chicken." Cash flow has increased almost fivefold in the last decade, and the company has been expanding by acquisitions. Earnings are expected to grow by 18 percent to 20 percent annually over the next few years. IPG has been aggressively buying competitors, and in 1999 it bought 55 ad agencies. Operations outside the United States account for 48 percent of revenues.

Top competitors: Bcom3, Omnicom, WWP Group

Revenues: $4.4 billion—#351 Fortune 500, S&P 500

Minimum DRIP number of shares or minimum direct investment: 1 share

Minimum OCP: $10

Phone #: 201/324-0498

Purchase, ACH, or initial setup fee: yes

10-year annual return: 28 percent

Increased dividends every year 1989–1999: yes

JEFFERSON-PILOT (JP)–FINANCIAL–INSURANCE–
LIFE & HEALTH

JP is mainly a life insurance company. It has been disposing of noncore financial sector assets, like its mortgage title company. JP has been gaining critical mass in the insurance business by buying smaller competitors, and it has made six major acquisitions since 1996. Utilizing independent agents, JP has developed an excellent distribution network. JP recently exited the difficult business of group health insurance. JP also owns radio and television stations and produces sports programming.

Top competitors: Citigroup, MetLife, Prudential

Revenues: $2.5 billion—S&P 500

Minimum DRIP number of shares or minimum direct investment: 1 share

Minimum OCP: $20

Phone #: 800/829-8432

Purchase, ACH, or initial setup fee: none

10-year annual return: 22 percent

Increased dividends every year 1989–1999: yes

JOHNSON & JOHNSON (JNJ)–NONCYCLICAL–HEALTH CARE–DIVERSIFIED

JNJ is the world's largest and most comprehensive health care company, offering a broad line of drugs, consumer products, and medical and dental products. Brand names include Tylenol and Band-Aid products. Pharmaceuticals account for 38 percent of revenues and 69 percent of profits. About 75 percent of revenues are generated in products where JNJ is either #1 or #2 in global market share.

Top competitors: Aventis, Merck, Proctor & Gamble

Revenues: $27.4 billion—#43 Fortune 500, S&P 500, DJIA

Minimum DRIP number of shares or minimum direct investment: 1 share

Minimum OCP: $25

Phone #: 800/328-9033

Purchase, ACH, or initial setup fee: yes

10-year annual return: 22 percent

Increased dividends every year 1989–1999: yes

JOHNSON CONTROLS (JCI)–CYCLICAL–MANUFACTURING–DIVERSIFIED

JCI is the leading producer of automotive interiors and batteries. In addition, JCI manufactures controls for industrial production and nonresidential fire, security, heating, and cooling. General Motors, Ford, and DaimlerChrysler are the company's biggest customers, accounting for about 40 percent of sales. JCI's battery group makes auto batteries for retailers such AutoZone and Sears. JCI has been aggressively expanding overseas and has more than 80 subsidiaries worldwide.

Top competitors: Exide, Lear, Magna Int'l

Revenues: $16.1 billion—#108 Fortune 500, S&P 500

Minimum DRIP number of shares or minimum direct investment: $50

Minimum OCP: $50

Phone #: 800/524-6220

Purchase, ACH, or initial setup fee: none

10-year annual return: 16 percent

Increased dividends every year 1989–1999: yes

KEYCORP (KEY)–FINANCIAL–BANK–REGIONAL

KEY is a multiregional bank holding company operating over 950 branches in 13 states. KEY is expanding in the full-service investment banking and securities brokerage business, looking to expand its product offerings to existing clients. KEY has announced several programs to reduce its efficiency ratio (the percent of revenue needed for noninterest expense) from 58 percent to 52 percent, which should continue to drive earnings higher.

Top competitors: Bank of America, Citigroup, Merrill Lynch

Revenues: $7.9 billion—#221 Fortune 500, S&P 500

Minimum DRIP number of shares or minimum direct investment: 1 share

Minimum OCP: $10

Phone #: 800/539-7216

Purchase, ACH, or initial setup fee: none

10-year annual return: 14 percent

LANCASTER COLONY (LANC)–NONCYCLICAL– CONSUMER (JEWELRY, GIFTS)

LANC produces specialized foods, automotive aftermarket products, glassware, and candles. Although not flashy, LANC has been a steady performer, increasing revenues and income every year for over 10 years. Since 1992, return on equity has exceeded 23 percent annually. LANC has a mere 39 million shares outstanding and is not followed closely on Wall Street. Institutional ownership is only 46 percent.

Top competitors: Blythe Inc, Kraft, Newell

Revenues: $1.1 billion—S&P 400

Minimum DRIP number of shares or minimum direct investment: 1 share

Minimum OCP: $50

Phone #: 800/278-4353

Purchase, ACH, or initial setup fee: none

10-year annual return: 20 percent

LOWE'S (LOW)—CYCLICAL—RETAIL—BUILDING PRODUCTS

LOW operates over 590 retail building material stores in 39 states. Much like Home Depot (with almost twice the revenues), LOW attracts contractors and do-it-yourself handypeople by offering great prices and excellent customer service. The business model of warehouse stores works well for both LOW and HD. LOW recently acquired Eagle Hardware and Garden in the western United States, expanding its store count and geographic reach. Earnings should continue to expand as LOW continues to grow in store count and realizes greater cost savings. During the past 5 years, revenues have increased annually by 19 percent and EPS by 25 percent.

Top competitors: Home Depot, Menards, Wal-Mart

Revenues: $15.9 billion—#109 Fortune 500, S&P 500

Minimum DRIP number of shares or minimum direct investment: $250

Minimum OCP: $25

Phone #: 877/282-1174

Purchase, ACH, or initial setup fee: none

10-year annual return: 33 percent

Increased dividends every year 1989–1999: yes

MCDONALDS (MCD)–NONCYCLICAL–RESTAURANTS

MCD is the leading fast food chain in the world, with nearly half of its 24,000 restaurants located outside the United States. MCD is one of the most widely known brand names. Long term, MCD faces the challenge of an aging US population that is more attuned to casual dining, which requires a fuller, more diversified menu. MCD is currently changing its image by offering meals made to order, rather than its historic premade sandwiches.

> Top competitors: Burger King, Tricon, Wendy's
> Revenues: $13.2 billion—#132 Fortune 500, S&P 500, DJIA
> Minimum DRIP number of shares or minimum direct investment: $500, waived for ACH
> Minimum OCP: $50
> Phone #: 800/621-7825
> Purchase, ACH, or initial setup fee: yes
> 10-year annual return: 18 percent
> Increased dividends every year 1989–1999: yes

MERCK & CO (MRK)–NONCYCLICAL–HEALTH CARE–DRUGS

MRK is one of the world's largest pharmaceutical companies, and its Medco division is a leading prescription-by-mail service. MRK is the leader in the high-profit margin cardiovascular drug business. However, several of its blockbuster drugs are set to have their patent expire over the next few years, causing investor concern over future revenues and profits as generic replacement will gain market share. To offset this, MRK has a host of new drugs in the R&D pipeline.

> Top competitors: Aventis, Bristol-Myers-Squib, Novartis
> Revenues: $32.7 billion—#34 Fortune 500, S&P 500, DJIA
> Minimum DRIP number of shares or minimum direct investment: $350, waived if ACH
> Minimum OCP: $50
> Phone #: 800/831-8248
> Purchase, ACH, or initial setup fee: yes
> 10-year annual return: 20 percent
> Increased dividends every year 1989–1999: yes

PAYCHEX (PAYX)–INDUSTRIAL–SERVICES– DATA PROCESSING

PAYX provides payroll accounting, processing, and human resource services to small and medium-size businesses. PAYX is the second largest payroll services firm and serves over 377,000 clients. PAYX expands its business by offering existing clients additional services, such as a tax filing, in addition to finding new clients.1999 was the ninth consecutive year of record revenues and earnings and the eighth year of over 36 percent income growth. Long term, management has set a goal of 17 percent to 19 percent revenue growth and 25 percent earnings growth.

> Top competitors: Administaff, ADP, Ceridian
>
> Revenues: $1.4 billion—S&P 500
>
> Minimum DRIP number of shares or minimum direct investment: 1 share
>
> Minimum OCP: $100
>
> Phone #: 800/937-5449
>
> Purchase, ACH, or initial setup fee: yes
>
> 10-year annual return: 44 percent
>
> Increased dividends every year 1989–1999: yes

PFIZER (PFE)–NONCYCLICAL–HEALTH CARE–DRUGS

After closing the merger with Warner Lambert in mid-2000, PFE is the largest drug company. Major drugs include Lipitor, the world's best-selling cholesterol-lowering drug, along with several cardio-vascular drugs. Surprisingly, PFE has very little long-term debt. Cost savings from the merger should drive earnings higher over the next few years. International operations are 39 percent of total revenue.

> Top competitors: Bristol-Myers-Squibb, Merck, Novartis
>
> Revenues: $16.2 billion—#107 Fortune 500, S&P 500
>
> Minimum DRIP number of shares or minimum direct investment: $500
>
> Minimum OCP: $50
>
> Phone #: 800/PFE-9393

Purchase, ACH, or initial setup fee: none

10-year annual return: 30 percent

Increased dividends every year 1989–1999: yes

PITNEY BOWES (PBI)–TECHNOLOGY–OFFICE EQUIPMENT–MAILING EQUIPMENT

PBI is the largest US manufacturer of mailing equipment and software and is expanding into the Internet. Focused on the mailroom, PBI offers postal meters, scales, mailing machines, and software. With the introduction of their ClickStamp Plus on-line postage service, PBI should expand rapidly in the small business market, which has been a weak market for PBI until now. Within a few years, e-commerce could add $300 million to PBI's top line.

Top competitors: Bell and Howell, Canon, E-Stamp

Revenues: $4.4 billion—#354 Fortune 500, S&P 500

Minimum DRIP number of shares or minimum direct investment: 1 share

Minimum OCP: $100

Phone #: 800/648-8170

Purchase, ACH, or initial setup fee: yes

10-year annual return: 18 percent

Increased dividends every year 1989–1999: yes

RPM, INC. (RPM)–BASIC MATERIALS–CHEMICALS–SPECIALTY

RPM manufactures chemicals used in coatings, structural waterproofing, and corrosion control. Consumer brand names include Rust-Oleum, DAP Product, and Bondex. RPM has rewarded long-term investors with 53 years of record earnings. In 1999, RPM restructured to improve profitability and charges broke the string at 53. RPM has had 54 years of record revenues. Dividends have been increased annually for the past 26 years. International revenue represents 23 percent of total revenue.

Top competitors: DuPont, PPG Industries, Sherwin Williams

Revenues: $1.9 billion—S&P 400

Minimum DRIP number of shares or minimum direct investment: 1 share

Minimum OCP: $25

Phone #: 800 / 776-4488

Purchase, ACH, or initial setup fee: none

10-year annual return: 8 percent

Increased dividends every year 1989–1999: yes

SCHERING-PLOUGH (SGP)–NONCYCLICAL–HEALTH CARE–DRUGS

SGP is a leading producer of prescription and over-the-counter pharmaceuticals, with a large market share in sun care, animal care, and foot care products. As a niche drug company, their brand names are familiar to most of us and include Coppertone, Afrin, Chlor-Trimenton, Coricidin, and Dr. Scholls. Claritin D is the company's largest product and the world's best-selling antihistamine. SGP will most likely offer an over-the-counter version prior to the expiration of the patent. SGP has virtually no long-term debt.

Top competitors: Aventis, Glaxo Wellcome, Roche

Revenues: $9.1 billion—#185 Fortune 500, S&P 500

Minimum DRIP number of shares or minimum direct investment: 1 share

Minimum OCP: $25

Phone #: 800 / 524-4458

Purchase, ACH, or initial setup fee: none

10-year annual return: 25 percent

Increased dividends every year 1989–1999: yes

SERVICEMASTER (SVM)–NONCYCLICAL– CONSUMER–SERVICES

Management is focused on killing bugs, cleaning houses, mowing lawns, and fixing broken appliances. SVM provides consumer and commercial services using the brand names Terminix, Merry Maids, ServiceMaster, ChemLawn-TruGreen, and American Home Shield. Through the strategy of acquisitions, SVM has built an impressive collection of branded services in a very fragmented industry. SVM has also built outstanding consumer awareness and brand loyalty.

Top competitors: Aramark, Ecolab, Rollins

Revenues: $5.7 billion—#295 Fortune 500

Minimum DRIP number of shares or minimum direct investment: 1 share

Minimum OCP: $25

Phone #: 800/858-0840

Purchase, ACH, or initial setup fee: yes

10-year annual return: 20 percent

SHERWIN WILLIAMS (SHW)—CYCLICAL—RETAIL—BUILDING SUPPLIES

SHW is the largest US manufacturer and distributor of paint and varnishes, and it is a major seller of wall coverings and related products. Over the past 3 years, SHW has been growing by acquisitions. The largest was its purchase of Pratt & Lambert Paint and Thompson's Minwax. Industry unit growth has been sluggish during the past few years, increasing only 1.5 percent to 2.0 percent annually. SHW should continue its acquisition strategy, expanding revenue and profit growth in this highly fragmented industry.

Top competitors: Akzo Nobel, DuPont, RPM

Revenues: $5.0 billion—#326 Fortune 500, S&P 500

Minimum DRIP number of shares or minimum direct investment: 1 share

Minimum OCP: $10

Phone #: 800/524-4458

Purchase, ACH, or initial setup fee: none

10-year annual return: 11 percent

STATE STREET CORP (STT)—FINANCIAL—FINANCIAL SERVICES—MONEY MANAGEMENT

SST is a leading provider of financial services worldwide, with $5.3 trillion in assets under custody, and directly manages $582 billion in assets. An asset under custody relates to posttransaction services provided to stock brokerage firms and mutual funds, in addition to trust management. STT focuses on services to institutional, lease finance, and global trade clients.

Top competitors: Bank of New York, Barclays, Citigroup

Revenues: $4.9 billion—#345 Fortune 500, S&P 500

Minimum DRIP number of shares or minimum direct investment: 10 shares

Minimum OCP: $100

Phone #: 800/426-5523

Purchase, ACH, or initial setup fee: yes

10-year annual return: 24 percent

Increased dividends every year 1989–1999: yes

SUNTRUST BANK (STI)—FINANCIAL— BANK—REGIONAL

STI operates banking operations in the southeast and has $93 billion in assets. As the ninth largest bank in the United States, STI has grown by timely acquisitions, with the largest being a recent merger extending their reach to the Washington, DC and Virginia areas. As a conservatively managed bank, STI has a great reputation in the consumer, commercial, and trust services businesses. STI owns approximately 50 million shares of Coca-Cola (KO). Each share of STI represents about one-sixth of a share of KO. STI's market extends from Washington, DC to Alabama to Florida.

Top competitors: Bank of America, First Union, Wachovia

Revenues: $7.6 billion—#234 Fortune 500, S&P 500

Minimum DRIP number of shares or minimum direct investment: 1 share

Minimum OCP: $50

Phone #: 404/588-7822

Purchase, ACH, or initial setup fee: yes

10-year annual return: 22 percent

Increased dividends every year 1989–1999: yes

WALGREENS (WAG)—NONCYCLICAL—RETAIL— DRUG STORES

WAG is the largest US retail drug store chain in terms of revenues and profitability; it operates over 2800 stores in 39 states. The largest concentrations of stores are in Florida, Illinois, and Texas. WAG has recently formed a pharmacy benefits management company using a mail-order service, and it is focusing on small to medium-size businesses and HMOs.

> Top competitors: CVS, Eckerds, Rite Aid
>
> Revenues: $17.8 billion—#95 Fortune 500, S&P 500
>
> Minimum DRIP number of shares or minimum direct investment: $50
>
> Minimum OCP: $50
>
> Phone #: 800/286-9178
>
> Purchase, ACH, or initial setup fee: yes
>
> 10-year annual return: 27 percent
>
> Increased dividends every year 1989–1999: yes

WAL-MART (WMT)—CYCLICAL— BROAD-BASED RETAILER

WMT is the leading retailer in the United States. WMT has more revenues than Kmart, J.C. Penney, and Sears combined. WMT operates 4000 stores, including discount stores (Wal-Mart), combination discount and grocery stores (Wal-Mart Supercenters and ASDA in the UK), and membership-only warehouse stores (Sam's Club). WMT is expanding internationally and is the #1 retailer in Canada and Mexico. WMT operates in South America, Asia, and Europe. Founder Sam Walton's heirs own about 38 percent of Wal-Mart stock.

> Top competitors: Costco, Kmart, Target
>
> Revenues: $165.0 billion—#2 Fortune 500, S&P 500, DJIA
>
> Minimum DRIP number of shares or minimum direct investment: $250, waived if ACH
>
> Minimum OCP: $50
>
> Phone #: 800/438-6278

Purchase, ACH, or initial setup fee: yes

10-year annual return: 29 percent

Increased dividends every year 1989–1999: yes

WRIGLEY (WM.) JR. (WWY)–NONCYCLICAL–FOODS

WWY is the leading producer of chewing gum, with about 50 percent US market share. Fifty-two percent of revenues comes from overseas operations. Brand names include Wrigley's, Spearmint, Doublemint, Juicy Fruit, and Big Red. The Wrigley and Offield families control 55 percent of the stock.

Top competitors: CSM, Nabisco, Pfizer

Revenues: $2.0 billion—S&P 500

Minimum DRIP number of shares or minimum direct investment: $250, waived if ACH

Minimum OCP: $50

Phone #: 800/438-6278

Purchase, ACH, or initial setup fee: yes

10-year annual return: 19 percent

DRIP and Direct Investing Companies, S&P Rated A

The following is a list of companies that offer DRIP and direct investing programs and are rated A for 10-year consistency in earnings and dividend growth. Company information is listed alphabetically.

AIR PRODUCTS (APD)—BASIC MATERIALS—CHEMICALS

APD is a major producer of industrial gases, and specialty and intermediate chemicals, including nitrogen, oxygen, argon, and hydrogen. APD is expanding into the medical and beverage markets. Gases account for 60 percent of sales. APD also makes systems that recover and process gases. APD operates in 30 countries and exports to more than 100.

> Top competitors: Airgas, AirLiquide, Praxair
> Revenues: $5.0 billion—#324 Fortune 500, S&P 500
> Minimum DRIP number of shares or minimum direct investment: $500, waived if ACH
> Minimum OCP: $100
> Phone #: 888 / 694-9458
> Purchase, ACH, or initial setup fee: yes

10-year annual return: 13 percent

Increased dividends every year 1989–1999: yes

AMERICAN WATER WORKS (AWK)—UTILITY—WATER

AWK is one of the largest investor-owned water companies. AWK serves 10 million consumers in 23 states. Pennsylvania and New Jersey operations comprise half the company's revenues. AWK's subsidiary, American Water Services, provides water and wastewater utility management, as well as leasing and commercial services.

Top competitors: Philadelphia Suburban, United Water Services, Vivendi

Revenues: $1.2 billion—S&P 400

Minimum DRIP number of shares or minimum direct investment: 1 share

Minimum OCP: $100

Phone #: 800/736-3001

Purchase, ACH, or initial setup fee: none

10-year annual return: 13 percent

Increased dividends every year 1989–1999: yes

BANK ONE (ONE)—FINANCIAL—BANK—REGIONAL

The merger of BancOne and First Chicago created ONE. ONE is the fourth largest bank in the United States (behind Bank of America, Chase Manhattan, and Citigroup) and the second largest issuer of credit cards (after Citigroup). However, ONE has experienced major trouble with its credit card division and profits have fallen. ONE is rumored to be a possible takeover candidate by other banks, such as Wells Fargo, seeking exposure in the midwestern markets. ONE operates 1800 branches in 14 states, mostly in the midwest and southwest.

Top competitors: Bank of America, Chase Manhattan, Citigroup

Revenues: $25.9 billion—#50 Fortune 500, S&P 500

Minimum DRIP number of shares or minimum direct investment: 1 share

Minimum OCP: $25

Phone #: 888/764-5592

Purchase, ACH, or initial setup fee: none

10-year annual return: 11 percent

BECTON, DICKINSON (BDX)–NONCYCLICAL–HEALTH CARE–MEDICAL PRODUCTS

BDX provides a wide variety of medical products and is the world's largest producer of needles and injection systems. International operations account for 46 percent of revenues and 33 percent of profits. With about 90 percent market share, BDX leads the industry in diabetes care, infusion therapy, and drug injection products. BDX also operates Biosciences segment (microbiology products, cellular analysis systems, labware and growth media, and test kits) and Preanalytical Solutions (specimen management systems, bar-code data capture, and consulting services).

Top competitors: Abbott Labs, Bristol-Myers-Squibb, Johnson & Johnson

Revenues: $3.4 billion—#451 Fortune 500, S&P 500

Minimum DRIP number of shares or minimum direct investment: $250, waived if ACH

Minimum OCP: $50

Phone #: 800/955-4743

Purchase, ACH, or initial setup fee: none

10-year annual return: 15 percent

Increased dividends every year 1989–1999: yes

BEMIS (BMS)–CYCLICAL–CONTAINERS AND PACKAGING–PAPER

BMS is a leading manufacturer of flexible packaging and pressure-sensitive materials. Its primary market is packaging for the food industry. BMS' focus is the food industry, with other customers in the agricultural, chemical, medical, personal care, and printing industries. BMS has production facilities and sales offices in North America, Europe, and Asia. The United States accounts for almost 85 percent of the company's sales.

Top competitors: 3M, Pechiney, Smurfit Stone Container
Revenues: $1.9 billion—S&P 500
Minimum DRIP number of shares or minimum direct investment: 1 share
Minimum OCP: $25
Phone #: 800/551-6161
Purchase, ACH, or initial setup fee: none
10-year annual return: 10 percent
Increased dividends every year 1989–1999: yes

BRISTOL-MEYER-SQUIBB (BMY)—NONCYCLICAL— HEALTH CARE—DRUGS

BMY is a leading manufacturer of personal health care items. Their products include market leaders Clairol and Excedrin. Seventy percent of revenues come from pharmaceuticals, with BMY's focus on cardiovascular treatments and related products. Pravachol, a cholesterol-reduction drug, is its best seller. BMY also makes baby formulas, wound treatments, and orthopedic products.

Top competitors: Aventis, Glaxo Wellcome, Merck
Revenues: $20.2 billion—#78 Fortune 500, S&P 500
Minimum DRIP number of shares or minimum direct investment: $50
Minimum OCP: $105
Phone #: 800/356-2026
Purchase, ACH, or initial setup fee: yes
10-year annual return: 20 percent
Increased dividends every year 1989–1999: yes

CENTURYTEL (CTL)—UTILITIES—TELEPHONE

CTL offers a wide variety of telephone services in 21 states, with a concentration in Wisconsin, Louisiana, Michigan, and Ohio. CTL's focus is in the rural and suburban markets where the larger telecom players do not tend to compete. CTL has acquired several smaller rural telecom companies over the past few years. Their largest purchase was PacificTelecom. CTL provides local exchange services for over 1.3 million access lines in 20 states and owns interests in cellular systems in 6 states. CTL also offers cable TV, long-distance, Internet access and business data services, and security monitoring in some markets.

Top competitors: AT&T, Verizon Communications, SBC Communications

Revenues: $1.6 billion—S&P 500

Minimum DRIP number of shares or minimum direct investment: 1 share

Minimum OCP: $25

Phone #: 800/969-6718

Purchase, ACH, or initial setup fee: none

10-year annual return: 17 percent

COCA-COLA (KO)—NONCYCLICAL— BEVERAGES—NONALCOHOLIC

KO is the world's largest soft drink company. KO has a sizable fruit juice business and owns 44 percent of bottler Coca-Cola Enterprises. KO is the largest producer of soft drink syrups, concentrates, juice, and juice-related products. Trademarked brand names include Coke, Fanta, Sprite, Barq's, PowerAde, Minute Maid, and Hi-C. In selected countries (except the United States, France, and South Africa), KO owns Schweppes, Canada Dry, Crush, and Dr. Pepper. KO, which does no actual bottling, sells more than 230 brands of beverages, including coffees, juices, sports drinks, and teas in some 200 nations. Sixty-seven percent of revenues come from outside the United States. KO commands a 50 percent global market share.

Top competitors: Cadbury Schweppes, Nestle, PepsiCo

Revenues: $19.8 billion—#83 Fortune 500, S&P 500, DJIA

Minimum DRIP number of shares or minimum direct investment: 1 share

Minimum OCP: $10

Phone #: 888/265-3747

Purchase, ACH, or initial setup fee: yes

10-year annual return: 21 percent

Increased dividends every year 1989–1999: yes

COLGATE PALMOLIVE (CL)–NONCYCLICAL–PERSONAL CARE

CL is the number one seller of toothpaste and a world leader in oral care products, which includes mouthwashes, toothpaste, and toothbrushes. CL is also a major supplier of personal care products, such as baby care, deodorants, shampoos, and soaps. Palmolive is a leading dishwashing soap brand worldwide. CL is a top producer of bleach and liquid surface cleaners (including Ajax). Subsidiary Hill's Pet Nutrition's Science Diet brand is a leading premium pet food worldwide. Foreign operations comprise 80 percent of CL's total revenues.

> Top competitors: Clorox, Gillette, Proctor & Gamble
>
> Revenues: $9.1 billion—#187 Fortune 500, S&P 500
>
> Minimum DRIP number of shares or minimum direct investment: 1 share
>
> Minimum OCP: $20
>
> Phone #: 800 / 756-8700
>
> Purchase, ACH, or initial setup fee: yes
>
> 10-year annual return: 26 percent
>
> Increased dividends every year 1989–1999: yes

COMERICA (CMA)–FINANCIAL–BANKS–REGIONAL

CMA is a Detroit-based bank with operations in Michigan, Texas, California, and Florida. This 150-year-old company has over 350 branches and is the 23rd largest bank with about $37 billion in assets. CMA's strength is in commercial loans, which comprise about 65 percent of its loan portfolio. CMA provides mutual funds and annuities, life insurance, trust products, investment banking, discount brokerage, and retirement services. CMA has operations in California, Florida, Michigan, and Texas, as well as banks in Mexico and Canada.

> Top competitors: Bank of America, Citigroup, Bank One
>
> Revenues: $3.3 billion—#455 Fortune 500, S&P 500
>
> Minimum DRIP number of shares or minimum direct investment: 1 share
>
> Minimum OCP: $10

Phone #: 800/468-9716

Purchase, ACH, or initial setup fee: yes

10-year annual return: 20 percent

Increased dividends every year 1989–1999: yes

ELECTRONIC DATA SYSTEMS (EDS)–TECHNOLOGY– COMPUTER SERVICES

EDS provides information technology services including business-processing management, systems management, and management consulting services. Spun off from General Motors (GM) in 1996, EDS has experienced almost stagnant revenue growth over the past few years, but its massive cash flow has allowed a reduction of its long-term debt by 50 percent. The largest independent systems consulting firm in the United States (IBM is number one overall), EDS offers systems integration, corporate outsourcing, data center management, and reengineering services. EDS also provides management consulting services through subsidiary A.T. Kearney. GM accounts for about 20 percent of EDS's revenues. EDS is building a substantial e-business consulting division, E.Solutions, with the 1999 acquisition of assets from MCI WorldCom.

Top competitors: Anderson Consulting, Computer Sciences, IBM

Revenues: $18.5 billion—#91 Fortune 500, S&P 500

Minimum DRIP number of shares or minimum direct investment: $250

Minimum OCP: $50

Phone #: 800/278-4353

Purchase, ACH, or initial setup fee: yes

10-year annual return: 19 percent

EQUIFAX (EFX)–INDUSTRIAL–SERVICES

EFX is the largest credit reporting company in the United States, with a growing credit card clearinghouse business. EFX has information on about 400 million credit holders worldwide. EFX also authorizes checks and provides credit card processing services. Equifax customers include banks and retail stores in the United

States, as well as in Canada, Latin America, and the UK. EFX is expanding into China and the Far East. In mid-2001, EFX will split into two companies.

Top competitors: Experian, First Data, Marmon Group

Revenues: $1.7 billion—S&P 500

Minimum DRIP number of shares or minimum direct investment: $500

Minimum OCP: $50

Phone #: 888/887-2971

Purchase, ACH, or initial setup fee: yes

10-year annual return: 14 percent

GILLETTE (G)—NONCYCLICAL—PERSONAL CARE

G is a global manufacturer of razors, razor blades, toiletries, and batteries. Brands include Duracell, Right Guard, Braun, and Oral B. Recently, G sold its stationery business to Newell (NWL) and its hair care products to Diamond Products. Manufacturing occurs in 25 countries, and international operations account for 63 percent of revenues. G's strong commitment to research and development has helped it become the world leader in most of its product categories.

Top competitors: Ralston Purina, Remmington Products

Revenues: $9.8 billion—#172 Fortune 500, S&P 500

Minimum DRIP number of shares or minimum direct investment: $1000

Minimum OCP: $100

Phone #: 888/218-2841

Purchase, ACH, or initial setup fee: yes

10-year annual return: 22 percent

Increased dividends every year 1989–1999: yes

MARSH & MCLENNEN (MMC)—FINANCIAL—INSURANCE BROKERS

MMC is the world's largest broker of insurance products and provides employee benefit packages and investment management services. MMC owns Putnam Investment, managing $294 billion in mutual fund assets. MMC also owns Mercer Consulting Group, which provides human resources and management consulting worldwide. Twenty-seven percent of revenues are generated overseas.

> Top competitors: AON, Arthur Gallagher, Willis Corroon
>
> Revenues: $9.1 billion—#186 Fortune 500, S&P 500
>
> Minimum DRIP number of shares or minimum direct investment: 1 share
>
> Minimum OCP: $10
>
> Phone #: 800/457-8968
>
> Purchase, ACH, or initial setup fee: yes
>
> 10-year annual return: 17 percent

MEDTRONIC (MDT)—NONCYCLICAL—HEALTH CARE—MEDICAL PRODUCTS AND SUPPLIES

MDT is a global manufacturer of medical devices and has a leadership role in the pacemaker, defibrillator, cardiac stent, and orthopedic markets. As our population ages, MDT is poised to continue to grow in both sales and profits. MDT's products help regulate erratic heartbeats, tremors, and incontinence. Fifty percent of revenue comes from defibrillators and pacing products, including devices for slow, irregular, or rapid heartbeats. MDT makes spinal implant devices, mechanical and tissue heart valves, catheters, stents, and guidewires used in angioplasties. MDT is committed to developing products for minimally invasive cardiac surgery and sleep apnea. Like many companies in the medical sector, MDT carries almost no debt.

> Top competitors: Baxter, Boston Scientific, Guidant
>
> Revenues: $5.0 billion—#387 Fortune 500, S&P 500
>
> Minimum DRIP number of shares or minimum direct investiment: 1 share
>
> Minimum OCP: $25
>
> Phone #: 651/450-4064
>
> Purchase, ACH, or initial setup fee: none

10-year annual return: 34 percent

Increased dividends every year 1989–1999: yes

MINNESOTA MINING AND MANUFACTURING (3M) (MMM)–INDUSTRIAL– MANUFACTURING–DIVERSIFIED

MMM is a diversified manufacturer with products ranging from Post It Notes to stethoscopes. MMM operates six divisions: industrial (advanced adhesives, tapes, and abrasives), transportation, graphics, and safety (reflective materials, respirators, and optical films), health care (drugs, dental, and skin products), consumer and office (tape), electro and communications (insulating products), and specialty material (gases and plastics). The company operates in more than 60 countries, and international operations account for about 60 percent of revenues.

Top competitors: Avery Dennison, ICI, Johnson & Johnson

Revenues: $15.6 billion—#110 Fortune 500, S&P 500, DJIA

Minimum DRIP number of shares or minimum direct investment: 1 share

Minimum OCP: $10

Phone #: 800/401-1952

Purchase, ACH, or initial setup fee: none

10-year annual return: 13 percent

Increased dividends every year 1989–1999: yes

MOTOROLA (MOT)–TECHNOLOGY– COMMUNICATION EQUIPMENT

MOT is the leading manufacturer of cellular telephone systems, semiconductors, two-way radios, and paging systems. Mobile phone usage worldwide is expected to double over the next 3 to 4 years, and MOT is well poised to expand sales and profits through its cell phone, satellite, and ground-based networking equipment. Cellular products make up nearly 40 percent of MOT's revenue. MOT is the sixth largest semiconductors manufacturer and also produces two-way radios, pagers, computers, and networking peripherals. MOT is providing wireless telecom services in developing nations. About 50 percent of MOT's revenues are generated overseas. MOT recently acquired General Instrument, a manufacturer of TV set-top boxes.

Top competitors: Ericsson, Lucent, Intel

Revenues: $30.3 billion—#37 Fortune 500, S&P 500

Minimum DRIP number of shares or minimum direct investment: $500

Minimum OCP: $100

Phone #: 800/704-4098

Purchase, ACH, or initial setup fee: yes

10-year annual return: 27 percent

NEWELL RUBBERMAID (NWL)– NONCYCLICAL–HOUSEWARES

NWL is a manufacturer of housewares, home furnishings, office products, and hardware. Its strategy is to expand through acquisitions, locating companies with strong brand names that are not generating their profit potential and then turning them around. Known within the industry as *Newellization*, NWL has been very successful with this strategy, buying more than 20 companies and growing its revenues to over $5 billion. In 1998, NWL acquired Rubbermaid and is currently restructuring this new business. In 2000, NWL purchased the stationery business from Gillette (G), adding to its Sanford pen product line. Major customers include retailers such as Home Depot. Brand names include Rubbermaid plastic products, Calphalon and Mirro cookware, Anchor Hocking glassware, Amerock cabinet hardware, Bulldog screws, Levolor blinds, Rolodex files, and Sanford markers.

Top competitors: Avery Dennison, Hunter Douglas, WKI Holdings

Revenues: $6.4 billion—#271 Fortune 500, S&P 500

Minimum DRIP number of shares or minimum direct investment: 1 share

Minimum OCP: $10

Phone #: 800/317-4445

Purchase, ACH, or initial setup fee: yes

10-year annual return: 12 percent

PENTAIR (PNR)—INDUSTRIAL— MANUFACTURING—DIVERSIFIED

PNR produces and markets professional power tools and machinery, water and fluid controls, and electric and electronic enclosures. PNR has recently expanded into the fast-growing business of water treatment pumps and equipment. The water and fluid technologies unit makes well pumps, sump pumps, and valves for water softeners. PNR's brands are well known within each industry: Delta and Porter-Cable power tools, Hoffmann and Schroff protective housings, Essef pool and spa equipment, and DeVilbiss air compressor equipment. Pentair has more than 80 plants and distribution locations in Asia, Europe, and North America. Twenty-eight percent of revenues are generated overseas. PNR has very little debt.

Top competitors: Black & Decker, IDEX, Stanley Works

Revenues: $2.3 billion—S&P 400

Minimum DRIP number of shares or minimum direct investment: 1 share

Minimum OCP: $10

Phone #: 800/468-9716

Purchase, ACH, or initial setup fee: none

10-year annual return: 18 percent

Increased dividends every year 1989–1999: yes

PEPSICO (PEP)—NONCYCLICAL— BEVERAGES—NONALCOHOLIC

PEP is the second largest producer of soft drinks and a major supplier of snack foods. Although historically behind Coca-Cola in the US soft drink market, PEP leads in many international markets. The Pepsi soft drinks (Pepsi, Mountain Dew, Slice) make up 25 percent of revenue and, like KO, bottling operations are run independently. Sixty percent of revenues come from Frito-Lay, the world's number one maker of snacks such as corn chips (Doritos, Fritos) and potato chips (Lay's, Ruffles, WOW!). Tropicana Products is the world leader in juices, and its Tropicana Pure Premium is a leading grocery brand. PEP also sells Aquafina bottled water, All Sport sports drinks, Dole juices (licensed), Grandma's cookies, Lipton ready-to-drink tea, and Rold Gold pretzels.

> Top competitors: Cadbury Schweppes, Coca-Cola, Proctor & Gamble
>
> Revenues: $20.3 billion—#76 Fortune 500, S&P 500
>
> Minimum DRIP number of shares or minimum direct investment: 5 shares
>
> Minimum OCP: $25
>
> Phone #: 800/226-0083
>
> Purchase, ACH, or initial setup fee: yes
>
> 10-year annual return: 14 percent
>
> Increased dividends every year 1989–1999: yes

PROCTOR & GAMBLE (PG)—NONCYCLICAL— HOUSEHOLD PRODUCTS—NONDURABLE

PG is a leading consumer products company marketing household and personal care items. Brand names total over 300 and include Crest toothpaste, Pampers diapers, Tide detergent, and Cover Girl cosmetics. PG is the number one US maker of household products in five main categories: laundry and cleaning (detergents, bleaches), beauty care (cosmetics, shampoos), food and beverages (coffee, snacks), paper goods (toilet paper, feminine products), and health care (toothpaste, medicine). PG also produces Iams premium pet food and PUR water filters. PG developed and markets olestra, a fat substitute used in snacks. PG operates in 140 countries, and about half of revenues come from international operations.

> Top competitors: Johnson & Johnson, Kimberly Clark, Unilever
>
> Revenues: $39.9 billion—#23 Fortune 500, S&P 500, DJIA
>
> Minimum DRIP number of shares or minimum direct investment: $250

Minimum OCP: $100

Phone #: 800 / 764-7483

Purchase, ACH, or initial setup fee: yes

10-year annual return: 22 percent

Increased dividends every year 1989–1999: yes

REGIONS FINANCIAL (RGBK)–FINANCIAL–
BANKS–REGIONAL

RGBK is a major southeast bank with total assets of $41 billion. It operates 700 branches in eight southeastern states. RGBK has grown by acquiring many smaller banks in Alabama, Arkansas, Florida, Georgia, Louisiana, South Carolina, Tennessee, and Texas. In addition to a broad range of consumer and commercial banking, RGBK offers mortgage banking, leasing, securities brokerage, and insurance.

Top competitors: American South, Bank of America, SunTrust Bank

Revenues: $3.3 billion—#453 Fortune 500, S&P 500

Minimum DRIP number of shares or minimum direct investment: $1000

Minimum OCP: $25

Phone #: 800 / 922-3468

Purchase, ACH, or initial setup fee: yes

10-year annual return: 16 percent

Increased dividends every year 1989–1999: yes

TARGET (TGT)–CYCLICAL–RETAIL–
GENERAL MERCHANDISE

TGT recently changed its name from Dayton Hudson, reflecting the growth of its Target stores. TGT operates 1250-plus stores with three retail concepts. They include Target, a discount chain with more than 920 stores. Mervyn's California operates midrange department stores found mainly in the midwest and west. Dayton's, Hudson's, and Marshall Field's are upscale department stores also focused in the midwest. Target Stores account for more than 75 percent of TGT's revenue. Target has recently focused its introduction in the northeast and midatlantic markets and is looking to aggressively expand in these areas. TGT is well received in the midwest, California, and Florida.

Top competitors: Federated, Kmart, Wal-Mart

Revenues: $33.7 billion—#32 Fortune 500, S&P 500

Minimum DRIP number of shares or minimum direct investment: $500, waived if ACH

Minimum OCP: $50

Phone #: 888/268-0203

Purchase, ACH, or initial setup fee: yes

10-year annual return: NA

Increased dividends every year 1989–1999: yes

TEXTRON (TXT)—TECHNOLOGY— MANUFACTURING—AEROSPACE

TXT makes the Cessna airplanes and Bell helicopters, along with automotive and general industrial components. International sales account for 35 percent of revenues. TXT is a diversified manufacturer and has four operating segments: industrial (fasteners, golf carts, lawn-care products), aircraft (Cessna and Bell), automotive (trim and fuel systems), and finance (term loans, revolving credit, and specialty finance). The US government accounts for 10 percent of TXT's revenues. TXT recently sold Avco, its consumers finance unit, and is using the proceeds for a stock buy-back program and acquisitions.

Top competitors: GE, Lear, United Technologies

Revenues: $11.5 billion—#154 Fortune 500, S&P 500

Minimum DRIP number of shares or minimum direct investment: 1 share

Minimum OCP: $25

Phone #: 201/324-1225

Purchase, ACH, or initial setup fee: yes

10-year annual return: 23 percent

WELLS FARGO (WFC)–FINANCIAL–BANK–REGIONAL

The merger of Norwest Bank and the old Wells Fargo formed WFC, now the seventh largest bank in the United States. WFC has over $205 billion in assets and over 6000 branches. Norwest was known for excellence in cross-marketing financial products to its clients. This expertise is expected to assist in driving profits higher as old Wells Fargo clients are targeted. WFC offers consumer and business banking services, as well as investment services, real estate loans, and consumer loans. WFC is one of the largest mortgage bankers in the United States. WFC is active in international trade financing through a joint venture with HSBC.

Top competitors: Bank of America, Citigroup, US Bancorp

Revenues: $21.7 billion—#68 Fortune 500, S&P 500

Minimum DRIP number of shares or minimum direct investment: $250, waived if ACH

Minimum OCP: $25

Phone #: 800/813-3324

Purchase, ACH, or initial setup fee: yes

10-year annual return: 25 percent

Increased dividends every year 1989–1999: yes

DRIP and Direct Investing Companies, S&P Rated A−, B+

The following is a list of companies that offer DRIP and direct investing programs rated A− or B+ for 10-year consistency in earnings and dividend growth. Company information is listed alphabetically.

ADVANTA (ADVNA)−FINANCIAL−SERVICES B+

ADVNA is in a transition period. After selling its consumer credit card business (it had been one of the largest credit card issuers), ADVNA focused on mortgages to the subprime market, or those with less than stellar credit histories. In mid-2000, ADVNA announced it would exit that business as well, mainly due to investors' dislike of higher risk loans, which has put downward pressure on its stock price. ADVNA is shifting focus onto the needs of small businesses. It is operating a growing credit card business along with equipment leasing, credit-related insurance services, and venture capital investments. ADNVA owns two banks—Advanta National Bank and Advanta Bank Corp.

> Top competitors: Aames Financial, The Associates, Household International
>
> Revenues: $572 million
>
> Minimum DRIP number of shares or minimum direct investment: $1500

Minimum OCP: $50

Phone #: 800/225-5923

Purchase, ACH, or initial setup fee: yes

10-year annual return: 20 percent

AMERICAN STATES WATER (AWR)—UTILITY— WATER B+

AWR's main subsidiary, regulated public utility Southern California Water, serves more than 244,000 customers in 75 towns, primarily greater Los Angeles and Orange County regions. AWR also distributes electricity to more than 21,000 customers. AWR operates in nonregulated industries, providing billing services, water delivery, and wastewater treatment.

Top competitors: California Water Service, Los Angeles Water and Power, Southwest Water

Revenues: $173 million—S&P 600

Minimum DRIP number of shares or minimum direct investment: $500

Minimum OCP: $100

Phone #: 800/482-7629

Purchase, ACH, or initial setup fee: yes

10-year annual return: 15 percent

Increased dividends every year 1989–1999: yes

AON CORP (AOC)—FINANCIAL—INSURANCE B+

AOC is the world's #2 insurance brokerage and consulting company, behind Marsh & McLennan, operating three major business segments: commercial brokerage, consulting services, and consumer insurance underwriting. The brokerage operations, which comprise more than half of revenue, includes retail and wholesale insurance for groups and businesses. Its consulting services focus on employee benefits. The underwriting segment offers supplementary health, accident, and life insurance and extended warranties for consumer goods. AOC has around 550 offices in about 120 countries around the world.

Top competitors: Arthur Gallagher, Marsh McLennen, Willis Corroon

Revenues: $7.0 billion—#248 Fortune 500, S&P 500

Minimum DRIP number of shares or minimum direct investment: 1 share

Minimum OCP: $20

Phone #: 800/446-2617

Purchase, ACH, or initial setup fee: yes

10-year annual return: 16 percent

Increased dividends every year 1989–1999: yes

AT&T (T)−UTILITY−TELEPHONE/CABLE B |

T is a long-distance carrier expanding into cable TV and Internet services. T is the United State's number one telecom company, with more than 80 million customers. T provides long-distance, wireless, and local telephone service, along with Internet access and a full range of telecom services for businesses. T's joint venture with British Telecommunications targets multinational corporations. T is the number one US cable operator after its acquisition of MediaOne. Over the next few years, T will split itself into four business units.

Top competitors: Sprint, Verizon, Worldcom

Revenues: $62.3 billion—#8 Fortune 500, S&P 500, DJIA

Minimum DRIP number of shares or minimum direct investment: 1 share

Minimum OCP: $100

Phone #: 800/348-8288

Purchase, ACH, or initial setup fee: yes

10-year annual return: 8 percent

BANK AMERICA (BAC)−FINANCIAL−BANK− REGIONAL A−

The merger of NationsBank and BankAmerica formed BAC. The combined firm has about 4500 retail branches in 21 states and almost 40 countries. BAC's operating units (consumer banking, commercial banking, global corporate and investment banking, and principal investing and asset management) also offer residential and commercial mortgages and insurance. BAC is expanding its on-line services to remain competitive.

Top competitors: Bank One, Chase Manhattan, Citigroup

Revenues: $51.6 billion—#11 Fortune 500, S&P 500

Minimum DRIP number of shares or minimum direct investment: $1000

Minimum OCP: $50

Phone #: 800 / 642-9855

Purchase, ACH, or initial setup fee: yes

10-year annual return: 12 percent

BRIGGS & STRATTON (BGG)—INDUSTRIAL— MANUFACTURING A–

BGG is the world's largest producer of 3 to 25 horsepower air-cooled gasoline engines used in lawn and garden equipment and snow throwers. Lawn- and garden equipment-related revenue account for about 75 percent of sales. BGG's three largest customers combined account for 42 percent of revenues. BGG manufactures in the United States, its primary market, and serves European customers through a regional office in Switzerland and a warehouse in the Netherlands.

Top competitors: Honda, Kohler, Tecumseh Products

Revenues: $1.5 billion, S&P 500

Minimum DRIP number of shares or minimum direct investment: 1 share

Minimum OCP: $25

Phone #: 800 / 637-7549

Purchase, ACH, or initial setup fee: none

10-year annual return: 15 percent

Increased dividends every year 1989–1999: yes

CALIFORNIA WATER SERVICE (CWT)—UTILITIES— WATER A–

CWT provides water services to over 50 communities in California. With increasingly stronger federal water quality regulation, the industry is in the midst of a huge consolidation. Local municipal water districts are selling out to public companies such as CWT. In addition, much larger companies have acquired many smaller publicly traded water utilities, and CWT may be a takeover target. Its main subsidiary, regulated utility California Water Service (Cal Water), serves more than 387,000 customers in 60 cities from Los Angeles to San Francisco. Subsidiary utility Washington Water serves about 15,000 customers in Washington State. CWS Utility Services unit provides nonregulated water utility services such as meter reading, billing, and water treatment.

Top competitors: American States Water, US Filter

Revenues: $206 million

Minimum DRIP number of shares or minimum direct investment: $500

Minimum OCP: $100

Phone #: 800/337-3503

Purchase, ACH, or initial setup fee: yes

10-year annual return: 14 percent

Increased dividends every year 1989–1999: yes

CHEVRON (CHV)—ENERGY—INTERNATIONAL B+

After its pending merger with Texaco, CHV will be the number two US integrated oil company, behind Exxon Mobil. CHV operates in more than 90 countries, runs about 8100 gas stations, and has proved reserves of 4.8 billion barrels of oil and 9.1 trillion cubic feet of natural gas. CHV is pursuing an exploration and production strategy in lucrative, but politically unstable, areas such as Kazakhstan and Angola. CHV has combined its petrochemicals operations with Phillips Petroleum. CHV holds a 50 percent stake in Caltex, a global refiner and marketer equally owned with Texaco.

Top competitors: BP Amoco, ExxonMobil, Royal Dutch Shell

Revenues: $31.5 billion—#35 Fortune 500, S&P 500 index

Minimum DRIP number of shares or minimum direct investment: $250, waived if ACH

Minimum OCP: $50

Phone #: 800/842-7629

Purchase, ACH, or initial setup fee: yes

10-year annual return: 14 percent

Increased dividends every year 1989–1999: yes

CLAYTON HOMES (CHM)–CYCLICAL–HOUSING A–

CMH is the third largest mobile home manufacturer with interests in marketing, finance, and insurance. Its homes range in size from 500 square feet to 2400 square feet, and prices range from $10,000 to $75,000. CMH sells 28,000 homes a year in 31 states through 300 company-owned retail centers and 700 independent dealers. The company provides financing and operates 75 manufactured home parks. Chairman James Clayton owns 27 percent of the company.

Top competitors: Champion Enterprises, Fleetwood Homes, Oakwood Homes

Revenues: $1.2 billion, S&P 400

Minimum DRIP number of shares or minimum direct investment: 1 share

Minimum OCP: $100

Phone #: 800/278-4353

Purchase, ACH, or initial setup fee: yes

10-year annual return: 20 percent

COMPUTER ASSOCIATES (CA)–TECHNOLOGY–SOFTWARE B+

CA is a leading developer of computer software for business applications. It is the world's third largest independent software company behind Microsoft and Oracle. CA offers more than 500 software products, from data access to network management tools. CA, which has grown by acquiring smaller software firms, changed tacks with the purchase of PLATINUM Software (1999) and Sterling Software (2000) for nearly $4 billion.

Top competitors: BMC Software, Compuware, Microsoft

Revenues: $6.1 billion—#315 Fortune 500, S&P 500

Minimum DRIP number of shares or minimum direct investment: 50 shares

Minimum OCP: $25

Phone #: 800/244-7155

Purchase, ACH, or initial setup fee: yes

10-year annual return: 35 percent

CRANE & CO (CR)−TECHNOLOGY−AEROSPACE B+

CR is a diversified manufacturer of a wide variety of industrial products, including valves and fluid control products, aerospace components and systems, control valves and regulating systems, fiberglass panels, plumbing fixtures, and vending machines. Aerospace products such as pressure sensors and braking systems account for 25 percent of revenues and almost 50 percent of operating profits.

Top competitors: BF Goodrich, Dover, IMI

Revenues: $1.5 billion—S&P 500

Minimum DRIP number of shares or minimum direct investment: 1 share

Minimum OCP: $10

Phone #: 201/324-1225

Purchase, ACH, or initial setup fee: none

10-year annual return: 9 percent

CROMPTON CORP (CK)−BASIC CHEMICALS− CHEMICALS B+

CK was formed in 1999 from the merger of Crompton & Knowles and Witco Chemicals. CK produces specialty chemicals and equipment used in manufacturing tires, textiles, and auto parts. CK also makes rubber chemicals and polymers, seed-treatment and crop-protection chemicals, dyes, additives for plastic and petroleum products, and process equipment. CK has expanded through acquisitions and joint ventures. The most important was the acquisition of Uniroyal Chemical.

Top competitors: BASF Corp, Ciba Specialty Chemicals, Struthers Industries

Revenues: $2.1 billion—S&P 400

Minimum DRIP number of shares or minimum direct investment: $50

Minimum OCP: $30

Phone #: 800/288-9541

Purchase, ACH, or initial setup fee: none

10-year annual return: 7 percent

DISNEY, WALT (DIS)–CYCLICAL–ENTERTAINMENT B+

DIS is the number three media conglomerate in the world behind AOL-Time Warner and Viacom. DIS has very diversified operations in television, film, theme parks, and the Internet. DIS owns the top-rated ABC network and several cable channels like ESPN (80 percent owned by DIS) and A&E Television Networks (38 percent owned by DIS). Walt Disney Studios produces films through Touchstone, Hollywood Pictures, and Miramax. DIS theme parks, Walt Disney World and Disneyland, are the most popular in North America. Walt Disney Internet Group (72 percent of tracking stock owned by DIS) oversees *ABC.com*, Disney Online, and *ESPN.com.*

Top competitors: Fox Entertainment, AOL-Time Warner, Viacom

Revenues: $23.4 billion—#66 Fortune 500, S&P 500, DJIA

Minimum DRIP number of shares or minimum direct investment: $1000, waived if ACH

Minimum OCP: $100

Phone #: 800/948-2222

Purchase, ACH, or initial setup fee: yes

10-year annual return: 13 percent

Increased dividends every year 1989–1999: yes

DOW CHEMICAL (DOW)–BASIC MATERIAL– CHEMICALS B+

DOW is a world leader in the production of plastics, chemicals, hydrocarbons, herbicides, and pesticides. Dow is the number two US chemical company. Almost 40 percent of revenue is from performance plastics (adhesives, sealants, and coatings). DOW also produces commodity chemicals and crude oil–based raw materials. DOW operates 123 plants in 32 countries and recently acquired competitor Union Carbide.

Top competitors: BASF, Bayer AG, DuPont

Revenues: $18.9 billion—#89 Fortune 500, S&P 500

Minimum DRIP number of shares or minimum direct investment: 1 share

Minimum OCP: $25

Phone #: 800/369-5606

Purchase, ACH, or initial setup fee: none

10-year annual return: 11 percent

Increased dividends every year 1989–1999: yes

DQE INC. (DQE)—UTILITY—ELECTRIC A−

DQE is one of the new utility companies flourishing in the world of deregulation. Its principal subsidiary, Duquesne Light, distributes electricity to about 580,000 customers in southwestern Pennsylvania, including Pittsburgh. DQE sold its seven power-generating plants to focus on electrical power distribution. DQE's AquaSource provides water and wastewater services to about 430,000 customers in 18 states. Other nonregulated subsidiaries are involved in natural gas, fiberoptic telecommunications, energy distribution management, energy investing, e-commerce for energy commodities, and energy outsourcing for industrial and institutional clients.

Top competitors: Allegheny Energy, American Water Works, PECO Energy

Revenues: $1.3 billion, S&P 400

Minimum DRIP number of shares or minimum direct investment: $105

Minimum OCP: $10

Phone #: 800/247-0400

Purchase, ACH, or initial setup fee: yes

10-year annual return: 13 percent

DUKE ENERGY (DUK)—UTILITY—ELECTRIC A−

DUK is the third largest US investor-owned utility, behind Enron and PG&E. DUK provides electricity to 2 million customers in North and South Carolina. DUK trades gas and electricity, with plans to move into European markets. In the United States, DUK operates an 11,000-mile interstate pipeline system and is a top natural gas producer and gatherer. DUK's Duke/Fluor Daniel venture is a leading builder of fossil-fuel plants. Duke's international projects are mostly in Australia and Latin America. Other services include telecommunications.

> Top competitors: Enron, PG&E, Williams Companies
> Revenues: $21.7 billion—#69 Fortune 500, S&P 500, Dow Jones Utility Index
> Minimum DRIP number of shares or minimum direct investment: $250
> Minimum OCP: $50
> Phone #: 800/488-3853
> Purchase, ACH, or initial setup fee: none
> 10-year annual return: 11 percent
> Increased dividends every year 1989–1999: yes

DUPONT (DD)—BASIC MATERIALS—CHEMICALS B+

Better known simply as DuPont, E. I. du Pont de Nemours, is the largest chemical company in the United States. DD is the inventor of Lycra, Dacron, and Teflon and has operations in about 65 countries. Its eight business units make products including coatings (automotive finishes and performance coatings), nylon, specialty polymers (flat panel displays and Teflon), and pigments and chemicals. Other units produce specialty fibers (Lycra and Kevlar), herbicides, pesticides, polyester, and biotechnology products such as food ingredients and seeds. Its pharmaceuticals are used to treat HIV, heart disease, nerve disorders, and cancer.

> Top competitors: BASF AG, Bayer AG, Dow Chemical
> Revenues: $26.9 billion—#42 Fortune 500, S&P 500, DJIA
> Minimum DRIP number of shares or minimum direct investment: 1 share

Minimum OCP: $20

Phone #: 888/983-8766

Purchase, ACH, or initial setup fee: yes

10-year annual return: 16 percent

Increased dividends every year 1989–1999: yes

ENRON (ENE)—ENERGY—NATURAL GAS A−

ENE is the world's leading marketer of natural gas. With the deregulation of electric utilities in the mid-1990s, ENE has been expanding its marketing of electricity as well and has grown to become the leading electric marketer. ENE has recently focused its marketing expertise to the communication, high-bandwidth market. ENE is leading the way for this industry to offer its system's reserves in a similar liquid market. ENE operates a 32,000-mile gas pipeline system in the United States.

Top competitors: American Electric Power, Duke Energy, Utilicorp

Revenues: $40.1 billion—#18 Fortune 500, S&P 500 Index

Minimum DRIP number of shares or minimum direct investment: $250

Minimum OCP: $25

Phone #: 800/662-7662

Purchase, ACH, or initial setup fee: yes

10-year annual return: 23 percent

EXXONMOBIL (XOM)—ENERGY—OIL— INTERNATIONAL INTEGRATED A−

XOM is the result of the merger of Exxon and Mobil; it is the world's largest nonstate-owned oil company. XOM explores, transports, refines, and markets oil and oil-related products. XOM has proven reserves of 21 billion barrels of oil equivalent and can refine more than 6 million barrels per day. XOM operates about 45,000 service stations in 118 countries under the Exxon, Esso, and Mobil brands. XOM also produces and sells petrochemicals and has interests in coal mining, minerals, and electric power generation.

Top competitors: BP Amoco, Royal Dutch Shell, Texaco

Revenues: $160.8 billion—#3 Fortune 500, S&P 500, DJIA

Minimum DRIP number of shares or minimum direct investment: $250

Minimum OCP: $50

Phone #: 800/252-1800

Purchase, ACH, or initial setup fee: none

10-year annual return: 17 percent

Increased dividends every year 1989–1999: yes

GATX (GMT)—INDUSTRIAL—RAILROAD/LEASING B+

GMT is the largest rail car leasing company in the United States with a growing aircraft and technology equipment leasing business. GATX Capital leases rail cars to railroads, provides equipment financing, and leases commercial jets and information technology equipment. GATX Rail owns a North American fleet of about 88,000 tank cars and leases rail cars in Europe through affiliates. GATX Integrated Solutions Group offers logistics and supply-chain services to chemical and petroleum companies.

Top competitors: CHR, GE Capital, TTX

Revenues: $1.7 billion—Dow Jones Transports, S&P 400

Minimum DRIP number of shares or minimum direct investment: 1 share

Minimum OCP: $25

Phone #: 800/851-9677

Purchase, ACH, or initial setup fee: none

10-year annual return: 11 percent

Increased dividends every year 1989–1999: yes

HARLEY DAVIDSON (HDI)—CYCLICAL—OTHER—MOTORCYCLE MANUFACTURER B+

HDI is the only US manufacturer of motorcycles and was recently added to the S&P 500 Index. HDI offers 24 models of heavyweight motorcycles through a worldwide network of more than 1300 dealers. With a world market share of over 20 percent of the heavy-weight motorcycle market, HDI has developed a brand loyalty envied by many.

Top competitors: Honda, Kawasaki, Suzuki

Revenues: $2.5 billion, S&P 500

Minimum DRIP number of shares or minimum direct investment: 1 share

Minimum OCP: $30

Phone #: 800 / 637-7549

Purchase, ACH, or initial setup fee: yes

10-year annual return: 39 percent

HAWAIIAN ELECTRIC (HE)−UTILITY−ELECTRIC B+

HE is a holding company for Hawaiian Electric Company (HECO) and nonutility subsidiaries. HECO, which is the parent of both Maui Electric and Hawaii Electric Light, serves more than 95 percent of the population on the islands of Hawaii, Lanai, Maui, Molokai, and Oahu. HE's utility businesses account for about 70 percent of sales. Nonutility businesses include American Savings Bank with 68 retail branches in the state and a subsidiary investing in power and energy projects throughout the Pacific Rim. Recently, HE was forced to write off its investments in China and the Phillipines. Note: HE's stock has rebounded from the approximate December 1999 price used for annual return calculations. In late 1999 and early 2000, HE's stock traded at 10-year lows. Having rebounded in price since, the annual return would be correspondingly higher.

Top competitors: BancWest, Citizens Communications, Pacific Century Financial

Revenues: $ 1.5 billion, S&P 400

Minimum DRIP number of shares or minimum direct investment: $250

Minimum OCP: $25

Phone #: 808 / 532-5841

Purchase, ACH, or initial setup fee: yes

10-year annual return: 3 percent

HEINZ (H.J.) (HNZ)—NONCYCLICAL—FOODS A–

HNZ produces a wide variety of human and animal food products. These include Heinz brand ketchup and condiments, Star-Kist tuna, and Weight Watchers frozen dinners. Animal food products include 9Lives, Kibbles and Bits, and Ken-L-Ration pet foods. HNZ is the #1 maker of private-label soup. HNZ generates 45 percent of revenues and 42 percent of profits outside North America, with strong overseas operations in Australia, Canada, New Zealand, the UK, and Northern Europe.

> Top competitors: Campbell Soup, ConAgra, Nestle
> Revenues: $9.4 billion—#183 Fortune 500, S&P 500
> Minimum DRIP number of shares or minimum direct investment: $250
> Minimum OCP: $50
> Phone #: 800/253-3399
> Purchase, ACH, or initial setup fee: none
> 10-year annual return: 9 percent

HILLENBRAND INDUSTRIES (HB)—NONCYCLICAL— HEALTH CARE—MANUFACTURING A–

HB is the largest casket and crematory urn manufacturer in the United States. HB also produces hospital equipment and offers burial insurance. Equipment includes hospital beds, infant incubators, and hospital room furniture. HB operates three subsidiaries, and Hill-Rom makes hospital beds, infant incubators, and gurneys in Europe and North America. HB's two funeral service companies are casket maker Batesville Casket and Forethought Financial Services, which provides insurance-based funeral planning. The Hillenbrand family owns 30 percent of the company.

> Top competitors: Invacare, Sunrise Medical, York Group
> Revenues: $2.0 billion, S&P 400
> Minimum DRIP number of shares or minimum direct investment: $250
> Minimum OCP: $100
> Phone #: 888/665-9611
> Purchase, ACH, or initial setup fee: yes

10-year annual return: 5 percent

Increased dividends every year 1989–1999: yes

INTEL (INTC)−TECHNOLOGY−SEMICONDUCTORS A−

INTC is the world's largest manufacturer of semiconductors, with more than 80 percent of the PC microprocessor market. INTC makes microprocessors, including the Pentium series and the lower end Celeron. INTC's largest customers, Compaq and Dell, each accounts for 13 percent of sales. Intel also provides flash memories and embedded chips for communications, industrial equipment, and military markets. INTC is expanding into networking services and communications infrastructure. Fifty-five percent of revenues are from outside the United States.

Top competitors: AMD, IBM, Motorola

Revenues: $29.3 billion—#39 Fortune 500, S&P 500, DJIA

Minimum DRIP number of shares or minimum direct investment: 1 share

Minimum OCP: $25

Phone #: 800 / 298-0146

Purchase, ACH, or initial setup fee: none

10-year annual return: 44 percent

KENNAMETAL (KMT)−INDUSTRIAL−TOOLS− DISTRIBUTION B+

KMT is the leader in the cutting tool industry. It produces metal-cutting tools and mining and highway construction equipment. KMT's products include cutting tools, milling and drilling tools, grader blades, and snowplow blades. It also supplies equipment and safety products to industrial companies. KMT operates primarily in North America and Europe. The company sells its products worldwide under the Drill-Fix, Fix-Perfect, Hertel, Kendex, Kenloc, Kennametal, and Kyon brands.

Top competitors: Allied Power, Bridgeport Machines, Milacron

Revenues: $1.8 billion, S&P 400

Minimum DRIP number of shares or minimum direct investment: 1 share

Minimum OCP: $25

Phone #: 800/756-3353

Purchase, ACH, or initial setup fee: none

10-year annual return: 20 percent

NORFOLK SOUTHERN (NSC)–CYCLICAL–
RAILROADS A–

NSC expanded its rail system by 50 percent in 1999 when it acquired
59 percent of Conrail. CSX, its main competitor, purchased the balance. Whereas other railroads have focused on east–west routes,
NSC concentrates on the north–south routes, especially along the
East Coast. NSC has experienced difficulty integrating Conrail, but
over time, the acquisition should boost carloads, revenues, and
profits. NSC operates Norfolk Southern Railway, a major freight
railroad that covers 21,800 route miles in 22 states, mostly east of the
Mississippi. NSC transports raw materials, intermediate products,
and finished goods. NSC offers intermodal services using a combination of rails and trucks through subsidiaries Triple Crown Services and Thoroughbred Direct Intermodal Services. NSC also manages coal, natural gas, and timber holdings in six states.

Top competitors: Burlington Northern Santa Fe, CSX, Union
Pacific

Revenues: $5.1 billion—#316 Fortune 500, S&P 500, Dow
Jones Transports

Minimum DRIP number of shares or minimum direct investment: 1 share

Minimum OCP: $10

Phone #: 800/432-1040

Purchase, ACH, or initial setup fee: yes

10-year annual return: 7 percent

OMNICARE (OCR)–NONCYCLICAL–MEDICAL A–

OCR is the largest pharmacy services company for nursing homes
and long-term care facilities. It provides services to some 8000 long-

term care facilities in more than 40 states. It dispenses drugs for nursing homes and provides computerized recordkeeping. OCR also offers drug therapy evaluation, drug administration monitoring, and regulatory compliance oversight. Related services include infusion therapy, medical supply, pharmaceutical research, and wellness maintenance programs. OCR is moving strongly into contract research to capitalize on its extensive data with geriatric health. With the lowering of Medicare reimbursements in 1999, OCR has been struggling to redirect its business to nongovernment-related clients.

Top competitors: McKesson HBOC, Owens Healthcare, PharMerica

Revenues: $1.8 billion, S&P 400

Minimum DRIP number of shares or minimum direct investment: 1 share

Minimum OCP: $10

Phone #: 800/317-4445

Purchase, ACH, or initial setup fee: yes

10-year annual return: 20 percent

Increased dividends every year 1989–1999: yes

PACIFIC CENTURY FINANCIAL (BOH)—FINANCIAL— BANK—REGIONAL A−

BOH is the holding company for the Bank of Hawaii, Hawaii's largest bank. BOH subsidiaries offer consumer and commercial banking services in Hawaii, on the US mainland, in Asia, in New Caledonia, and in Saipan. BOH is in the process of merging its banks and trimming operations. BOH's earnings have been hurt by a tourist slump in Hawaii, Asia's economic troubles, and rising interest rates.

Top competitors: BancWest, Bank of America, Wells Fargo Bank

Revenues: $1.3 billion, S&P 400

Minimum DRIP number of shares or minimum direct investment: $250

Minimum OCP: $25

Phone #: 808/537-8239

Purchase, ACH, or initial setup fee: yes

10-year annual return: 9 percent

Increased dividends every year 1989–1999: yes

PHILADELPHIA SUBURBAN (PSC)–UTILITY– WATER A–

PSC is a water utility operating in Pennsylvania, New England, Illinois, and Ohio. PSC services 1.8 million customers. PSC is one of the largest investor-owned water companies in the United States and has grown largely by acquisitions. It has acquired nearly 40 small water or wastewater companies since 1992, including the 1999 purchase of Consumers Water. PSC also contracts with municipalities to operate their water systems. France's Vivendi, the world's #1 water company, owns about 17 percent of PSC's outstanding stock.

Top competitors: American Water Works, United Water Resources

Revenues: $257 million, S&P 600

Minimum DRIP number of shares or minimum direct investment: $500

Minimum OCP: $50

Phone #: 800/205-8314

Purchase, ACH, or initial setup fee: none

10-year annual return: 17 percent

PROGRESS ENERGY (PGN)–UTILITY–ELECTRIC A–

In late 2000, Carolina Power and Light merged with Florida Progress, making PGN the ninth largest utility in the United States. PGN has 2.6 million electric customers in North Carolina, South Carolina, and Florida. Even though the Carolinas' electricity markets have not been deregulated yet, PGN is expanding in anticipation. PGN's nonutility business includes power marketing and trading, Internet and telecommunications services, and energy services and management. PGN also owns NC Natural Gas, with 180,000 gas customers.

Top competitors: Duke Power, Southern Company, TVA

Revenues: (premerger) $3.3 billion—#459 Fortune 500, S&P 500

Minimum DRIP number of shares or minimum direct investment: 1 share

Minimum OCP: $20

Phone #: 800/633-4236

Purchase, ACH, or initial setup fee: yes

10-year annual return: 8 percent

Increased dividends every year 1989–1999: yes

RAYTHEON (RTN.B)—TECHNOLOGY—ELECTRONICS—DEFENSE A−

RTN.B is the third largest defense contractor to the Pentagon. US government contracts account for 58 percent of revenues. Almost 30 percent of revenues are generated from overseas clients. RTN.B provides electronic products and services and builds aircraft for general, commercial, and military use. Electronic products account for about 75 percent of revenue and include such diverse products as air-combat infrared imaging systems, commercial fish finders, and the Hawk and Patriot missile systems. RTN.B manufactures Hawker and Beech jets and turboprop aircraft. Over the past few years, RTN.B has acquired several of their competitors. RTN.B has struggled to integrate these acquisitions, but in the long term these acquisitions should provide substantial revenue and profit potential. RTN.B is restructuring, reducing debt, and cutting costs to improve profitability.

Top competitor: Boeing, Lockheed Martin, Northrop Grumman

Revenues: $19.8 billion—#82 Fortune 500, S&P 500

Minimum DRIP number of shares or minimum direct investment: 1 share

Minimum OCP: $25

Phone #: 800/360-4519

Purchase, ACH, or initial setup fee: none

10-year annual return: 7 percent

SBC CORP (SBC)—UTILITY—TELEPHONE A–

SBC is one of the Baby Bells and is the local phone company for customers in the southwest and midwest. SBC is the #2 local phone company in the United States after Verizon. SBC operates 61 million network access lines in 13 US states, and its biggest markets are California, Texas, and Illinois. SBC is beginning to offer long-distance service in Connecticut and Texas. SBC has about 12.2 million wireless phone subscribers in 24 states and is combining operations with BellSouth. SBC also has financial stakes in telecom operations in 22 countries outside the United States.

> Top competitors: AT&T, Verizon, Worldcom
> Revenues: $49.4 billion—#12 Fortune 500, S&P 500, DJIA
> Minimum DRIP number of shares or minimum direct investment: $250, waived if ACH
> Minimum OCP: $50
> Phone #: 800/351-7221
> Purchase, ACH, or initial setup fee: yes
> 10-year annual return: 15 percent
> Increased dividends every year 1989–1999: yes

TYSON FOODS (TSN)—NONCYCLICAL—FOODS B+

TSN is the largest producer of chickens in United States. In an effort to boost profits, it is divesting noncore businesses and redeploying assets. TSN breeds, processes, and markets chickens and Cornish game hens. TSN also produces tortillas and chips (Mexican Original) and animal and pet food. TSN sells its products in more than 60 countries. Commercial customers account for nearly half of revenues. Don Tyson controls nearly 90 percent of the company's voting power.

> Top competitors: ConAgra, Gold Kist, Perdue
> Revenues: $7.3 billion—#241 Fortune 500, S&P 400
> Minimum DRIP number of shares or minimum direct investment: $250
> Minimum OCP: $50
> Phone #: 800/822-7096

Purchase, ACH, or initial setup fee: yes

10-year annual return: 7 percent

TYCO INT'L (TYC)—INDUSTRIAL—
CONGLOMERATE B+

TYC believes in growth through acquisitions. The company's largest group of businesses, Telecommunications and Electronics, produces electrical connectors, printed circuit boards, and undersea fiberoptic cable. The Healthcare and Specialty Products group makes Curity bandages, patient-monitoring equipment, crutches, and adhesives. The Fire and Security Services group is the world leader in security and fire-protection systems. The Flow Control group makes pipe, pipe fittings, tubing, flow meters, and other steel equipment for commercial and industrial applications. In addition to acquisitions, internal sales growth has been strong and should continue to propel TYC shares ahead.

Top competitors: Honeywell, Johnson & Johnson, 3M

Revenues: $22.4 billion—#76 Fortune 500, S&P 500

Minimum DRIP number of shares or minimum direct investment: 1 share

Minimum OCP: $25

Phone #: 800/685-4509

Purchase, ACH, or initial setup fee: yes

10-year annual return: 31 percent

VERIZON COMMUNICATIONS (VZ)—UTILITY—
TELEPHONE B+

VZ was formed in 2000 when Bell Atlantic bought GTE. It is the number one local phone company in the United States and the number two telecom services provider behind AT&T. VZ has 63 million local-access lines in 31 states and 4 million long-distance customers. Verizon Wireless, the company's joint venture with Vodafone, is the number one US wireless company with 25 million mobile phone customers and 4 million paging customers nationwide. Outside the United States, VZ affiliates serve 6 million wireless customers and operate 4 million local-access lines.

Top competitors: AT&T, SBC Communications, Sprint
Revenues: $22.1 billion—#33 Fortune 500, S&P 500
Minimum DRIP number of shares or minimum direct invest-
ment: $1000
Minimum OCP: $50
Phone #: 800/631-2355
Purchase, ACH, or initial setup fee: yes
10-year annual return: 13 percent

WASHINGTON MUTUAL (WM)–FINANCIAL–SAVINGS AND LOAN B+

WM is the largest savings and loan in the United States and is expanding into commercial banking. WM operates more than 2000 facilities across the west and south. California accounts for about 75
percent of its deposits and 60 percent of its loans. Washington Mutual offers a range of financial services, including traditional commercial and consumer banking as well as mutual funds and brokerage services.

Top competitors: Bank America, Gold West Financial, Wells
Fargo
Revenues: $13.5 billion—#127 Fortune 500, S&P 500
Minimum DRIP number of shares or minimum direct invest-
ment: 1 share
Minimum OCP: $50
Phone #: 206/461-3187
Purchase, ACH, or initial setup fee: none
10-year annual return: 20 percent
Increased dividends every year 1989–1999: yes

DRIP and Direct Investing Companies, S&P Rated NR, B, B−

The following is a list of companies that offer DRIP and direct investing programs rated NR, B or B− for 10-year consistency in earnings and dividend growth. Information is listed alphabetically by rating. (NR [Not Rated] usually means the company does not have a 10-year stock trading history and may not be an indication of poor performance. If rated Below Average or Low, these companies may be of interest as potential turnaround situations, and investors could anticipate the ratings to improve over time.)

INTIMATE BRANDS (IBI)−CYCLICAL−SPECIALTY RETAIL NR

IBI is a leading retailer of women's intimate apparel and personal care products. It operates more than 2100 stores under the names Victoria's Secret (lingerie, cosmetics, and fragrances) and Bath & Body Works (personal care products). Victoria's Secret also sells apparel on-line and mails 350 million catalogs a year. IBI sells candles through White Barn Candle Co. stores. The Limited (LTD) owns 84 percent of IBI.

> Top competitors: Body Shop, Maidenform, Sara Lee
> Revenues: $4.5 billion
> Minimum DRIP number of shares or minimum direct investment: $500, waived if ACH

Minimum OCP: $50

Phone #: 888/426-6700

Purchase, ACH, or initial setup fee: yes

10-year annual return: NA

LUCENT TECHNOLOGIES (LU)—TECHNOLOGY— COMMUNICATION EQUIPMENT NR

LU is the leading manufacturer of telephone communication equipment, which includes semiconductors, networking equipment, and software. LU was spun off from AT&T and is the old Bell Labs Division. LU has a rich history as a world leader in communications technology. LU also produces integrated circuits and telecommunications power systems and is a major supplier to the personal communications services market. Through acquisitions, LU has become a leader in the broadband (voice, data, and video) networking market. Most of LU's customers are telecom providers like AT&T (12 percent of sales). Lucent has recently spun off to shareholders its slower growth PBX, cabling, and microelectronics businesses to focus on high-growth areas.

Top competitors: Alcatel, Cisco Systems, Nortel Networks

Revenues: $38.3 billion—#22 Fortune 500, S&P 500

Minimum DRIP number of shares or minimum direct investment: $1000, waived if ACH

Minimum OCP: $100

Phone #: 800/727-7033

Purchase, ACH, or initial setup fee: yes

10-year annual return: NA

MCGRAW-HILL PUBLICATIONS (MHP)— NONCYCLICAL—PUBLISHING NR

MHP is one of the world's largest producers of textbooks, tests, and related materials serving the elementary, secondary, and higher education markets. MHP is also a leading supplier of financial and business information services and provides indexes and ratings for both domestic and overseas markets through Standard & Poor's. It publishes *BusinessWeek* magazine and a number of industry trade journals (*Aviation Week, Engineering News-Record*). MHP owns four television stations in three states.

> Top competitors: Dunn & Bradstreet, Harcourt General, Pearson
>
> Revenues: $3.9 billion—#401 Fortune 500, S&P 500
>
> Minimum DRIP number of shares or minimum direct investment: $500, waived if ACH
>
> Minimum OCP: $100
>
> Phone #: 800/842-7629
>
> Purchase, ACH, or initial setup fee: yes
>
> 10-year annual return: 19 percent

MORGAN STANLEY DEAN WITTER (MDW)— FINANCIAL—STOCK BROKERAGE NR

MDW is the #2 retail broker in the United States behind Merrill Lynch, with more than 560 branches in 25 countries. MDW's Discover unit is a leading credit card issuer, and Morgan Stanley Dean Witter Online is a top on-line broker. MDW offers asset and investment management services to individuals and institutions. Institutional services include securities underwriting, corporate finance, and research services. MDW, which is forming an on-line trading system in Europe, is also an investor in Primex Trading, an electronic communications network (ECN). As an alternative to the standard trading exchanges, ECNs utilize the growing capabilities of Internet and electronic-based stock trading.

> Top competitors: Goldman Sachs, Merrill Lynch, Soloman Smith Barney (Citigroup)
>
> Revenues: $33.9 billion—#50 Fortune 500, S&P 500
>
> Minimum DRIP number of shares or minimum direct investment: $1000
>
> Minimum OCP: $100
>
> Phone #: 800/228-0829
>
> Purchase, ACH, or initial setup fee: none
>
> 10-year annual return: NA

NOKIA (NOK)—TECHNOLOGY— COMMUNICATIONS NR

NOK is the world's largest manufacturer of cellular phones and is located in Finland. Its products are divided into three divisions: mobile phones (66 percent of sales), networks (wireless and Internet protocol infrastructure), and other operations (TV set-top boxes, Internet software and services, home networking, and mobile displays). NOK is focusing on high-speed data connections through third-generation wireless systems, digital subscriber lines, and interactive television networks.

> Top competitors: Lucent, Motorola
>
> Revenues: $19.9 billion
>
> Minimum DRIP number of shares or minimum direct investment: $250, waived if ACH
>
> Minimum OCP: $50
>
> Phone #: 800/483-9010
>
> Purchase, ACH, or initial setup fee: yes
>
> 10-year annual return: NA

APACHE OIL CORP (APA)—ENERGY—NATURAL GAS B

APA is a fast-growing independent producer of oil and natural gas. It has onshore and offshore operations in Australia, China, Egypt, Poland, and North America. The company has proven reserves of more than 860 million barrels of oil equivalent, mainly located in North America. APA is known for buying and developing oil fields from its much larger competitors, especially when the price is cheap.

> Top competitors: BP Amoco, ExxonMobil, Royal Dutch Shell
>
> Revenues: $1.3 billion, S&P 500
>
> Minimum DRIP number of shares or minimum direct investment: 1 share
>
> Minimum OCP: $50
>
> Phone #: 800/468-9716
>
> Purchase, ACH, or initial setup fee: yes
>
> 10-year annual return: 9 percent

CHICAGO BRIDGE AND IRON (CBI)—CYCLICAL—OIL-RELATED INFRASTRUCTURE B

CBI is a leading specialty construction company focused on oil tanks and oil terminals. CBI specializes in flat-bottom tanks (44 percent of sales), cryogenic tanks, pressure vessels, and elevated tanks for the water industries. Specialty products include vacuum facilities for aeronautic testing. CBI has been aggressively expanding into process piping systems used in microelectronics and pharmaceutical applications. CBI recently acquired one of its major construction competitors, Pitt-De Moines. CBI is headquartered in the Netherlands and has a worldwide presence.

Top competitors: Halliburton, Matrix Service

Revenues: $674 million

Minimum DRIP number of shares or minimum direct investment: $200

Minimum OCP: $50

Phone #: 888/BNY-ADRS

Purchase, ACH, or initial setup fee: yes

10-year annual return: NA

CORNING (GLW)—TECHNOLOGY—MANUFACTURING B

GLW was primarily a kitchenware and lab products manufacturer, but has transformed itself into the world's top maker of fiberoptic cable, with twice the market share of #2 Lucent. GLW invented fiberoptics cable 20 years ago. GLW's telecommunications unit generates about 60 percent of revenues. The Advanced Materials unit produces industrial and scientific products, including emission controls and semiconductor materials. CLW's Information Display segment makes glass products for televisions, VCRs, and flat-panel displays. Its joint ventures include beleaguered breast implant maker Dow Corning.

Top competitors: Alcatel, JDS Uniphase, Pielli SpA

Revenues: $4.2 billion—#334 Fortune 500, S&P 500

Minimum DRIP number of shares or minimum direct investment: 1 share

Minimum OCP: $10

Phone #: 800/255-0461

Purchase, ACH, or initial setup fee: none

10-year annual return: 22 percent

Increased dividends every year 1989–1999: yes

FORD (F)–CYCLICAL–AUTOMOTIVE B

F is the world's largest truck maker and the #2 maker of cars behind General Motors. F manufactures vehicles using the Aston Martin, Ford, Jaguar, Lincoln, Mercury, and Volvo brands. Two of its biggest successes are the Ford Taurus and the F-series pickup. F owns a controlling (33 percent) stake in Mazda and has purchased BMW's Land Rover SUV operations. Ford Motor Credit is the top auto finance company in the United States. F also owns 81 percent of Hertz, the top car rental firm in the world. The Ford family owns about 40 percent of the firm's voting stock.

Top competitors: DaimlerChrysler, General Motors, Toyota

Revenues: $ 162.5 billion—#4 Fortune 500, S&P 500

Minimum DRIP number of shares or minimum direct investment: $1000

Minimum OCP: $50

Phone #: 800/955-4791

Purchase, ACH, or initial setup fee: yes

10-year annual return: 14 percent

GENERAL MOTORS (GM)–CYCLICAL–AUTOMOTIVE B

GM continues to be the world's #1 maker of cars, including the Buick, Cadillac, Chevrolet, GMC, Oldsmobile, Pontiac, and Saturn brands. GM also produces cars through its Holden, Opel, and Vauxhall units, and through affiliations with Isuzu, Saab, and Suzuki. Nonautomotive interests include Hughes Electronics (satellites, communications), Allison Transmission (medium- and heavy-duty transmissions), and GM Locomotive (locomotives, diesel engines). GM has spun off Delphi Automotive Systems, the world's top auto parts maker, and has agreed to take a 20 percent stake in Fuji Heavy

Industries (Subaru) and Fiat Auto (Alfa Romeo, Lancia). GMAC also provides auto financing.

Top competitors: DaimlerChrysler, Ford, Toyota

Revenues: $ 176.5 billion—#1 Fortune 500, S&P 500, DJIA

Minimum DRIP number of shares or minimum direct investment: 1 share

Minimum OCP: $25

Phone #: 800/331-9922

Purchase, ACH, or initial setup fee: yes

10-year annual return: 9 percent

IBM (IBM)—TECHNOLOGY—COMPUTER— DIVERSIFIED B

IBM is the world's top provider of computer hardware. IBM manufactures a broad range of computers, including PCs, notebooks, mainframes, and network servers. IBM is the #2 software developer behind Microsoft. IBM generates 35 percent of sales from its computer services units, which is the largest in the world. IBM owns software pioneers Lotus Development and Tivoli Systems. About 60 percent of revenues are to customers overseas. IBM continues to revamp its product line and is focusing heavily on Internet business.

Top competitors: Compaq, Hewlett-Packard, Microsoft

Revenues: $87.5 billion—#6 Fortune 500, S&P 500, DJIA

Minimum DRIP number of shares or minimum direct investment: $500, waived if ACH

Minimum OCP: $50

Phone #: 888/426-6700

Purchase, ACH, or initial setup fee: yes

10-year annual return: 20 percent

NATIONAL DATA CORP (NDC)—TECHNOLOGY— SERVICES B

NDC is a leading Internet-based medical office services company. NDC's health division (about 60 percent of sales) provides patient eligibility, claims processing, billing, and other services to doctors, pharmacists, and health care firms. NDC also specializes in the transfer of financial information, including credit and debit transaction processing and check verification. NDC continues to expand through acquisitions and plans to reorganize into separate health and e-commerce companies.

> Top competitors: CorVel, First Data, First USA Bank
> Revenues: $685 million, S&P 600
> Minimum DRIP number of shares or minimum direct investment: 1 share
> Minimum OCP: $25
> Phone #: 800/568-3476
> Purchase, ACH, or initial setup fee: yes
> 10-year annual return: 6 percent

SEARS (S)—CYCLICAL—BROAD-BASED RETAIL B

S is the second largest retailer after Wal-Mart and is growing its business on the Internet. S operates 850 US mall-based stores. Specialty store operations include nearly 1400 automotive and hardware stores using the names NTB National Tire & Battery, Sears Auto Centers, Sears Hardware, and Orchard Supply Hardware. There are also over 700 independently owned Sears stores serving smaller communities.

> Top competitors: JC Penney, Target, Wal-Mart
> Revenues: $41.0 billion—#16 Fortune 500, S&P 500
> Minimum DRIP number of shares or minimum direct investment: $500, waived if ACH
> Minimum OCP: $50
> Phone #: 800/732-7780
> Purchase, ACH, or initial setup fee: yes
> 10-year annual return: 1 percent

TEKTRONICS (TEK)—TECHNOLOGY—EQUIPMENT B

TEK is the second leading manufacturer of testing equipment for semiconductor producers behind Agilent Technologies. TEK's test equipment (45 percent of sales) features oscilloscopes and various types of multimeters and analyzers.

Top competitors: Agilent Technologies, LeCroy, Teradyne

Revenues: $1.1 billion, S&P 500

Minimum DRIP number of shares or minimum direct investment: $500

Minimum OCP: $100

Phone #: 800/842-7629

Purchase, ACH, or initial setup fee: yes

10-year annual return: 15 percent

COMPAQ COMPUTER (CPQ)–TECHNOLOGY– COMPUTERS B–

Although still the #1 PC maker in the world and the second largest computer seller behind IBM, CPQ is reorganizing to prop up its profitability. CPQ has greatly reduced its number of resellers, cut jobs, and established direct sales operations through its Custom Edge unit in an effort to better compete. CPQ offers corporate servers, handheld systems, and technology services. CPQ derives most of its revenues from business customers.

Top competitors: Dell, Hewlett-Packard, IBM

Revenues; $ 38.5 billion—#20 Fortune 500, S&P 500

Minimum DRIP number of shares or minimum direct investment: $250

Minimum OCP: $50

Phone #: 888/218-4373

Purchase, ACH, or initial setup fee: yes

10-year annual return: 26 percent

Increased dividends every year 1989–1999: yes

Glossary

ACH   Automated Clearing House; see Automatic Debit.

Accrued Principal   When referring to Treasury Inflation Protection Securities (TIPS), the value of the bond at maturity. TIPS index the amount redeemed at maturity to the inflation rate over the life of the bond.

Acquisition   Purchase of one company by another company using cash or stock.

ADR   see American Deposit Receipt.

Affinity Group   Some direct investing plans require that investors belong to a specific group to participate, and specifics of each requirement are disclosed in the DRIP materials. Examples include a requirement that an investor be a resident of a particular state. Used mainly by utility companies, Affinity Groups are being phased out by companies offering DRIPs.

After-Tax Income   Income remaining after income tax is paid.

Aggressive   Investment strategy that focuses more on capital gains as an investing priority than on price stability or income. Aggressive investments usually involve more investment risk.

American Deposit Receipts (ADRs)   Certificates consisting of shares of a foreign corporation that are being held in custody. Although ADRs have the same currency and economic risks as the underlying foreign shares, they are much more convenient for US shareholders to own versus buying on the overseas exchange. Using ADRs, there are few difficulties in transferring securities or currency conversion. ADRs are traded on major stock exchanges just like common stock.

Amortization   Repayment of a loan, or the depreciation of an intangible asset such as corporate goodwill, by installments.

Analyst (also known as a Financial Analyst or Security Analyst)   Analysts have expertise in evaluating companies and investments. Brokerage firms, investment advisors, or mutual funds typically employ analysts. They make buy, sell, and hold investment timing recommendations and may specialize in industries or sectors.

Annual Report   A corporation's annual statement of financial operations. An annual report usually includes a balance sheet, income statement, auditor's report, and description of a company's operations. The Securities and Exchange Commission requires that publicly traded companies file an annual report (Form 10-K) and make it available to all shareholders.

Appreciation   The increase in value of an asset.

Asset Allocation   Separating investments by overall asset category, such as stocks, bonds, or money market accounts.

Assets   Assets include cash, accounts receivable, inventory, or anything of value that a corporation owns. The total financial resources of a corporation.

Asset Turnover   Ratio of net corporate revenues to average assets.

Authorized Stock   The maximum number of shares permitted to be issued by the corporate charter. The number of authorized shares can be changed only by a vote of the company's shareholders.

Automatic Debit (also known as ACH or Electronic Funds Transfer, EFT)   The process for automatically debiting an investor's cash accounts, such as a bank account, for DRIP investments.

Automatic Monthly Withdrawals   Once enrolled in a DRIP, companies may allow you to purchase additional shares through OCPs and may allow automatic debit from your bank account via EFT. Most commonly, these withdrawals are processed on a monthly basis.

Basic Materials Sector   Industrial sector focused on providing raw materials for other manufacturers.

Beta   Statistical difference between the price performance of a specific stock and a market index over a specific time period. Useful in evaluating investment risks.

Bond   A loan to the government or a company. Usually provides investors with steady income and high capital preservation.

Bond Maturity   See Maturity.

Broker Consensus Recommendation   The median of all broker recommendations for the investment timeliness of a specific stock.

Capital   Permanent money invested in a business or asset. Can also refer to the long-term assets of a business.

Capital Appreciation   The rise in the market value of an asset.

Capital Asset   The sum of all a company's tangible property. Includes securities, real estate, and other property.

Capital Expenditures   Funds used by a company to acquire or upgrade physical assets such as property, plant, or equipment.

Capital Gain The profit made when an asset is sold for more than its original cost basis.

Capitalization On a corporate balance sheet, indicates stockholders' equity plus bonds outstanding. Sometimes refers to a corporate expense that is considered an asset on the corporate balance sheet. Not to be confused with Market Capitalization.

Capital Loss The loss realized when an asset is sold for less than its cost basis.

Cash and Cash Equivalents Assets that are cash or can be converted into cash immediately, such as bank accounts, marketable securities, and Treasury Bills.

Cash Dividend A dividend paid in cash to a corporation's shareholders. The amount is normally paid from a company's net income and is taxable as income to the shareholders.

Cash Flow The amount of cash that flows into or from a company. The most widely used method of calculating cash flow is net income plus depreciation.

Commission The fee paid to a broker to buy or sell securities. Increases the tax basis of a purchased security, reducing the eventual capital gain.

Commissions Per Share on Purchases A fee charged by a DRIP administrator for each share purchased.

Commissions Per Share on Sales A fee charged by a DRIP administrator for each share sold.

Common Stock The class of owners who have residual claims on the assets and earnings of a corporation after all debt and preferred stockholders' claims have been met.

Community Property Nine states use the community property system to determine the interest of a husband and wife in property acquired during marriage. If investors now live or previously lived in one of these states, they should review these special rules.

Compound Interest Interest earned on previously paid interest that has remained in an account.

Confirmation A written acknowledgment provided when a trade has been completed. It includes details such as the date, price, commission, fees, and settlement terms.

Conservative Investment strategy that focuses on price stability or income as an investing goal versus increasing the value of the original investment.

Contributed Capital The amount of money raised from the stockholders by selling common stock.

Convertible Bonds Bonds that can be converted into common stock.

Corporation A form of business organization in which the company is divided into shares of stock. A corporation is a legal entity.

Corporate Ethics Statement List of moral and social objectives of a corporation.

Corporate Mission Statement A few sentences that clearly explain the purpose of a corporation.

Cost Basis   The original cost, including fees or commissions, to acquire an asset.

Cost of Goods Sold   The cost of production of goods and services that were sold in a specific operating period. Found on a company's earnings statement.

Current Assets   Cash, accounts receivable, inventory, marketable securities, prepaid expenses, and other assets that can be converted to cash within 1 year. Appears on a company's balance sheet.

Current Liabilities   Amounts owed for interest, accounts payable, short-term loans, expenses incurred but unpaid, and other debts within 1 year. Appears on a company's balance sheet.

Current Ratio   Current assets divided by current liabilities; measures corporate liquidity.

Current Yield   The average annual rate of cash income received from an investment, income received during a year, divided by the security's current market price.

Custodial Account   Investment accounts opened for the benefit of minors.

Custodian   An adult who manages the property of a minor until the minor reaches legal age of control.

Cyclical Industry   Industrial sector whose performance is closely tied to the business cycle of the general economy, such as manufacturers of durable goods.

Debt   Informal term for corporate liabilities.

Debt/Equity Ratio   Total liabilities divided by total equity.

Debt Financing   Issuance of bonds or notes to individuals or institutions.

Debt Ratio   Total debt to total assets.

Debt Service   The repayment of interest and principal of a debt.

Deferred Income Taxes   A liability that results from income already earned and recognized for accounting purposes but not for tax purposes. Used in a company's balance sheet.

Deferred Revenue   Money received from customers in advance of delivery of goods or services.

Depreciation   Reduction in the book value of corporate assets over their useful lifetime and in compliance with IRS regulations.

Devaluation   A significant fall in the value of a currency as compared to gold or another country's currency.

Dilution   Reduction in a company's earnings per share caused by the issuance of additional shares of stock.

Direct Purchase Stock Plan (DSP; also known as Direct Enrollment Stock Plan [DESP])   A company that has registered with the Securities and Exchange Commission to sell shares of its stock directly to investors.

Diversification   Reduction of risk by investing in unrelated companies or business activities.

Dividend   Payment per share by a company to its stockholders, either in cash or stock.

Dividend Payout Ratio   Stock dividend divided by net income; used to evaluate the percentage of corporate income paid out as dividends.

Dividend Reinvestment   The use of cash dividends to purchase additional shares of the identical security.

Dividend Reinvestment Plan (DRIP)   Program offered by a corporation for the reinvestment of cash dividends by purchasing additional shares on the dividend payment date. The company or its transfer agent usually administers the DRIP.

Dividend Yield   The annual cash dividend per share paid by a company divided by its current stock price.

Dollar Cost Averaging   An investment strategy of buying a fixed dollar amount of an investment on a regular schedule. More shares are purchased when prices are low, and fewer shares are purchased when prices are high.

DRIP   see Dividend Reinvestment Plan.

Earnings   Net income for a company during a specific period. Usually refers to after-tax income.

Earnings Per Share (EPS)   Net corporate income divided by the number of common shares outstanding for a specified period (usually a year or quarter). Companies usually use a weighted average number of shares outstanding over the reporting term. Primary Earnings Per Share (or Fully Diluted Earnings Per Share) uses all the shares currently outstanding and all common stock equivalents, such as convertible preferred stock and stock options. The result is the number of shares that would be outstanding if all convertible securities were converted into common stock. Basic earnings per share are calculated on only those shares that are currently outstanding, and basic earnings per share are usually slightly higher than primary earnings per share.

Electronic Funds Transfer (EFT)   Funds automatically transferred from a bank account directly to the Plan Administrator for DRIP processing.

Enrollment Fee   A one-time fee charged to investors when the plan administrator opens a DRIP account.

Equity   The ownership interest of common and preferred stockholders in a corporation.

Equity Financing   The process of selling common or preferred stock to raise working capital.

Equity Investors   Investors who are owners of the business through ownership of common or preferred stock.

Ex-Dividend Date ("Ex-Date")   The date after which the seller, and not the buyer, of a stock is entitled to a recently announced dividend. It is usually 4 business days before the record date indicated in newspaper listings with an "x."

Exchange Market where securities, commodities, options, and futures are traded, such as New York Stock Exchange and American Stock Exchange.

Financial Leverage Use of debt to increase the anticipated return on equity, measured by the ratio of assets to equity.

Financial Sector Industrial sector focused on providing financial services, such as bank and insurance companies.

Financial Statements A balance sheet, income statement, statement of changes in financial position, and statement of changes in owners' equity accounts usually available in a company's annual report.

Float The total number of outstanding shares available to trade on the exchange.

Form 10K A company's annual audited report filed with the Securities and Exchange Commission; due within 90 days of the end of the company's fiscal year.

Form 10Q A company's quarterly report filed with the Securities and Exchange Commission; due within 45 days of the end of the company's quarter.

Fundamental Analysis A method of evaluating stocks based on basic factors such as revenues, earnings, future growth, return on equity, and profit margins to determine a company's underlying value and potential for future earnings and dividend growth.

Funds Corporate working capital or current assets less current liabilities. Sometimes used to refer to cash or cash and marketable securities.

Gift Account Allows an individual to establish an account for another person (not a minor). The recipient of the gift account is responsible for all management of the account as well as any taxes incurred as a result of the account.

Goals Specific objectives that relate to specific time periods.

Going Public The process of initially selling shares to new investors for the first time (see IPO).

Gross Margin Gross profit as a percentage of sales.

Gross Profit Sales revenue minus the cost of goods sold.

Growth Rates The compounded annualized rate of growth of a company's revenues, earnings, or dividends.

Income Statement The statement of company revenues, expenses, gains and losses, and net income for a specific period of time.

Indicated Dividend The total dividends that would be paid on a share of stock in the next 12 months if each dividend were the same amount as the latest payment.

Indicated Yield The yield that a share of stock would return based on its current indicated dividend. Calculated by dividing the indicated dividend by the current share price.

Individual Retirement Account (IRA)   Allows individuals to invest up to a specified dollar amount each year and pay no taxes on the earnings or capital gains until retirement.

Industrial Sector   Industrial sector focused on manufacturing products for other manufacturers.

Industry   A category used to describe a company's primary business activity; usually determined by the largest source of the company's revenues.

Inflation   The increase in the cost of identical products or services over time. Usually expressed as a percentage per year.

Initial Investment Fee   The fee charged by the direct investing plan administrator when establishing an account through an initial investment.

Initial Investment Minimum   See Minimum Initial Investment.

Initial Minimum Waived   Some direct investing plans allow investors to submit initial investment through recurring automatic debits from a bank account rather than in one lump sum.

Initial Public Offering (IPO)   The first sale of stock by a company to the investing public.

Intangibles   Patents, goodwill, and other nonphysical, hard-to-measure costs.

Interest   The cost for borrowing money; usually expressed as an annual percentage rate.

Interest Coverage   Corporate earnings, before interest and taxes, divided by interest expense. Helps investors evaluate the overall financial strength of a company.

Inventory   Physical assets held for future use in production or sales. Inventory on a corporate balance sheet is the cost of these assets.

Inventory Turnover   Number of times the average inventory has been sold during a period; measured by the cost of goods sold for a period divided by the average inventory for the period.

Invested Capital   The money that investors have put into a business. It is equal to long-term liabilities plus owners' equity.

Investment Risk   See Risk.

Investment Unit Trust (Closed-End Fund)   Invest in other securities (like a mutual fund), but have a fixed number of shares and are traded similarly to stocks. Most trade on the American Stock Exchange and do not usually offer DRIPs or direct investing programs.

Joint Account Registration   When registering a stock certificate, it allows for both spouses to be named on the certificate. (See also Joint Tenants with Right of Survivorship, Tenants by Entirety, and Community Property.)

Joint Tenants with Rights of Survivorship (JTWROS)   Both spouses are named on a stock certificate. On the death of one of the joint tenants, the surviving tenant acquires sole title to the shares.

Keogh Plan   A qualified tax-deferred retirement plan for self-employed individuals.

Letter to Shareholders   Part of an annual report that addresses the recent performance of the company.

Leverage   See Financial Leverage.

Leverage Ratios   See Solvency or Leverage Ratios.

Liabilities   Total value of financial claims on a firm's assets. Equal to current liabilities plus long-term liabilities, and total assets minus stockholders' equity.

Liquidity   The ease and certainty with which an asset can be converted into cash.

Liquidity (short-term)   Sufficient cash to meet maturing short-term claims.

Liquidity Ratios   Measures the firm's ability to meet maturing short-term obligations. Includes current ratio and quick ratio.

Long-Term Assets   The value, based on cost, of a company's property, equipment, and other capital assets less depreciation; found on the balance sheet.

Long-Term Debt   Loans with obligations of over 1 year.

Long-Term Debt to Capitalization Ratio   A ratio that indicates a company's financial leverage. It is calculated by dividing long-term debt by the total capital of the company.

Long-Term Liabilities   Liabilities for leases, bond repayments, and other items due in more than 1 year.

Market Capitalization   The total dollar value of all outstanding shares, calculated by multiplying the number of shares times the current market price.

Market Timing   An attempt to increase trading profits by forecasting the market's next move up or down.

Market Value or Market Price   The prices at which investors buy or sell a security.

Maturity   The length of time for which a particular amount of money is loaned, such as a bond.

Maturity Date   The exact date when repayment of loans or bonds are expected to be repaid.

Merger   When two or more business enterprises are joined to form a single company.

Minimum Initial ACH   Some DRIP and direct investing programs allow investors to meet the minimum initial investment, or the minimum number of shares required to enroll, through preauthorized withdrawals from a bank account of a specified amount for a determined length of time.

Minimum Initial Investment   The minimum dollar amount required to begin participation in a direct stock purchase plan.

Minimum Number of Shares Required   To participate in a DRIP, an investor may be required to first be a registered shareholder of a specific number of shares to enroll.

Minimum Optional Cash Investment   Optional cash investments are subject to the minimum and maximum limits set forth in the plan details.

Minor   A child who has not yet reached the age of majority (18 or 21, depending on the state).

Money Market Securities   Short-term securities that pay some income and focus on price stability.

Moving Average   The average price of a security for a particular period, charted for the purpose of determining recent stock pricing trends.

Municipal Bonds (Muni Bonds)   Bonds issued by local and state governments, whose interest payments are exempt from US federal income taxes.

Mutual Fund   An open-ended investment company that manages a portfolio of securities and offers shares to investors.

NASDAQ (National Association of Securities Dealers Automated Quotation System)   A nationwide computerized quotation system for current bid and asked quotations on over 5500 over-the-counter stocks. A competitive stock market exchange to the New York Stock Exchange (NYSE).

Net Assets   Book value of a company's common stock, surplus, and retained earnings.

Net Asset Value (NAV)   The value of a mutual fund's investments calculated each day and usually expressed as a per-share amount.

Net Income   The amount of money remaining after all corporate expenses have been subtracted from revenue; the "Bottom Line."

New York Stock Exchange (NYSE)   The major marketplace to buy and sell stocks of usually larger market capitalization and better-known companies.

Noncyclical Sector   Industrial sector focused on consumer products and services that are not affected by overall economic cycles.

Objectives   Broad statements of direction to achieve a specific goal.

On-line Synthetic DRIP   An Internet-based broker account that specializes in dollar-denominated, rather than share-based, investing. On-line synthetic DRIP brokerage firms duplicate the investment benefits of DRIPs and direct investing.

Operating Expenses   The day-to-day costs of running a business.

Operating Income   The amount of revenue remaining after the Cost of Goods Sold and Selling and General and Administrative costs have been subtracted from sales revenue.

Operating Margin   Operating profit (before interest and taxes) divided by sales.

Optional Cash Purchase (OCP)   The voluntary purchase of additional shares through a DRIP.

Optional Cash Purchase Fee   The fee charged by a DRIP administrator when additional shares are purchased through the plan.

Overbought or Oversold   Terms that define when a stock price has moved higher or lower than justified by the fundamentals.

Overhead   Costs incurred in providing a business facility, but not directly associated with identifiable units of products or services. Costs that cannot be directly applied to production expenses.

PEG (P/E Ratio to EPS Growth)   Calculated by dividing a stock's P/E ratio by its long-term earnings per share growth rate. A fundamental investing tool used to evaluate a stock's price.

Payout Ratio   See Dividend Payout Ratio.

Personal Portfolio Tracking Service   Stock value tracking service provided by most financial Internet websites; allows investors to upload a basket of stocks and follow their value.

"Phantom" Capital Gains   The capital gains realized by a mutual fund, but undistributed to the fund investors.

Plan Administrator   An organization overseeing the purchase and sale of shares in a DRIP. Handles statements, transfers, and other administrative transactions, and can be a bank, transfer agent, or the company itself.

Plant and Equipment   The value of factories and equipment recorded on a corporate balance sheet. Shows original cost less accumulated appreciation.

Position   An investor's ownership of an asset.

Preferred Stock   Stock class with fixed dividend payment. Takes priority over common stock in claims against a company's asset.

Pretax Income   Corporate profit before income taxes have been deducted.

Price to Book Ratio   Compares a stock's market value to its book value. Calculated by dividing the current price by common stockholders' equity per share (book value). Used in the fundamental evaluation of stock prices.

Price to Cash Flow Ratio   Compares a stock price to the company's cash flow. Calculated by dividing a stock's price per share by its cash flow per share. Used in the fundamental evaluation of stock prices.

Price to Earnings Ratio (PE)   Compares a stock's price to the company's earnings. Calculated by dividing the stock price by the earnings per common share for the past year. The most important stock ratio used in fundamental analysis.

Price to Sales Ratio   Compares a stock's price to the company's revenues. Calculated by dividing a stock's current price by its revenues per share. Used in the fundamental evaluation of stock prices.

Productivity   The process by which a greater amount of output is generated from the same amount of input. Measured as sales volume per employee or sales dollar per employee wage dollar.

Profitability The degree to which a company earns the highest possible return from resources used or capital employed.

Profit Margin Net income as a percent of sales.

Prospectus A formal written statement that discloses the terms of a public stock offering or mutual fund. The prospectus is required to reveal essential information to investors about the proposed offering.

Proxy A formal document signed by a shareholder to authorize another shareholder, or commonly the company's management, to vote the holder's shares at the annual meeting.

Quick Ratio Liquid assets divided by current liabilities. Liquid assets include cash, short-term marketable securities, and accounts receivable.

Quotation or Quote The current price being offered by sellers for a particular stock.

Range The difference between the high and low price of a stock during a particular period.

Ratio A number resulting when one number is divided by another. Used to assess aspects of profitability, solvency, liquidity, and efficiency.

Real Rate of Return Investment returns after adjusting for inflation.

Receivables Any money owed to the corporation from the sales of its products or services, regardless of whether they are currently due. Long-term receivables appear as a long-term asset.

Recession A period of general economic decline.

Registered Shareholder An individual who owns stock that is held by the individual directly, and not through a broker.

Reinvest The purchase of additional shares instead of receiving interest or dividend payments in cash.

Research and Development Research is an activity aimed at discovering new knowledge in hopes it will be useful in creating a new product, process, or service or improving a present product, process, or service. Development is the implementation of research findings into a new or improved product, process, or service.

Resource Allocation The process and decision of designating money to a specific asset, project, or business unit.

Retained Earnings The cumulative amount of corporate income not paid out as dividends by the corporation.

Return The percentage gain or loss for a security in a particular period. The real rate of return is the annual return on that investment, adjusted for changes due to inflation.

Return on Assets A profitability ratio measured by net income divided by assets. Helpful in evaluating management's performance.

Return on Capital   A profitability ratio measured by net income divided by invested capital. Helpful in evaluating management's performance.

Return on Equity   A profitability ratio measured as net income divided by equity. Helpful in evaluating management's performance.

Return on Sales (Profit Margin)   A profitability ratio measured by net profit divided by revenues.

Revenue   The price of a product multiplied by the number of units sold.

Risk   The chance an investor will lose some or all invested capital in an asset or a group of assets.

Sale Fee   A fee charged by a DRIP administrator when selling shares through the plan.

Secondary Market   All stock exchanges where investors buy securities from other investors rather than directly from the company. The NYSE, ASE, and NASDAQ are secondary markets.

Securities and Exchange Commission (SEC)   The federal government agency responsible for the regulation of the securities industry.

Security (Securities)   Documents that show ownership or indebtedness.

Share Repurchase   A company's plan to buy back its own shares, reducing the number of outstanding shares. Usually an indication that company management believes the shares are undervalued.

Shares   Certificates representing ownership in a corporation.

Solvency or Leverage Ratios   Measure a firm's ability to meet long-term obligations, including debt to assets, debt to equity, and financial leverage ratios.

Standard Deviation   Statistical difference between a stock's high and low price and the average price over a specific time period; useful in evaluating investment risks.

Standard & Poor's 500 Index (S&P 500)   Standard & Poor's is a widely recognized unmanaged index of 500 larger capitalized common stocks.

Standard & Poor's Equity Ranking   A rating system developed by S&P to evaluate consistency in earnings and dividend growth during the most recent 10 years. Useful in evaluating management's ability to increase shareholder value for long-term investors.

Start-Up Fees   See Initial Investment Fee.

State of Residence   The state in which a permanent home is established.

Statement of Changes in Financial Position   Sources of funds and uses of funds during a period of corporate operations; found in annual reports.

Statement of Changes in Owner's Equity   A statement comparing the beginning and ending balances for contributed capital and retained earnings. Focuses on the changes that occurred during the year; found in annual reports.

Statement of Changes in Retained Earnings   Reconciles the beginning-of-period and end-of-period balances in the retained earnings account; found in annual reports.

Statements of Cash Flows Summarizes corporate activities that generate and consume cash; found in annual reports.

Stockbroker A licensed representative who facilitates orders to buy and sell securities for clients.

Stockholders' Equity (Book Value) The value of a company's assets after deducting its liability, usually on a per-share basis.

Stock Dividend A dividend paid in additional shares of a company's stock rather than in cash.

Stock Option The right to purchase a specific number of shares of stock for a specified price at a specified time; usually granted to key employees.

Stock Split A proportional increase in a company's outstanding shares. After the stock split, the market value of the total shares remains the same, although the number of shares held by each shareholder is proportionally increased while the market price per share is proportionally decreased.

Stock Symbol A unique symbol, usually up to four letters, assigned to a company's stock.

Strategic Financial Analysis Analyzing competitors' financial statements with the goal of determining their financial strengths and weaknesses.

Strategic Planning Corporate planning that focuses on longer-range objectives and goals. It is essentially direction-setting and focuses on new corporate opportunities.

Synthetic DRIP An account at a third party, such as a broker, where dividends received are reinvested.

Technical Analysis A method of evaluating stocks by analyzing data of its market activity, generally price, and volume. Technical analysts use charts to identify patterns that can suggest future trends.

Technology Sector Industrial sector focused on technology, such as computers and aerospace.

Tenants by Entirety In some states, stock certificates are registered for a married couple by this designation. Have the same characteristics as the standard JTWROS account.

Tenants in Common Tenants in common stock registration makes both spouses equal owners unless they agree otherwise. Allows the right to transfer ownership while living or at death.

Termination Fee A fee charged by a DRIP administrator for terminating participation in a plan; it is in addition to the cost of selling shares through the plan.

Total Debt to Total Assets Calculated by adding short- and long-term debt and dividing by the corporation's total assets. Used to measure a company's overall financial strength, as determined by how much of the company's assets have been financed by debt.

Total Return Expressed as a percentage, this calculation informs investors how much has been made or lost on an investment over time. It assumes that all dividends and capital gains have been reinvested.

Total Revenue   Total sales and other revenue for a particular period.

Trading Range   The spread between the high and low stock prices traded during a period of time.

Treasury Bills (T-bills)   Short-term US government securities with maturities of no more than 1 year.

Treasury Inflation Protected Securities (TIPS)   A bond issued by the US Treasury Department that increases in maturity value equal to the compounded inflation rate over the life of the bond.

Trust Account Registration   A trust is a legal mechanism by which a "trustee" holds shares for the benefit of another. A living trust allows an individual to establish a trust for his or her own benefit for life and provides for the distribution of assets on his or her death.

Uniform Gifts or Transfers to Minors Act (UGMA and UTMA)   With an UGMA account, adults generally maintain control over the investment until the child reaches the age of majority (18 or 21, depending on the state). UTMA accounts work in the same way as UGMA accounts, except that UTMA accounts let the parent maintain control over the account for a longer period of time. Although UGMA assets are transferred to the child at the age of majority, UTMA accounts permit postponing transfer until age 18, 21, or 25, depending on the state.

Utilities Sector   Industrial sector focused on providing basic services such as electricity, water, and telephone.

Yield   The annual distribution, either dividends or interest, paid on a share of stock or a bond.

Endnotes

CHAPTER 5

[1]Grebler, Daniel, "Indian Motorcycles revs up brand effort." *Reuters Limited*, June 6, 2000

CHAPTER 6

[1]Ferrell, Paul, "Market Timing is bad for your health," *cbs.marketwatch.com*, May 15, 2000

[2]*Worth.com*

[3]Pond, John, "The Harsh Reality of Market Timing," *Worth Magazine*, May 1995

[4]*quicken.com*

[5]*Texnews.com*

[6]*Charlesschwab.com*

[7]Ferrell, Paul, "Market Timing is bad for your health," *cbs.marketwatch.com*, May 15, 2000

CHAPTER 8

[1]*University.smartmoney.com*

[2]*University.smartmoney.com*

[3]*Forbes.com*

CHAPTER 9

[1]*Ibbotson.com*

[2]*Sunamerica.com*

CHAPTER 10

[1]American Association of Individual Investors, April 2000

SOURCES

2000 U.S. Master Tax Guide, CCH Editorial Staff Publications, CCH pp. 11, 217–222, 510–538

Barron's Financial Weekly, Dow Jones Publications, April 19, 1999

Cable Network News, April 14, 2000

Downes, John, & Jordan Elliott Goodman, *Barrons Finance and Investment Handbook, 5th Edition*, 1998, pp. 89–116

Faerber, Esme, *All About Bonds*, 2000, McGraw-Hill

Faerber, Esme, *All About Stocks*, 2000, McGraw-Hill

Forbes Magazine, May 2000

Harley Davidson 1999 Annual Report

Home Depot 1999 Annual Report

Ibbotson Associates, *Stocks, Bonds, Bills and Inflation: Historic Returns 1926–1999*

Ibbotson Associates, *Stocks, Bonds, Bills and Inflation: Historic Returns: 1926–2000*

Kolojeski, Gregory, "Required Minimum Distribution for Traditional and Roth IRAs"

Lowe, Janet, *Benjamin Graham on Value Investing: The Lessons from the Dean of Wall Street*, 1994, Dearborn Financial Publishing, pp. 139–144

S&P 2000 Directory of Dividend Reinvestment Plans, McGraw-Hill

S&P Stock Reports, Feb/March 2000, S&P Consumer Investment Services, McGraw-Hill

Sea Containers 1998 Annual Report

Smart Money, June 2000, Hearst Communications and Dow Jones Publishing, p. 133

Tigule, Joseph, & Joseph Lisanti, *The Dividend Rich Investor,* 1997, McGraw-Hill, p. 95

Value Line Investment Survey, Value Line Publications, May 2000

Warfiled, Gerald, *How to Read and Understand the Financial News,* Harper & Row Publishers, 1986 pp. 54–79

WEBSITES

401kafe.com

Aol.com/personalfinance

Bankofny.com

cbs.marketwatch.com

Chicago-bridge.com

Dripwizard.com

Directinvesting.com

Djinteractive.com

Dtonline.com

Fairmont.com

Fenis.com

Hec.ohio-state.edu

Hoovers.com

Ibbotson.com

Marketguide.com

Money.com, Michael Sivy, March 2000

Multexinvestor.com

Netstockdirect.com

Rplanner.com

Savewealth.com
Smartmoney.com
Spglobal.com
Tecumseh.com
University.smartmoney.com
Yahoo.com
Zacks.com
Zpub.com

INDEX

ABOUT THE AUTHOR

George C. Fisher is a graduate of Williston Academy and Ohio Wesleyan University, and has held several management positions in a top Fortune 50 company. Mr. Fisher has also successfully managed smaller companies specializing in manufacturing and export. Starting with his first DRIP investment in 1970, Mr. Fisher has been an active direct investor and currently publishes *Power Investing with DRIPs Newsletter*. His weekly investment commentary is available at *www.netstockdirect.com*, the leading resource for direct investing information on the Internet.

I would like to subscribe to *Power Investing with DRIPs Newsletter*. Published bimonthly, *Power Investing with DRIPs Newsletter* offers unique commentary and specific DRIP stock recommendations. Available for just $99 a year, *Power Investing with DRIPs Newsletter* provides a comprehensive resource of up-to-date information concerning the fast-growing trend of direct investing. Complete and return this form to North Shore Associates, Box 97, Winnetka, Illinois 60093, or visit our website at *www.powerinvestdrips.com*.

Name:

Address:

City, State, Zip Code:

We accept checks, Visa, Mastercard, or American Express

Credit Card Type:

Credit Card #:

Expiration Date: